Margaret McWilliams

Margaret McWilliams

An Interwar Feminist

MARY KINNEAR

Mary Kinnear (signature)

McGill-Queen's University Press
Montreal & Kingston • London • Buffalo

Legal deposit third quarter 1991
Bibliothèque nationale du Québec

Printed in Canada on acid-free paper

This book has been published with the help of a grant
from the Social Science Federation of Canada, using
funds provided by the Social Sciences and Humanities
Research Council of Canada.

Canadian Cataloguing in Publication Data

Kinnear, Mary, 1942–
    Margaret McWilliams
    Includes bibliographical references and index.
    ISBN 0-7735-0857-0
    1. McWilliams, Margaret, 1875–1952. 2. Feminists–
    Canada–Biography. 3. Social reformers–Canada–
    Biography. 4. Women social reformers–Canada–
    Biography. I. Title.
    HQ1455.M38K46 1991   305.42′092   C91-090123-6

Typeset in Palatino 11/13 by Caractéra inc.,
Quebec City.

Contents

Acknowledgments

Margaret McWilliams's career as a public woman began in 1910, just before the enfranchisement of women in Canada, and continued until her sudden death in 1952. With a degree in political economy from the University of Toronto, she earned her living as a journalist for five years before her marriage. Working for the community in women's organizations, she was a founder and first president of the Canadian Federation of University Women. Through her vice-presidency of the International Federation of University Women, McWilliams came to meet educated women from Europe and the English-speaking world, forming associations that would contribute to the strengthening of her feminist views as she grew older. An historian and political analyst, she was dedicated to the notion of an informed democracy and continually stressed the obligation of university graduates to serve society. During the Depression years, she was elected as alderman for the city of Winnipeg, only retiring when her husband was appointed lieutenant-governor of the province of Manitoba.

The public record of her career is documented in the four books McWilliams wrote, in newspaper reports of her activities, and in the minutes of the many organizations in which she participated. I found considerable material to support my theme that hers was one of the faces of feminism during the interwar years. Less easy to come by was material that would provide insight into her feelings. McWilliams left no diary, memoir, or collection of letters. Still, members of her family kept some correspondence, and many people who knew her retain vivid memories of her personality.

To McWilliams's great-nephew Jack Stovel of Williamstown, Massachusetts, to her great-niece and namesake Margaret Stovel of Montreal, and above all, to her niece by marriage, Velma McWilliams, of Peterborough, Ontario, I am immensely grateful for their generosity in sharing letters, photographs, and impressions. Their material supplemented the public record and allowed me to begin to understand McWilliams's continuing reputation, forty years after her death. I am also indebted to the many other women and men who shared their memories with me. Their names are in the bibliography, and I want especially to acknowledge the comments of Doris Saunders, Douglas Campbell, and Mrs W.L. Morton. I would also like to thank the archivist of the University Women's Club, Joyce McFarland, who showed me the McWilliams library and memorabilia kept at the clubhouse.

Librarians and archivists facilitated my research, and I am particularly grateful to Patrick Wright of the St. John's College library, Vera Fast and Jocelyn McKillop of the Provincial Archives of Manitoba, Sharon Larade of the University of Toronto Archives, Mary Jacomb of the City of Winnipeg Archives, and David Fraser at the National Archives of Canada in Ottawa. I thank Kate Hamerton and Wendy Parker for their research assistance. Betty Jane Wylie, Helen Norrie, and Rosemary Malaher, who had already worked on aspects of McWilliams's career, gave me their insights into her character.

I have been fortunate in my colleagues. My department head, Ed Moulton, encouraged me from the outset, and A.M.C. Waterman, Angela Davis, Jean Friesen, John Kendle, Michael Kinnear, and Karen Ogden critically commented on various parts of my study. Above all, I benefited from the forthright comments of Susan Jackel of the University of Alberta, who read the penultimate draft.

I am grateful to the editors of McGill-Queen's University Press for their painstaking editorial work.

I acknowledge the financial help of the Social Sciences and Humanities Council of Canada, particularly for its award of a research time stipend, which allowed me to devote a year full-time to the completion of my project.

Finally, I thank my family for their companionship and good humour.

Tassie Callaway Stovel with Russell, Hodder, and Margaret. Courtesy of Jack Stovel.

Tassie Callaway Stovel. Courtesy of Velma McWilliams.

Margaret Stovel (seated on left) with the other members of the Executive Committee of the Harbord Collegiate Institute Literary Society. Courtesy of Harbord Collegiate Institute.

Harbord Collegiate Institute graduating class. Margaret Stovel is in the second row, second from left. Courtesy of Toronto Board of Education.

Ladies' Glee Club, University College, University of Toronto, 1897–98 with Margaret Stovel, its president, third from left. University of Toronto Archives.

Board of *Torontonensis*, University of Toronto, 1898. Margaret is in the front row, third from right. University of Toronto Archives.

Margaret Stovel in Montreal, *ca.* 1900. Courtesy of Margaret Stovel (great-niece of Margaret McWilliams).

Margaret Stovel in her wedding dress, 1903. Courtesy of Velma McWilliams.

Margaret and Roland McWilliams, hiking, 1912. Courtesy of Velma McWilliams.

McWilliams, front row, fourth from left, with the Canadian delegation to the 1922 conference of the International Federation of University Women (IFUW), Paris. Provincial Archives of Manitoba.

McWilliams, seated, third from right, with other IFUW delegates, Paris, 1922. Courtesy of University Women's Club, Westgate, Winnipeg.

IFUW conference, Paris, 1922. Vice-President McWilliams (on left) with President Caroline Spurgeon and Secretary Theodora Bosanquet. Courtesy of University Women's Club, Westgate, Winnipeg.

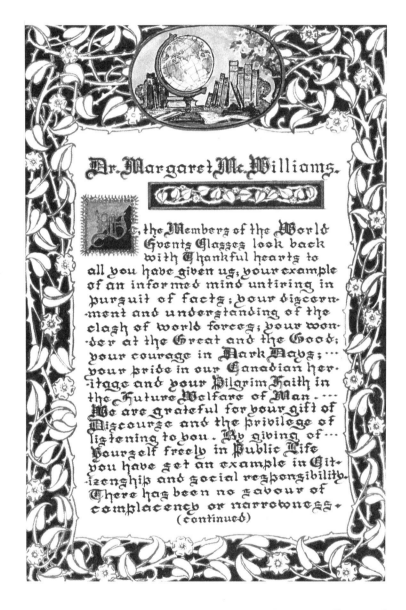

Dr. Margaret Mc. Williams.

the Members of the World Events Classes look back with Thankful hearts to all you have given us; your example of an informed mind untiring in pursuit of facts; your discernment and understanding of the clash of world forces; your wonder at the Great and the Good; your courage in Dark Days; ... your pride in our Canadian heritage and your Pilgrim Faith in the Future Welfare of Man. ... We are grateful for your gift of Discourse and the privilege of listening to you. By giving of ... yourself freely in Public Life you have set an example in Citizenship and social responsibility. There has been no savour of complacency or narrowness.
(continued)

Scroll presented to McWilliams by her current events class in 1948. Courtesy of University Women's Club, Westgate, Winnipeg.

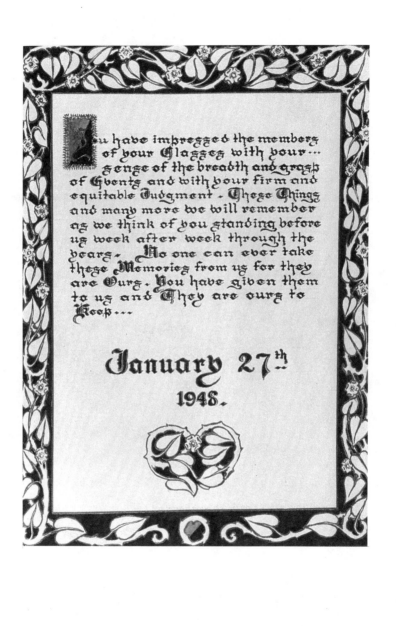

You have impressed the members of your Classes with your... sense of the breadth and grasp of Events and with your firm and equitable Judgment. These Things and many more we will remember as we think of you standing before us week after week through the years. No one can ever take these Memories from us for they are Ours. You have given them to us and They are ours to Keep...

January 27th 1948.

IFUW conference, Christiania (Oslo), Norway, 1924. McWilliams is in the front row, sixth from left. Courtesy of Velma McWilliams.

Margaret McWilliams

Margaret McWilliams:
An Interwar Feminist

Margaret McWilliams was recognizable to her contemporaries as a public woman. From the perspective of the 1990s, she can be seen as an interwar feminist.

McWilliams's career was launched when, at the age of thirty-five, she arrived in Winnipeg with her husband in 1910. It was built on the firm foundation of a university education: in 1898 she was the first woman to graduate with a degree in political economy from the University of Toronto. For five years she earned her living as a journalist in Minneapolis and Detroit, then married a barrister, an old university friend. She spent seven barren and unproductive years in Peterborough, Ontario, but on arrival in Winnipeg, she joined the Women's Canadian Club (WCC) and the Local Council of Women (LCW). A charter member of the Winnipeg University Women's Club, she was first president of the Canadian Federation of University Women (CFUW) and first vice-president of the International Federation of University Women (IFUW). She produced a book of women's history, *Women of Red River*, in 1923, a book on her impressions of Russia in 1927, a history of Manitoba in 1928, a blueprint for Canadian social and economic reform in 1931, and a book on the political institutions of Canada in 1948.[1]

During the 1930s, McWilliams served four consecutive terms as Winnipeg's second woman alderman, becoming chair of the important Health and Unemployment Relief committees. During the 1940s, after her husband was appointed lieutenant-governor of the province, she helped revitalize the Manitoba Historical Society, serving as its president when it sponsored more research than at any other time, before or since. She chaired the Subcommittee on the Post-war Problems of Women, a subcommittee of the federal Advisory Committee on Reconstruction. For over thirty years, until 1947, she maintained a unique Winnipeg institution – her "current events" classes for women, which involved continuing education in politics. She died in 1952 at the age of seventy-seven.

Margaret McWilliams's career as a public woman spanned forty-two years. Her feminism developed slowly until about 1922, and then more urgently thereafter. At first, with enormous confidence, she appeared to recognize no effective barriers to women's participation in public life. Writing of the period around 1910, she noted that "things were prospering and there was plenty to occupy [women's] minds and hands. They did not see the necessity for the suffrage – the world was theirs anyway."[2] McWilliams's practical experience working with and for other women soon brought the realization that the public world by no means belonged to women. Her career is the story of her growing feminist consciousness, and it is also a window onto the little-known scene of interwar feminism in Canada.

The nineteenth-century women's movement sought to open public life to women, although participants embraced a variety of causes and were rarely united on priorities. Some feminists were concerned with the problems women were experiencing in the labour force, where young and single working-class women worked mainly as domestic servants and factory workers. Other feminists were concerned with women's control over their own sexuality, believing they should have access to birth control. Some worked to eliminate the dual sexual standard whereby women were punished more severely than men for sexual transgression. The early feminists' overall lack of unity was masked by an apparent unanimity over the claim that each woman had the right to serve society, to be involved in public life.

Most activists were middle class and understood the public sphere in terms of politics, property, and the professions. The slogan "Votes for Women" constituted both a symbol and a major practical tool of the movement. In a modern parliamentary democracy, the vote signified the acknowledgment of the full identity of an individual person. In acquiring political power, women might be able to promote legislation that would allow them to own and control their own wages and property. The male preserve of universities could be required to admit women into courses that trained doctors, lawyers, and other professionals.

Most of Margaret McWilliams's thoughts and hopes for women were concentrated on women like herself. "College women, in their respective countries, occupy a strategic position. They may be divided generally into three groups – those teaching the children in the schools, the 'merely married,' but with sufficient leisure to work through clubs to make their influence felt in their communities, and those pioneering in the various professions."[3] She wished to rouse the privileged numbers of university graduates to be leaders of their communities, both local and national: "pilgrims of peace abroad and pilgrims of understanding at home."[4] She believed that for this task they should use their trained intelligence and accept the responsibility to keep themselves continually informed – hence her current events classes. The students of these classes paid tribute to McWilliams in 1948 – "By giving of Yourself freely in Public Life you have set an example in Citizenship and social responsibility"[5]

Gradually McWilliams came to the view that women should run for political office. In 1920 *Saturday Night* reported that she was "not yet opening that kind of account with the public." She had "a large following of women [who] look to her for direction. This may seem a bigger work to her hand than a seat in legislative halls. She has earned the right to work in her own way."[6] In 1923 McWilliams wrote to Saskatchewan feminist Violet McNaughton: "Nix on the Parliamentary career to use slang. It is not for me unless some day some moral issue arises which it seems my job to fight for in that way."[7] In 1926 she was urging women to "show more courage in accepting office." By 1938 she had come to the view that "women must be elected to public offices before we can be truly effective in our gifts to civilisation."[8]

In 1933 she was prepared to take the plunge herself. The risks were minimized. The Local Council of Women, its officers well connected with politicians and businessmen, agreed in principle to draft two candidates for the municipal elections. McWilliams was chosen to run in the south Winnipeg ward where most women affiliated with the LCW resided. The council organized public meetings and had an array of committees in charge of publicity and finance. Of the two sponsored candidates, only McWilliams was elected.[9]

Behind her respect for public service was the notion that this was the appropriate way for a university graduate to repay society for her endowment of wits and opportunity.[10] Hers was a meritocratic vision tinged with a sense of obligation. She believed that particularly those women fortunate enough to be economically supported by a husband should consider serving in the public sphere.

Community leadership was not the only occupation she envisaged for women. Involvement with the University Women's Club and the Canadian and International federations of University Women acquainted her with the problems faced by new professional women. Women academics, for instance, did not find jobs easily. At the 1921 triennial meeting of the CFUW, delegates heard a guest from the American Association of University Women report on a survey investigating difficulties faced by women working in universities. One male academic had explained why so few women were appointed: "It is psychologically impossible for men entirely to ignore in their dealings with women the fact that they are dealing with persons that are not men ... Men find life simpler in its workaday aspects when one's colleagues and instructors are men."[11]

The university women's organizations also dealt with the problems of married women working in the labour force. McWilliams always considered that domestic responsibilities ought not to be a barrier to work outside the home, even though they had priority. "A married woman's first job is to run her house and family, and not until she has learned to do that so smoothly that her absence for a meal does not upset the comfort of the home, should she take an outside job."[12] By 1943 she had concluded that a woman herself was the only proper judge of whether she would work outside the home. The state should provide social services, including nursery schools integrated into the educational system, to enable any woman, single, married, or a mother, to choose to work without disadvantage.[13]

Moreover, by 1943 McWilliams was imagining a new postwar society where the public world of politics and work was less segregated. Her 1943 report for the Subcommittee on the Post-War Problems of Women was not uninfluenced by prewar society and employment patterns for women. For example, her subcommittee expected domestic service to continue to employ large numbers. However, in regard to the sort of work women would do, McWilliams hoped for postwar integration of women into practically all fields, a position in contrast to that of both the provincial Manitoba Commission on Rehabilitation Training of 1944 and the federal National Selective Service Women's Division, both of which expected a massive return of women into traditional female occupations.[14] McWilliams also advocated that household work be established on a more professional footing, with standardized training, minimum wages, and integration into governmental social security schemes.[15]

Though McWilliams gave less attention to the problems of women in the family, this was nevertheless an area she did not neglect. She always appreciated the hard work and managerial skills of the housewife, which she thought qualified women for the tasks of political leadership.[16] In 1915 she promoted "the principle of Mothers' Pensions" when as secretary, then president, of the Local Council of Women, she supported the proposal that Manitoba give mothers' allowances to eligible women to help raise their children.[17] She was an early advocate of state-supplied welfare benefits that would help to reduce the burdens of women's family responsibilities.[18] When she was a city alderman, she reorganized the Relief Department so that women recipients would be served by a section under a woman supervisor.[19] In 1943 she reasserted that homemaking was "a vital economic value to the community."[20] These initiatives benefited women in the family, but her main focus was on women in the service of society.

McWilliams believed in a beneficent and socially aggressive state with the power and obligation to do good. Her experience with "Leninism" during her visit to Russia in 1926 modified, but never eradicated, her enthusiasm.[21] She was not a socialist, but in *If I Were King of Canada,* she and her husband, writing under the pen-name Oliver Stowell, advocated a wide range of centralized and universal social services much like those proposed later by the new socialist Co-operative Commonwealth Federation (CCF).[22] Similarly, in her comments on the 1943 *Report on Social Security for Canada* (the Marsh Report, by Leonard Marsh, research adviser on the federal Advisory Committee on Reconstruction), she promoted social security in the form of unemployment and sickness insurance, pensions, family allowances, and nursery schools, whose outcome, if implemented, would reduce the financial burdens on individual families, enhance the choices of wives and mothers, and assert the economic value of household work.[23]

McWilliams's preoccupation with the adult woman as an individual, as distinct from a "relational" human being, reflected her own personal situation. She had no children, and although she enjoyed happy relationships with younger people, with one niece especially, she never experienced at first hand the limitations children could impose on a mother's freedom of action. She rarely referred publicly to questions of sexuality. When she was president of the Women's Canadian Club in the early 1920s, she concurred with the executive's decision to turn down a speaker who was to discuss birth control, "considered not suitable for a Canadian Club audience."[24] McWilliams's mission was to demonstrate and exhort women to take a more prominent part in public life, primarily in politics but also in the labour force, and she gave less consideration to the domestic conditions under which the majority of women lived, conditions that tended to restrict their freedom of action. An efficient housekeeper herself, she tended to be impatient with women who were unable to organize their households in such a way as to release time for public-spirited work.

Worthy causes, for McWilliams, were not confined to women's issues. Though not a pacifist, she thought women could be "pilgrims of peace." In 1922 she justified the existence of the International Federation of University Women as an organization "primarily for aiding in promoting international unity and unbreakable peace."[25] In 1924 she joined the League of Nations Association,[26] and in 1930 she was proud to be appointed a Canadian government adviser at an International Labour Organization (ILO) conference.

By 1938 she was troubled by "a black and deadly cloud. That cloud is Fascism ... if Fascism comes, [women] will be regimented back to the old kitchen, church and children, which will effectually stop us offering our gifts to the nation."[27] She maintained her current events classes during the Second World War, and in January 1942 she presented to her students an analysis of the League of Nations' failure while declaring that the world must in future organize for peace: "Peace cannot be maintained without police ... One cannot reason with wolves ... some form of world government is essential."[28] This idea became even more important after the discovery of atomic energy, and in 1947 she was a passionate supporter of the United Nations. Most of all, McWilliams put her faith in the informed intelligence of individual citizens in a democracy.[29]

Contemporaries credited her with a powerful personality. "Mrs McWilliams is a very fluent speaker, with a command of forceful language and a charming platform personality that won the abiding attention of her hearers, even while she discoursed on such dry subjects, from a woman's viewpoint, as the transportation and marketing problems of the Western Provinces," wrote the *Peterborough Examiner* in 1925.[30] She was inclined to solemnity, and knew it. "There are those of us who are too earnest. I used to be like that myself," she said in 1938. By then she had come to realize "it doesn't do to be too earnest."[31]

McWilliams applied immense energy to her personal mission and was helped by a superb physical constitution. A colleague in the Canadian Federation of University Women attributed McWilliams's success and stamina to her "newspaper woman's temperament" and noted moreover that she "was not born to doubt." Dr Ursilla MacDonnell, CFUW president in 1946–50, added that McWilliams derived great support from her home: Roland McWilliams was proud of his wife's attainments at a time when it was commonly thought appropriate for the husband to take the lead and the wife to follow.[32]

In January 1916 Manitoba was the first province in Canada to legislate votes for women. The single unifying aim of nineteenth-century feminists was achieved. Thenceforward, different women had different visions of what was best for women.

Such views were to a large extent framed by class. Both "feminism" and "class" are disputed terms.

"Feminism" has been a much-contested term during its century of usage, making it necessary for "scholars ... to invent their own definitions of feminism."[33] I use the following definition. *Feminism* is a set of beliefs and attitudes about the rightful place of women in society that contains at least three elements. First, the assumption is made that females are equal to males, in the sense that women in general ought not to be treated as inferior to men in general. Secondly, it is presumed that the condition of women is socially constructed: it is not predestined by God or "nature" but rather can be altered by human choice. Thirdly, it is assumed that women experience a consciousness of identification with other women as a social group.[34]

In this definition, paradoxes abound. Feminism implies a sexual equality that at the same time permits sexual difference. Feminism wants individual freedoms for women – each woman should be free to determine her own fate – yet, at the same time, feminism calls on women to work with other women, which usually means a subordination of individual priorities to those of a group, at least for certain aims and at certain times. There is thus a comprehending of both individualism and collectivism.

The definition is general enough to allow comparisons between different time periods and countries, but not so minimal as to admit all those who believe only that "women suffer from systematic social injustice because of their sex."[35] It has the merit of including the notion of a woman as both an individual and a relational human being, with responsibilities to and for other human beings as well as herself.[36]

The notion of identity, of what it means to be a woman, is problematic. The American historian Gerda Lerner elucidates the term "women's emancipation." Literally, "emancipation" means to be free from dominance, and with reference to women, it means freedom from oppressive restrictions imposed by men on women. But emancipation goes beyond the acquisition of civil rights and the abolition of gender-determined barriers. In the context of Western societies, emancipation comprehends also the positive notion of autonomy, which includes the freedom to make decisions concerning one's own body and the responsibility to arrange for self-support. For women at the beginning of the twentieth century, this insistence on self-definition required political and economic opportunities that implied a radical transformation of society.[37]

By the time of the First World War, some progress had been made. Before the end of the nineteenth century, women had been admitted to universities and property laws were reformed. In western Canada, the dower law, entitling a widow to occupy the family home at her husband's death, was under consideration at the time of the First World War. By the end of the war, most new democratic countries had enfranchised women. Thereafter, women in most Western societies worked in a variety of ways towards greater autonomy.

In the United States, the major issue to divide feminists was protective legislation. Egalitarian feminists wanted an equal rights amendment. They interpreted equal rights for women as meaning that women would enjoy the same legal and civil privileges and responsibilities as men. Consequently, they opposed legislation that would apply only to women. Supporters tended to be middle class, working and living in a context where they were, or expected to be, the professional colleagues of men. Insofar as they had, or expected to have, the domestic responsibilities of housekeeping and child rearing, their assumption was that they could purchase the services of other women to reduce their own direct involvement.[38]

Distinguished from these women were those whose acquaintance with the labour force was marked by monotony and toil and whose family responsibilities were direct and unremitting. Insofar as feminism was to offer a prospect of improvement in their lives, it could only be interpreted to be in terms of a reduction in drudgery and an increase in control over the means by which they managed their households. For such women, protective factory legislation could be seen as a practical improvement, and where such legislation was easier to obtain for women than for workers generally, they did not hesitate to support it. Feminists concerned with the immediate problems of women working in the segregated labour force were therefore reluctant to support an equal rights amendment that might prohibit the targeting of legislation designed to benefit women in the labour force or family.[39]

In England there was a similar division between the "'old' feminists who wanted to concentrate on individualist and egalitarian reforms and the 'new' feminists who favoured discriminatory welfare reforms as the way of bringing 'real' equality to woman in her distinctive role as mother."[40] The dilemma was described in a Fabian tract of 1914: middle-class feminists objected to the "parasitism" associated with women who were economically supported by a man, and tended to romanticize the nature of paid employment, which they saw as a panacea; working-class women, on the other hand, were chafing against their hard domestic work, augmented as it often was by work in the labour force, frequently as domestic servants, and they for their part tended to romanticize the attraction of being protected by a male breadwinner earning a satisfactory family wage. Both points of view had emerged in a society with few social services provided by the state and in a context where it was difficult, if not impossible, to imagine how motherhood could be combined, to women's benefit, with their wide-scale paid employment.[41]

A specific break in the feminist movement came in 1926 and 1927 when a split occurred in the National Union of Societies for Equal Citizenship (NUSEC), the successor organization to the National Union of Societies for Women's Suffrage. Egalitarian feminists left to form the Open Door Council or joined the Six Point Group in order to fight protective legislation and to remove what they deemed to be artificial barriers to women's progress. Feminists who remained in the NUSEC supported the efforts of its president, Eleanor Rathbone, to promote the idea of state-provided welfare payments to mothers in a scheme of family support. Women should be recognized as different, she thought. Rathbone was scornful of those in the habit of "continually measuring women's wants by men's achievements," a habit she said was "out of date, ignominious and intolerably boring."[42]

As debates in the United States and Britain reveal, "class" is central to an understanding of women in society. Yet "class" is a term that eludes precise definition when applied to women, especially in the context of an economically dynamic and ethnically mixed society such as Canada's in the early years of the twentieth century. The notion of an upper class, for a start, was difficult to apply to western Canada, where European sensibility to birth and nobility was scorned or ridiculed. The terms "middle class" and "working class" were more useful, at least when applied to men. The economic determinants of a man's class were the level of his income and its origin. Someone whose income was derived from investment, from a profession, or from the management of an enterprise was middle class. A man whose income was derived from manual labour was working class. Men who worked as salesmen or clerks were not so easy to categorize, nor were men who had a skilled trade, requiring apprenticeship and formal tests of admission. Occupation was the major, if not conclusive, determinant of class, but anomalies could arise with respect to income level.[43] It was not easy to classify low-paid white-collar workers.

In a society where factors besides income buttressed the primary categorization, where, for example, a person's education, location of housing, accent, and leisure pursuits tended to reinforce a distinction between middle and working class, then class might considerably influence the attitudes and aspirations of individuals. In the large industrial cities of nineteenth-century Western Europe and in the long-established villages of Eastern Europe, the opportunities realistically available were limited by resources not only of money but also of imagination. These societies were neither closed nor static, and there was considerable class mobility. Nevertheless, class-consciousness inevitably grew in conditions of class oppression. The few with wealth could live in relative ease and comfort, and the many without had little opportunity to acquire capital assets. The desire to live in a society untrammelled by old mentalities, together with the perceived chance to acquire wealth, inspired many to migrate to the New World. Immigrants to western Canada brought with them cultural baggage inherited from the Old Country, but the fact of emigration freed such people from some shackles of the old mind-set. In some immigrants, attitudes to class survived the journey intact. In others, class-consciousness was diluted or dissolved in a country where the most coveted asset of all, land, was there for the clearing, and work was to be had in most years before the Great Depression.

In Manitoba, ethnicity complicated the class structure. In the century 1870–1970, immigrants of Ontario-British origin controlled political and economic power. The lower class included working-class immigrants from Britain, other immigrants of non-British origin, and the province's aboriginal and Métis (mixed-blood) inhabitants. In rural Manitoba, members of the first group occupied most of the productive arable land in the southwest, and this division was mirrored in Winnipeg, which became "two distinct cities." The prosperous families of Ontario-British origin lived in the south and west of the city, while the "north end ... became a noisy, crowded ghetto."[44]

The ethnic division had obvious political and economic significance for the men who dominated public life. Early twentieth-century immigrants from Britain, together with East European and Jewish socialists, determined the provincial and municipal politics of the interwar years, beginning with the dramatic achievement of the Winnipeg General Strike of 1919.[45] In the 1920 provincial election, eleven Labour candidates were returned to the fifty-five–member Legislative Assembly. Ten of the eleven were of British origin.[46] In municipal politics, there was a city council of eighteen, of whom half were usually Labour in the interwar years. Most were recent British immigrants, but there were also one or two East European Jews.[47] Economically, ethnicity was as much a determinant of success, or, in the thirties, of survival strategy, as previous education and work experience. For Ukrainians, Poles, and Jews in 1931, "Winnipeg was far from being a city of 250,000 in which they ... were free to search for work. As much as two-thirds of it was barred and bolted against them."[48] For new immigrants, class and ethnicity tended to be directly related, but the connection grew looser in subsequent generations.[49]

Women did not experience class in the same way as men. To begin with, women had fewer options anyway. Most, if not all, women who came to western Canada were not expecting to be either homesteaders or wage earners, nor did they contemplate participation in politics. They were not as free as men to choose between alternative occupations, nor were they treated as independent agents by immigration officials. A woman was almost invariably linked to a man, who provided economic support in return for her "reproductive" services of housekeeping, childbearing, and child rearing. Most women therefore were viewed, and viewed themselves, as part of the family of the man. Their class was determined, as was their livelihood, by their husband's class or, in the case of unemployed single women, by their father's. Insofar as their husband's class wavered in any way between the old and the new countries, women's lot in life was parallel to the men's. There was a small number of women who migrated as single women: domestic servants, nurses, and teachers for the most part. The main determinant of their class was their occupation for so long as they were single. At the time of their marriage, their status tended to sink, or rise, to the level of that of their husband.[50]

In such circumstances, *class* is a shorthand term for what has been described as follows: "For women, class describes their relationship to the means of production *as mediated* through the man to whom they render sexual and reproductive services and/or the man on whom they are dependent in their family of origin. In the case of women who enjoy economic independence, 'class' still describes not only their relationship to the means of production, but their control (or lack thereof) over their reproductive capacity and their sexuality."[51]

During the interwar period, prominent feminists in the United States and Britain tended either to the idea that in all relevant ways a woman was the same as a man and therefore should enjoy the same rights and responsibilities, or to the idea that she was different and that her difference justified her enjoying rights and responsibilities that in some instances would be the same as a man's but in some others would be different but equivalent. The first of these positions was straightforward. The second carried more nuances and was also vulnerable to manipulation by antifeminists, who could argue that a woman's difference made her inferior. Nevertheless this second notion corresponded more to women's actual experience and future opportunities. Only recently have feminist scholars begun to articulate this position with care.[52]

Most leading Canadian feminists in McWilliams's time believed, as she did, in equal rights without the jettisoning of safeguards for women's unique reproductive functions.[53] Inter-war feminists were to be found in political, church, and welfare organizations, professional associations and trade unions, journalism, and, most visibly, in women's organizations like the local councils of women and other volunteer women's groups. Their major concerns were ideals "of service and caring for community and family," objectives that applied as much to middle-class women as to working-class women activists even though there was less unanimity among the former over how to achieve such goals.[54]

The Canadian historian Eliane Silverman has called for "many more biographical studies" of women in order to map a new "landscape" of Canadian history.[55] The recovery of these women's experiences would allow us to "redefine the meaning of being a woman and discover what masculine history has suppressed: how women make history and therefore who women are."[56] In Margaret McWilliams's life, we can see how she applied her personal resources of energy and intellect to the improvement of women's social conditions so that they would have more control over their lives. Her achievements and failures show one woman's way of formulating a new world. They also throw light on the society that gave women opportunities for public service but at the same time maintained barriers in their way.

Across Canada, the name of Margaret McWilliams is known to those students who are familiar with the scholarship established in her memory by the Canadian Federation of University Women in 1952, as well as to the members of that organization. She was one of twenty Canadian women selected for a series of brief biographies by the federation in 1966. Nevertheless, relatively few people are acquainted with that interwar generation of women active in the public sphere. This book is a contribution to a more complete comprehension of Canadian society through an analysis of one woman's understanding of feminism in action.

Writing a biography without being able to refer to a diary, memoir, or collection of letters is like making a journey without a clear itinerary. The place of certain milestones along the way is known, but it is often difficult to discern how, and above all why, the traveller chose one direction rather than another. In this case, the observations of other people were critical, as were the visible relics left behind by Margaret McWilliams herself.

McWilliams made occasional attempts to keep a systematic collection of things that were important to her. In 1924 she compiled a scrapbook of memorabilia and correspondence concerning her visit to Christiania (Oslo), Norway, where she attended the International Federation of University Women's meeting. Her travelling companion was Elsie Moore, an old friend from the Winnipeg University Women's Club. Together they produced for the scrapbook daily itineraries, postcards, a few snapshoots, and McWilliams's notes for a speech she delivered in London en route for the continent. McWilliams also included the letters she and her husband exchanged.

A similar effort to maintain a record was started in 1929, when the McWilliamses moved to a new house. Margaret bought a scrapbook with a printed frontispiece: "Margaret McWilliams, Her Book, 500 Stradbrooke Avenue, 1929." A few pages contain handwritten entries, but for the most part, in the form it has survived, it is a haphazard collection of news clippings, her husband's draft articles on politics and economics, and a few personal references.

When the McWilliamses moved to Manitoba's Government House in 1940, they both were seized with the intention to keep a "journal of happenings," in Margaret's words. She bought a locked journal. However, in April 1941 she wrote, "The days have gone by too swiftly to allow me to make even a single entry," and that pattern persisted. The heavy red-leather volume became the repository of notes for wartime current events classes, interspersed with a few narratives written by Roland of notable visits to Government House. These volumes offer no evidence that Margaret McWilliams ever felt the need to put her own life in perspective.[57]

We therefore lack mundane details that might elaborate upon events, and we rarely see self-expressed motivation. Her considered judgment on what was significant, and what was not, is unavailable to us in a direct form. The only way to know McWilliams is through her deeds and through the perceptions of others. Perhaps she found a memoir impossible to write.

Her life can be seen as an example of "a brave attempt to live a life for which there was no pattern."[58]

Gerda Lerner reminds us that an historian attempts to "recreate the life and times of her subject from within the consciousness of her subject and from within the context of her time."[59] Yet a biographer can only select from available evidence.

The first retrospectives were the obituaries. McWilliams died on a Saturday, and on the following Monday both the *Winnipeg Free Press* and the *Winnipeg Tribune* carried long news items, beginning on the first page, describing her career, and additionally, each devoted an editorial to her.[60] Subsequent days carried tributes, and her funeral was given extensive coverage. Appreciations were printed in other publications, such as the *Chronicle* of the Canadian Federation of University Women and *Canadian Welfare*.[61]

Other written overviews of her entire life can be found. Less than a year before McWilliams's death, Kathleen Strange published an article, "Margaret McWilliams of Manitoba," in the *Canadian Home Journal*. Strange lived in Winnipeg and was able to use her personal acquaintance to inform an exuberant account: "Margaret McWilliams of Manitoba? Is it not truer to say, Margaret McWilliams of Canada? Or, perhaps, Margaret McWilliams, good citizen of the world!"[62] After McWilliams's death, Amy Roe produced for the *Country Guide* "a personal sketch in tribute to one who lately moved among us, who because of her talents and work became truly a leader of women and a great Canadian."[63]

Interviews with intimate friends enlivened the longest and best of these overviews, Betty Jane Wylie's chapter in Mary Quayle Innis's *The Clear Spirit* (1966). Finally, there are two tributes produced by members of the Winnipeg University Women's Club. The first, a slide-tape show produced by Bernice Cunnington and Helen Norrie in 1974, is a summary of her career, and the second, by Rosemary Malaher in 1985, is an examination of some of McWilliams's interests.[64] Together, these retrospects provide a guide, with places and dates, for the new traveller.

None of these accounts analyses McWilliams's writings. Besides the two books she co-authored with her husband and the two she wrote alone, she left the unfinished typescript of a history of the wheat pools, "The Battle of Wheat" or "The Battle of the Giants."[65] In addition, "an incessant stream of unsigned newspaper articles and editorials about Europe flowed from her pen."[66] It is not possible to identify all her writing, but the articles on China published by the *Manitoba Free Press* in 1931 were clearly hers, as were her contributions to *Canada and Her Great Neighbour* (1938).[67] She also wrote the report of a royal commission subcommittee in 1943.[68]

McWilliams spent much of her time in committees, where at least decisions, and sometimes discussion, were recorded in the minutes. Committee work began in high school, and there is some documentation of her career both at Harbord Collegiate Institute and at the University of Toronto.[69] Minutes afford evidence of her actions and frequently her attitudes. Prime archives of this sort are the minutes of the University Women's Club, the Women's Canadian Club, the Local Council of Women, the Canadian Federation of University Women, the Council of the City of Winnipeg, and the Manitoba Historical Society.[70]

There are also reports of meetings where she spoke as an officer or guest of an association. Her connection with the National Council of Education was documented in the *Western School Journal*.[71] Some of her work as vice-president of the International Federation of University Women was reported in that organization's *Chronicle*.[72] One set of minutes that provides an exhilarating exception to the somewhat solemn recording of business is that of the CFUW for the year 1936.[73] The recorder transcribed the conversation of those present, along with their frequent interruptions. Irritation and impatience leap off the page. This gives one of only a few opportunities we have to pierce the facade of controlled serenity emanating from McWilliams's public persona.

Once or twice newspaper reports of her activities and speeches manage to get under the surface. In 1938 Alderman McWilliams was fined for illegal parking, and later a City Council meeting was enlivened by her wondering whether the police had nothing better to do in their leisure time than tag cars on side streets.[74] Most news reports give the impression of a woman attracting respect, recognized by her community, and highly regarded for her efforts. Winnipeg newspapers conducted feature interviews with her.[75] As noted, at her death, obituaries appeared across Canada.[76] This press coverage provides an invaluable source of information on her public appearances.

Although there is no single collection of correspondence, nevertheless some has been preserved, both in formal archival collections and by members of her family. Her letters belie the impression of pomposity occasionally implied by the press. She rarely employed platitudes and was concise both in substantive communication and in her invocation of the immediate circumstances of writing. One letter to her brother Russell, just before her death in 1952, had to do with books but it was interspersed with a running commentary on the interruptions she was experiencing. First, she noted, she had a telephone call from a young man "on his way to see me about an accident we had with the car the other evening." Three paragraphs later she wrote, "At this moment the young man arrived and I have spent a good twenty minutes with him."[77] The few letters that remain have been liberally used in this book to give a firsthand impression of her character.

Finally, an informal archive exists in the recollections of people who knew her. Women and men who worked with her in clubs, organizations, or on City Council, and who attended current events classes continue to carry their own personal memories. These sometimes grow dim and have been influenced by what others have said and written, but this memory bank has proved most useful. Conversations and interviews with people, some of whom knew her as early as the 1920s, have provided me with invaluable information.

Three months after her marriage, Margaret McWilliams wrote a parable, "The Land of the Heart's Desire," which she bound in leather as a Christmas gift for her husband. Describing in biblical tones "a quest made by two true lovers" for happiness together, she declared they had now "entered into the land we have greatly sought, even the land of the Heart's Desire. Let us dwell in it and possess it nor ever depart therefrom."[78] From this enclave of personal trust and security, Margaret McWilliams launched her career. She rarely revealed her feelings, but her activities became a matter of record, making a story that depicts interwar feminism as much as her own life history.

CHAPTER TWO

Foundations

Maggie May Stovel was born 27 January 1875. Her father was Samuel Stovel, a successful Toronto tailor, and her mother, Tomasina ("Tassie") Callaway, was the daughter of Margaret Rodger Callaway. The Rodgers were "all Scotch," and a family legend spoke of an ancestress aiding Bonnie Prince Charlie to escape from England after his defeat in the 1745 Rebellion. Another relative was the engineer in charge of the bridge over the Firth of Forth, a construction marvel of its time. One of three sisters, each of whom was deserted by her husband, Grandmother Callaway was a woman of energy and ability who established "the most fashionable dressmaking establishment in Toronto" on Temperance Street. A pious Presbyterian, she was clever and brainy, like Margaret, who bore a physical resemblance to her. Grandfather Callaway, originally from Newmarket, England, went off with another woman to the southern United States. Grandmother Callaway raised three children: two sons, Sam and Will, who started to work in the railroad business at the ages of eleven and thirteen, and Tassie, who married Samuel Stovel.[1]

Samuel Stovel's father, Henry Stovel, was born in 1800, son of a kitchen carpenter in Goodwood, Sussex.[2] He was a dispatch rider to one of the Duke of Wellington's staff, and family lore relates that he served at the Battle of Waterloo. He married Sarah Carr, from a London fishmonger's family, and their first child was born in 1824.[3] Samuel, Margaret's father, born in 1841, was the tenth of Henry and Sarah's eleven children. They moved around: the first child was born in Boulogne, France, and the next eight were born at six different addresses in London. The last two, Samuel and his younger brother, Ebenezer, were born in the countryside at Faversham, Kent.[4]

In 1850 Henry Stovel migrated to Canada. One of his brothers, Joseph, had settled already in Toronto. Joseph Stovel, referred to as "the Governor" and known for being "pretty much of a dandy in dress," had built the "Stovel Offices" on King Street, Toronto, and occupied part of this impressive three-storey building with his tailoring business.[5] When Henry came to Canada with his children, he settled on a farm near Mount Forest, northwest of Toronto. Eventually members of his large family dispersed to all parts of Canada and the United States. Two who were later important in Margaret's life were Henry junior, whose sons settled in Winnipeg and established a printing firm, and David, who went to Detroit and practised medicine. Her own father, Samuel, joined his Uncle Joseph's tailoring business, and when Joseph died, Samuel became part owner and manager. He also invested in bank stock.[6]

Samuel Stovel married Tomasina Callaway in 1874. They lived at 51 Wellesley Street East, and this was where the three Stovel children were born. One evening in September 1880, Samuel died at the age of thirty-nine. Maggie May (Margaret) was five, her brother Russell was two, and baby Hodder was six months old. Tassie described the event in a letter to her aunt: "We had eaten supper together after he had returned from his business and I went to attend to some household duties. When next I saw him sitting in the chair on the verandah (some few moments after I left him) I thought he had fainted or something of the kind. We had Drs here as soon as possible but all of no avail – his spirit had gone back to God who gave it and I was alone, a widow, in this poor world. Drs said he had no consciousness of anything but going to sleep and as my little girl was with him all the time playing around – he could have had no idea of danger or he would have called for me."[7] Tassie's nearest relative was her mother's sister, Mrs Brown. She was sent for and arrived to find Tassie in hysterical tears. Mrs Brown later told the story of this episode to an impressionable Hodder, pronouncing as well her unsympathetic judgment that his mother had made a fool of herself. "Young as I was, I never forgave her for talking of my mother, whom I had never really known, in that way," wrote Hodder in his memoirs.[8]

Samuel's estate was worth $40,000, a considerable asset for a young man of thirty-nine to have built up. However, some of this was invested in the stock of a bank that failed, and the estate was reduced by a half.[9] Margaret never remembered her mother smiling after Samuel's death. Hodder attributed this lack of joy partly to his parents' religion. Samuel had been raised a Baptist and Tassie a Presbyterian, but they had both become ardent Plymouth Brethren.

The children were raised by their mother for only a further five years. In 1885 she too died. They were then orphans, and until Margaret was twenty-one, they were under the guardianship of Tassie's brother Bill and his wife, Emma, who lived at 40 Willcocks Street in Toronto.[10] This "very modest" neighbourhood in the vicinity of the University of Toronto is "a stone's throw from where College Street crosses Spadina Avenue." As a young man, Uncle Bill had snow white hair and dark eyebrows. Short and not handsome, "his face certainly caught the eyes." Though kindly, he was a stern disciplinarian. This could mean the strap for Hodder and Russell, but not for "Sis." Punishment could also include memorizing parts of the Bible. When Hodder called Russell a fool, he had to recite "He that calleth his brother a fool is in danger of hellfire and damnation" every Sunday morning for three months.

Aunt Emma was a placid woman, but she had quarrelled with her sister-in-law Tassie, and the boys felt that Emma did not welcome their entry into the household. They were together at the house on Willcocks Street for less than three years, but Hodder credited this experience as a formative period in his life. "If I have had a certain amount of success in my life" (which he did, as a mining engineer and executive) "quite a lot of that was due to the principles [Uncle Bill] tried to induce in me."[11] We do not have Margaret's direct testimony, but we know she preferred living with the Bill Callaways to an alternative presented in 1887.

Hodder's memories of this time were by no means all grim. The three Stovel children visited their Grandfather Stovel, whom Margaret remembered as "a very good looking old man, pink cheeks and white hair and beard. Always well groomed and sitting in an arm or rocking chair smoking a pipe." They also visited the youngest Stovel uncle, Eb. Eb's wife, Harriet, known as Aunt Harry, was very kind and "the loveliest memory" of Hodder's childhood.[12] Uncle Eb for a brief time managed what had been Samuel's tailoring business but then became a manufacturer's agent handling English woollens and silks. He and Aunt Harry lived in Rosedale in a house that had a dumb waiter, "often kept busy raising and lowering children." Outside, the children could roam on the farmland that extended immediately beyond the house. Aunt Harry sang, painted watercolours, went riding, and was an enthusiastic fisherman. After supper she would sit with the children in front of the fire and tell goblin tales, and as an extra treat she might play on her harp.[13]

The Stovel orphans spent most of the rest of their childhood separated from one another. In 1887 Bill Callaway's brother Sam and his family came to spend Christmas in Toronto. Uncle Sam had done very well in railways, and by his mid-thirties he was president of the Southern Pacific Railroad, with headquarters in Omaha. He suggested that Margaret move in with his family rather than continue living with Uncle Bill. At the same time it was proposed that Hodder should live in the countryside, which would be good for his failing health, and that their brother Russell should attend boarding school. Russell was sent to Upper Canada College, and Hodder, to Selwyn, near Peterborough, to board with Tassie's cousin Mrs Manning, daughter of the Mrs Brown whom Hodder so resented for her unkind comment on his mother. Hodder and Russell accompanied Margaret on her exploratory trip to the Sam Callaway household in Omaha. Sam sent his private railway car to fetch the Bill Callaways and the Stovel orphans. It was the most luxurious trip Hodder ever made, but Margaret decided to return to Toronto.[14]

Margaret made a very close friend who lived on the same street, Helen Grant Easson. Their friendship lasted a lifetime and was reinforced by ties of marriage. Russell married Helen in 1901. Hodder further strengthened the bonds when he married Helen's sister, Margaret Grant Easson, in 1907.[15] On Margaret Stovel's part, the connection extended to the next generation through her great affection for the daughter of Russell and Helen, also named Helen.

As soon as she could, Margaret abandoned the diminutive "Maggie May" in favour of the more dignified "Margaret."[16] When she started school at the age of fourteen, she rapidly became a star pupil, according to Hodder.[17] Harbord Collegiate Institute opened in January 1892, and Margaret attended in the academic years 1892–93 and 1893–94. In June 1893 she passed the Junior Leaving Examination, and the following summer she was one of seven to gain first-class honours in the Senior Leaving Examination. In the subject examinations, she gained first-class standing in English, history, and geography, and second-class standing in French, German, and mathematics.[18] She was an associate editor of the *Harbord Collegiate Review* for both 1893 and 1894, and treasurer of the Literary Society. In the *Review,* under the prescient heading "Among the Disputative Young Ladies," Margaret was noted as president of the Girls' Debating Society for 1893–94.[19]

At Harbord, Margaret "came under one of the formative influences of her life in the personality and teaching of Miss Gertrude Lawler."[20] Lawler was a judge for the Girls' Debating Society and taught English.[21] Margaret was grateful to her for "breeding or stimulating within [her pupils] that power to think for themselves, which is the true test of the value of a genuine educator."[22] Two of Margaret's four colleagues in the Debating Society were later Winnipeg neighbours, Amy Morison and W.T. Allison. Amy Morison became head of Havergal College Day School in Winnipeg and a charter member of the Women's Canadian Club. W.T. Allison became an English professor at the University of Manitoba and literary editor of the *Winnipeg Tribune.*[23]

Through school and family, Margaret had come to know several women of strong personality and unusual independence. Lawler was a well-educated single professional, and there were women in the Rodger and Stovel families whose reputation accustomed Margaret to the importance of self-sufficiency. That was a lesson she rapidly learned through her own experience in any case. Orphaned at the age of ten, she became used to fending for herself. In the life of her imagination, she enjoyed the novels of George Eliot, with their strong female protagonists. These impressive female role models reflected, too, the new opportunities for women in education and the professions – options introduced in response to feminists of the nineteenth-century women's movement.

The University of Toronto had only recently opened its doors to women. In the early 1880s women were permitted to compete for scholarships, and by 1884 they were attending classes at University College. Ten years later, in 1894, when Margaret entered the university, 19 women graduated from University College along with 139 men.[24] They were not universally welcome. Charles W. Gordon, who was to be Margaret's pastor at the Presbyterian St. Stephen's, Broadway, Church in Winnipeg, confessed to "a secret feeling ... that something of the lofty splendour of university life had departed with the advent of women ... Though we found the young ladies charming, if somewhat exclusive in their ways, there remained an indefinable regret at the passing of a certain virility from university life at the coming of 'the skirts.'"[25]

The honour course in political science was in 1894 under the "monarchical" direction of its second professor of political economy and constitutional history, James Mavor. He considered that governments would have to rely on the advice of applied social scientists, who should be trained in economics, constitutional and economic history, modern history, public finance, political philosophy, jurisprudence, and law. Margaret's interest in all these subjects remained with her the rest of her life. During her four years at University College, she (and her fellow students, including Roland McWilliams and future prime minister Mackenzie King) studied the political economy of Adam Smith, Malthus, and Ricardo, and the political philosophy of Plato, Aristotle, Hobbes, Locke, Rousseau, Burke, Bentham, Herbert Spencer, and T.H. Green. John Stuart Mill was not included in the curriculum.[26]

Without Margaret's own account of her intellectual development, we cannot be sure whose ideas made the most impact. In retrospect, T.H. Green's philosophy seems to have provided a guiding light for her own behaviour. Green was a British philosopher suspicious of John Stuart Mill's individualism and "hedonistic theory."[27] He considered that Mill's understanding of freedom was too negative, objecting to Mill's belief that the state should refrain from limiting the freedom of individuals. Green thought this was a mockery of the conditions under which the vast majority of the population lived. Freedom required power, and Green thought the state should provide positive opportunities for citizens to fulfil themselves and do good for society.[28] In his 1882 *Prolegomena to Ethics*, Green described a civic idealism in which "the life of citizenship is a mode of divine service": the life most worth living was that "which finds its nurture and its sphere of realisation in that supreme institution, the organised State." Although he agreed with Mill that the state should not unduly restrict the individual, he nevertheless believed the state should legislate, for example, the control of drinking "in order that [citizens] may become more free to exercise the faculties and improve the talents which God has given them."[29] Green's ideas had a powerful effect on the intellectuals who formulated the social gospel of Margaret's youth, and were part of the air she breathed in Toronto in the 1890s.[30]

Always eager for debate, Margaret joined the Women's Literary Society of University College, "the most prominent organisation among the women undergraduates," and by the beginning of her second year, she was the society's corresponding secretary. It met regularly on alternate Saturday evenings, occasions that "afford the girls ... their rare glimpses into that very distant promised land, the gymnasium." Its work "embraces all sides of student life, from grave to gay." The executive arranged debates, enacted scenes from plays, had "musical numbers," and heard literary, scientific, or political reports. The society entertained at two receptions, one for new students and one in honour of the faculty. At the final session, elections were held for the next year's officers.[31] This same variety of activities was to recur in the programs of the Winnipeg University Women's Club.

As corresponding secretary, Margaret made regular reports to the university newspaper, the *Varsity*.[32] She also wrote a spirited defence of the executive, which was attacked for developing "aesthetic tastes" above "sterner mental training." Margaret supported the program of dramatic re-enactments: "Is not the act of interpreting and personating one of the creations of a master mind, such as Tennyson or Shakespeare, just as much an act of mental training as the arguing of such questions as are usually argued before such a Society?" There was also a practical benefit: "It is much easier to persuade the members to take part in the dramatic selections than to get them to argue on a debate; and it has been thought that the first act would probably make the second seem easier." She concluded: "Never have the meetings been so largely attended as now."[33]

She was not without her own critics. One such critic, "R," reported on the "Representation of the Women of George Eliot," in which Margaret took the role of Mrs Bede, "furnishing the comedy of the piece." "R," whose acquaintance with the society had been limited to the "soul-starving reports in *Varsity*," was surprised to discover the society actually was "a more civilising agent to the University" than many lectures.[34]

In 1896 Margaret was active not only in the Women's Literary Society but also in the Modern Languages Club, to which she presented a paper reviewing Mrs Humphrey Ward's novel *Marcella*. The plot concerned problems of labour and capital, but its main appeal for Margaret lay in the delineation of Marcella, like herself an orphan, "deprived of her mother." Margaret unfavourably compared Ward with George Eliot, for whom she had great respect, believing her to be "perhaps the very greatest English novelist."[35]

Margaret chose to impersonate Dorothea Brooke of Eliot's *Middlemarch* when the Women's Literary Society accepted the invitation of the new governor general's wife, Lady Aberdeen, to attend her 1897 Historical Ball in costumes of characters taken from well-known novelists. *Sesame*, "the annual publication of the women graduates and undergraduates of University College," originating in 1897, published a five-page account of the ball.[36] The students designed their own clothes, and "Miss M.M. Stovel in plain grey-blue gown and white fur, hair very simply braided," joined colleagues in costumes of characters from other novels by Eliot and from works by Swinburne, Browning, and Gilbert and Sullivan.[37] Margaret was later to become more intimately acquainted with the work of Lady Aberdeen, founder of the National Council of Women.

In December 1897 Margaret was elected as one of the two students to debate with Victoria University women on the motion "Resolved, that the training received from the study of Natural Sciences is more beneficial than the training received from the study of literature." The debate was held two months later, and the University College women lost.[38]

Margaret graduated third in her class, with an honours degree in political economy.[39] She gained more than a degree from the University of Toronto. She learned success and failure in running for office. She was active in the Ladies' Glee Club and became its president. There, "she learned to handle people."[40] Although she was nominated as president of the Women's Literary Society in her final year, she was not elected.[41] She gained practical experience as a journalist, publishing reports in the *Varsity* and working on its editorial board. She served on the board of *Torontonensis,* the first year book that she helped to found, and from October to December 1897 she wrote a weekly column, "The College Girl," in the *Varsity* under the pen-name "Carr." Distinctively presented under a chequered arch, most of the copy was written by Margaret, who identified herself in the last issue.[42] She discovered, too, that she shared many interests, in public affairs, debating, and journalism, with a fellow student, Roland McWilliams, who also contributed to the *Varsity* before his graduation in 1897.[43]

Until 1896 Margaret continued to live with the Callaways, but then the Canadian Pacific Railway, for whom Bill worked, transferred him to Minneapolis as general passenger agent. In the same year, Margaret's younger brother, Hodder, came back from the Manning farm to attend Harbord Collegiate Institute. She then lived in a boarding house at 70 Brunswick Avenue run for women students, and Hodder moved into the attic. He later recalled that he and his sister were "poor as church mice," living off the interest from their father's depleted estate. Hodder considered that these young days as an orphan accentuated his own independent ways.[44]

Margaret graduated in 1898. In those days women university graduates had few career choices. The first women graduates of the University of Manitoba in 1889 could "think of nothing for women but teaching school," and similarly, nineteenth-century Dalhousie graduates went mainly into teaching.[45] But "teaching, as a profession, did not attract [Margaret], so she turned her mind to a journalistic career."[46]

Margaret had already some experience in journalism. Yet there were few openings, and editors were reluctant to hire women. One regular feature of most newspapers by the 1890s was a woman's page, and women reporters were generally confined to this. However, with extensive public interest in the women's movement, which embraced issues of employment and education as well as suffrage, many newspapers augmented fashion and society reporting with discussion of more contentious issues.[47]

Margaret was fortunate in getting work in Minneapolis, where she could live again with the Bill Callaways. The woman's editor of the *Minneapolis Journal* was spending a year in Europe, and Margaret took her place.[48] In 1901 she secured a permanent position with the *Detroit Journal*, and boarded with her father's brother, David Stovel.[49]

The *Minneapolis Journal* had a regular Saturday page, "Womankind," and during the week frequently published a column under the title "In Woman's World." Some columns carried the name of the writer, but none carred the byline of Margaret Stovel. One feature whose form she was later to duplicate was the Saturday supplement, "The Journal Junior." This carried pages of letters written by children from school addresses, puzzles, poems, "Books for Young People," a feature, "Feathered Friends of Field and Forest," and a leader page on domestic and international politics. There was also information on how to form "Journal Junior" clubs.[50]

On the *Detroit Journal* Margaret was the society and music editor.[51] As well as noting the pastimes of the Detroit elite, her job involved reporting on the programs and participants of the many women's organizations, such as the Detroit Woman's Club, the Twentieth Century Club, Tuesday Musicale, Hypatia, the Woman's Historical Club, the Home Study Club, and Per Gradus.[52] Every Saturday there was a regular page, "Music, Art and Society," and this included reviews of concerts and recitals and often interviews with performers. She was rarely named, but in two consecutive years "M.S." reported from the annual music festival in Ann Arbor.[53] Her colleagues said that "every piece of work that she handled was well and effectively done … A good deal of Miss Stovel's strength lay in her originality and her executive ability."[54]

Her flair for organization, if not her originality, was tested when she introduced the "Journal Junior" in 1901. Beginning in September 1901, the Detroit "Journal Junior" took one page, in the Saturday edition. Its sections paralleled those of the *Minneapolis Journal:* "The Editor's Word," "Constance Gets Curious," "Roosevelt Stories," "The Puzzle Corner," "Letters," and "Books." "The Editor's Word" rendered domestic and international politics accessible, foreshadowing her current events classes of some fifteen year later. Margaret instituted an essay contest, and an early topic was, "Which would you rather be, a man or a woman, when you grow up? Why?"[55] After January 1902 the "Journal Junior" progressed to a weekly four-page supplement.[56] When she left Detroit, the newspaper noted that "for the first two years of its existence Miss Stovel and The Journal Junior were synonymous to the thousands and thousands of children and teachers who read the little sheet every week."[57] Her colleagues, too, expected to miss her. At the time of her marriage, Margaret's "fellow newspaper workers" gave her "a complete chafing dish outfit in silver."[58]

In 1903 Margaret married Roland Fairbairn McWilliams. Roland was from Peterborough, where his great-grandparents, all Ulster Presbyterians, had migrated to Canada in the 1820s. His father was J.B. McWilliams, an inspector of Crown timber agencies for the province. J.B. McWilliams was on the Board of Education, an official in the Orange Lodge, and a member of the Peterborough Council for some years.[59] In 1888 he built an elaborate house on Water Street, where Roland grew up.[60]

Peterborough at the end of the nineteenth century was being transformed from a lumbering centre into an industrialized city based on hydroelectricity produced by the rapids on the Otonabee River. The two chief companies were Canadian General Electric, established there in 1890, and Quaker Oats, in 1900.[61] Roland attended local schools and the University of Toronto, graduating two years earlier than Margaret with an honours degree in political science in 1896. He then studied law at Osgoode Hall, graduating in 1899. He returned to practise law in Peterborough.

By the time of his marriage, Roland had already made a political name for himself. "I was introduced to the political platform at the age of nineteen when I was thrown into the middle of a Conservative meeting." The McWilliams family was Liberal and Roland continued the tradition. "From that time on, I campaigned constantly in every election."[62] Elected as an alderman for the first time in January 1903, he topped the poll with a margin of over 100 votes over the next candidate.[63] His wedding was announced in the summer. Roland later recalled "with amusement" that there was criticism in Peterborough when it became known he was to marry Margaret Stovel. "For one thing, his fiancée was reputed to be extremely clever ... she was thought to be an American ... and she was not an accomplished homebody ... but had concentrated her efforts on a successful livelihood in the business world."[64] They were married at the Callaway home in Minneapolis in the evening of 3 September 1903 by a Congregationalist pastor.

Margaret wore her mother's wedding dress. Her uncle Bill Callaway gave her away and her aunt was matron of honour.[65] The occasion also marked the twenty-fifth wedding anniversary of the Callaways, and about a hundred friends were invited to a later reception. There, a quartet sang "many of the sweet old ballads and folk songs," and guests heard appropriate wedding music played by a stringed orchestra. The bride and groom left at midnight for a tour to the Pacific Coast and planned to return to Peterborough by 1 November.[66]

Roland resumed his law practice and involvement in municipal politics, again heading the poll in January 1904. Almost immediately he was one of four hopefuls seeking the Liberal Party nomination for the federal election in Peterborough West, but failed. In the Peterborough Council he tried to have all committee meetings opened to the press, but was defeated. The mayor said "members of the committees would talk for publication ... time would be consumed and business retarded." Roland was also unsuccessful in an atttempt to reform the system of municipal government and ensure that the council was "representative of all classes."[67] Roland McWilliams was already earning a reputation for talking a lot.

In the autumn of 1904 Roland stood briefly as an independent candidate in Peterborough West, thereby making a mistake that was to haunt his subsequent Peterborough career. Withdrawing long before the federal election, he reverted to the Liberals with prominent work on behalf of their candidate in the neighbouring constituency of Peterborough East, who won the seat.[68] A provincial election was expected to come soon, and hot on the heels of this Liberal victory Roland succeeded in being chosen the provincial Liberal candidate for Peterborough West, replacing the retiring member, J.R. Stratton, businessman and publisher of the *Peterborough Examiner*. Election day was announced as 25 January 1905. Throughout the campaign the *Examiner* gave Roland enthusiastic support. When, however, he was defeated, the newspaper bluntly blamed not only the "inopportune time" but his previous "unpardonable disloyalty."[69]

In January 1906 he was again elected alderman.[70] The next year, "in 1907, I was elected Mayor in the teeth of bitter opposition from both party organisations and both newspapers."[71] He had a majority of 221 in the largest mayoralty vote ever polled.[72]

Great was his fall, therefore, when after only a year in office, he was denied the customary courtesy of a second term. "Never … in the history of the city, was there a more spontaneous and general demand for a change as expressed in both the mayoralty candidature and in giving it effect."[73] This humiliating defeat was a key to the McWilliamses' departure from Peterborough in 1910.

The Tory *Review*, while acknowledging that Roland meant well, blamed his "method of conducting civic business." He spent too much time trying "to induce every representative to see eye to eye with him."[74] The Liberal *Examiner*, which greeted Roland's defeat with "profound satisfaction," agreed. In an editorial three days before the election, it wrote of the mayor as follows: "He may speak with the tongue of men and angels, if he has not good business abilities, it profiteth nothing."[75] Roland was hampered by two difficulties during his mayoralty. One was a tax reassessment, which meant that most taxes, business as well as personal, increased. The Canadian General Electric Company, for instance, complained that its assessment had been increased by 90 percent since the previous year.[76] Secondly, a program of sewer expansion resulted in much shoddy work and the discovery, for example, that there were gaps where pipes were supposed to be joined.[77]

Roland later considered that his defeat was due to "a political combination, both parties to which were afraid of my becoming a candidate in the coming Dominion election."[78] At the time, he interpreted it as a personal blow delivered by the *Examiner's* publisher, J.R. Stratton, whose election practices were considered dubious by Roland.[79] Roland's resentment was made explicit when Stratton sought the federal Liberal nomination for Peterborough West in the fall of 1908. At a public meeting, Roland declared his opposition and exposed himself in turn to public denunciation from a Liberal official who reminded the audience that Roland McWilliams "offered his services to the Conservatives" in 1904.[80] Forty years later Roland depicted Peterborough politics as a story "of gross political corruption and dishonesty."[81]

Roland had burned his bridges. He continued to work as a captain with the 57th Regiment Peterborough Rangers and to practise law, but as a politician he had no future, at least for the short term.[82] Alienated from the most powerful Liberal in Peterborough and mistrusted by the Conservatives, he would have difficulty remaining in public life. His law business as well was not particularly successful. In retrospect he acknowledged that "my interests were too many and took up so much of my time and interest that I did not make the success in law that I might have made."[83] Besides his political involvements, he had captained the rugby football team and had worked with the Young Men's Christian Association (YMCA).

"By the Spring of 1910 I had made up my mind to leave Peterborough." Roland first thought of Toronto, but friends and associates advised against it. "Toronto was somewhat stagnant, and the profession much overcrowded."[84] Western Canada beckoned in the popular imagination. As recently as April 1907, another Peterborough lawyer, R.M. Dennistoun, had left for Winnipeg, "which, he believed, in a short time, would be the commercial metropolis of Canada."[85] At Dennistoun's suggestion, Roland visited Winnipeg and arranged to enter the law firm of Sir James Aikins.

"There was one other consideration which greatly influenced my leaving Peterborough" – the reception accorded his wife. "I brought to Peterborough the ablest woman the town has ever known but the animosities toward me were carried into social life against her as well and she spent seven years without being given an opportunity to put her talents to any use whatever."[86] When "Aunt Marg" married, according to family legend, she was disappointed in giving up her career but determined to become the best cook in Peterborough.[87] Immediately on return from their honeymoon, she said that "she would receive" her first week back, and thereafter on the third and fourth Fridays of the month. In the spring, she announced an end to receiving in May.[88] She reappeared in the newspaper's social column occasionally, note being made of her holiday visits to the McWilliams cottage, "Tecumseh Lodge," at Stony Lake, where she sometimes entertained friends, including the Toronto Eassons.[89]

Margaret was not altogether subdued. When the annual report of the public library was presented in 1906, she attended the meeting and contributed to "General Business." "Speaking on behalf of the ladies," she complained about the magazines supplied for their use. "She pointed out that many magazines which the ladies would like to read were found in the men's reading room and suggested that some arrangement might be made by which these might be supplied to the ladies. She also spoke of the difficulty experienced in obtaining the new books that came into the library."[90]

She was made an honorary member of the new Woman's Art Association, probably as she was the mayor's wife. She became secretary of the Protestant Home of Management and then became active in the Children's Aid Society.[91] When the McWilliamses left Peterborough in 1910, "The North End Reading Circle" gave a tea for Margaret and presented her with a silver entree dish.[92] Indeed, she seems to have fared better than her husband. The *Peterborough Examiner*, then under instructions from Stratton that Roland McWilliams's name should never appear in it, noted no farewell presentation to Roland.[93] The Tory *Review* reported an informal banquet, organized by the officers of the 57th Regiment, to honour Roland. At that event, the commanding officer "referred in most commendatory terms" to the "active part taken by Captain McWilliams in civic, political, social, educational, and religious affairs."[94]

Roland's nephew later recalled that "of course, Aunt Margaret attempted to start discussion groups – and these were resented." He thought there was "little understanding or advantage taken of her talents while they lived in Peterborough."[95] Roland later wondered, "How, in face of what she had done and subsequently did, she stood the seven years in Peterborough, I do not know ... it must have been purgatory."[96] Margaret left no stories of her Peterborough past. Winnipeg was the start of a new life.

The McWilliamses moved west in late summer, 1910. They took with them a personal life described by a close friend and colleague of Margaret's as her "anchor and personal fufilment ... sweetened with married affection."[97] Euphorically described by Margaret in 1903 as "The Land of the Heart's Desire," the McWilliamses' marriage was considered by Roland as a "haven." He was confident that its "love, truth, sympathy, joy," would always be waiting through future "trouble and strife ... defeat and victory, and the heartburning that must surely come."[98] They were fortunate: their marriage remained successful.

When Margaret sent engagement congratulations to her niece Helen in 1932 and her nephew Bruce in 1947, she referred both obliquely and directly to her own experience. "If you are surprised now how love can grow miraculously," she wrote to Helen, "I think you will find yourselves more astonished after a time for it comes to be something of which you cannot even think of as being separate from yourself. Oh, my dears, I hope it may be so with you. You are enough like me, Helen, to be very unhappy if it is not."[99] Three weeks later she told Helen that her wishes and hopes were for "the days, and weeks and months and years that follow after" and added "Oh well, we're pretty much alike, you and I, and if you and Lawrence can make as good a job of it as Roly and I have done, you'll be quite ready to cheer other young people along the way as hopefully and happily as we do you."[100]

To Bruce, fifteen years later, she spoke of her fear that he had been settling into "bachelordom." "Having experienced a happy marriage" herself, she wished him to have "as long and close and happy companionship as Roly and I have had and are still having after all the years with their ups and downs."[101] She was corroborated in a vivid letter to Bruce from Roland:

That was great news that overtook us while we were in the mountains. All the more appreciated because we spent our honeymoon in the mountains and, as we travelled through them, we renewed the memories of 1903. I am delighted to hear that you are going to be married. A marriage partnership adds immensely to the life of anyone and you have wisely waited long enough to use judgment as well as feeling in place of what may only be a passing passion when you are young. I was almost twenty-nine when I was married.

I like, too, what you tell us about the girl. That might be taken for granted, but it is all the better to know that she has grown up in University circles and that consequently you two will have a large stock of experiences and ideas in common. That's what makes married life a permanent success. I was impressed when I was young with the fact that many couples seemed only one-half married for their interests were entirely different outside of their homes and families.[102]

The McWilliamses took pleasure in each other's company. Family members noted how much time they spent together.[103] Others noticed that Roland and Margaret shared the same interests. Roland once explicitly described it approvingly as an "intellectual rather than romantic" marriage.[104] But there was room for some romance. They regularly exchanged gifts on St. Valentine's Day,[105] and they enjoyed canoeing and hiking together.[106] They were "much more alike than most married couples are" reflected Douglas Campbell, Manitoba premier for five of the years Roland was lieutenant-governor. "They were both well educated academically, both very interested in a wide variety of subjects, both erudite and outstandingly public spirited." Each respected the ability, intellect, and character of the other, and they got along together very well.[107]

More distant observers sometimes remarked that Margaret was the more dominant of the pair.[108] Roland became more reticent than she when they were together. Repeated comments on her "strong-mindedness" testify as much to the common expectation that women should remain subordinate as to the marital relationship of the McWilliamses. One cousin of Russell Stovel's recognized her skill after Roland's appointment as lieutenant-governor. "I always felt that Margaret was particularly clever in the way she kept herself in the background to push her husband to the fore – he never would have got to first base without her. Few women could restrain their ego, as she did."[109]

Margaret's letters to Roland express confidence, trust, and affection. Moreover, they contain humour, as did her letters to her niece.[110] Not unaware of their Winnipeg reputation, Margaret wrote to Helen in December 1941 reflecting on a year in Government House. "We have not long finished the first year of the five of our appointment ... As some of my more outspoken friends say, I have been kept busy during this first year learning to be the wife of my husband."[111]

Margaret's relationship with Roland's mother was a cause of poignant regret. When Helen mentioned her fiancé's mother in a letter of July 1932, Margaret replied: "I am so glad that you like one another and that you feel she is really your friend. It makes more difference than you can well imagine, and I am very happy, indeed, that it is so. You know my mother-in-law is a fine woman and I am confident she would tell you that I am a fine woman, and mean it. But we have never talked to each other except over a very high and wide wall. I have always felt that I was a bit cheated in that; that not having had my own mother since I was a little child, I had a sympathetic mother-in-law coming to me. So I am very glad for you that you have found one for whom you can have such nice warm feelings."[112]

Margaret and Roland regarded Helen almost as a daughter. After Helen's mother died – an occasion of deep grief for Margaret, since Helen Easson Stovel had been her bosom friend from high school days – she wrote to her niece, "I think you know I have a deep feeling for you and that it always seems to me that if I might have had a daughter of my own, I should have been entirely content and happy had she been just like you."[113] In Margaret's will, Helen headed the list of beneficiaries.[114] Avis Clark, whom Roland married after Margaret's death, recognized the bond between Margaret and Helen when in December 1959 she sent Helen "the most significant article of Margaret's that I can think of. She loved it. I pass it on to you with her love." This was a cigarette case. "Rollie had given it to her when they were on holiday … He would not give it away before but kept what few cigarettes we smoked in it. There were no other personal things that she treasured more than that. I am sure she would be happy for you to have it."[115]

Margaret, Roland, and Avis formed a companionable trio. Avis attended Harbord Collegiate Institute after Margaret left.[116] She was a school teacher, teaching Latin and English at Kelvin and Daniel MacIntyre high schools. She lived in Devon Court, the McWilliamses' appartment block. When they moved into a house, Avis moved with them.[117] The *ménage-à-trois* was considered remarkable by contemporaries mainly in this: that the McWilliamses had a "roomer" contributing to expenses, for they were known to be careful with their money.[118]

Eight years younger than Margaret, Avis shared many of Margaret's club interests and was directly instrumental in 1938 when the University Women's Club acquired its own clubhouse from C.W. Gordon's estate and furnished it. Avis followed Margaret in becoming president of the club.[119] Living with the McWilliamses put her and Roland in a curious position at Margaret's death. Roland was seventy-eight, Avis sixty-nine. She had made her home with them for twenty-eight years. Odd though a three-member household might have appeared, it was less so than a man and woman living together unmarried. Roland retired as lieutenant-governor in the summer of 1953, a year after Margaret's death. He and Avis were married in October.[120] When he died in 1958, Avis wrote to Helen, expressing how happy she was to have had "these long years with him – and especially the last when I could care for him and discovered other sides to his nature which were very dear."[121]

Helen cherished her Aunt Margaret's letters, "those letters that chanced to be kept," which are now woven through this biography.[122] They provide an occasional chronicle for her public life, which began with the move to Winnipeg, where "the Canada of tomorrow is being moulded."[123]

CHAPTER THREE

Initial Forays

In 1910 Roland McWilliams joined the law firm of Sir James Aikins, "the unquestionable leader in every sense of the Western Canadian Bar."[1] After a year living in the house of a physician, Dr Rorke, the McWilliamses took up residence in one of the newest and most fashionable apartment blocks, Devon Court, at 376 Broadway, only a few blocks away from the legislature and law courts. Built in 1909, the complex was designed by John Atchison, who incorporated advanced notions of heating, ventilation, and light into each of the forty-four apartments.[2] Apartment blocks, department stores, businesses, and homes were under construction everywhere. The Eaton's department store, four blocks west of Main, was completed in 1905.[3] In 1910 the tallest skyscraper, fourteen storeys, or 165 feet high, had just been built.[4] Near Devon Court, the new Union Station for the Canadian Northern and Grand Trunk Pacific railways was completed in 1911.[5] These were the days "when Winnipeg was believed marked out by Providence to be the chief city of the Dominion."[6]

In 1912 the *Canadian Annual Review* devoted a special supplement to Winnipeg, "gateway" to the West. The town "has become the greatest grain market on the continent, the chief distributing, industrial and financial city of the Canadian West."[7] With series of statistics the *Review* documented the evolution of water, rail, and street railway transport, Winnipeg's growth as an investment and banking centre, and the expansion of manufacturing. The population of Winnipeg and its suburbs in 1911 was 155,563.[8] There were institutions of higher learning and an expanding school system to teach 22,500 students in 1912, three times the number of 1900.[9] Reflecting the booming economy, the *Winnipeg Telegram* identified at least twenty millionaires residing in the city in 1910.[10]

Compared with what it had been in 1881, "the old Red River Settlement ... had been almost totally engulfed by a thriving commercial centre." The growth of the provincial civil service further boosted the population. As the city grew, certain districts became predominantly working class and others managerial or professional.[11]

Superimposed on the economic division was an ethnic division reflecting the East European immigration of the decades before 1910. The "North End" population in 1916 was 40 percent British, 30 percent Slavic, and 20 percent Jewish in origin. In contrast, the population of south and west Winnipeg was predominantly British (86 percent), with only 3 percent Slavic and 2 percent Jewish representation. The non-British groups each had thriving newspapers, churches, and clubs, including debating and drama groups. Some maintained their own schools.[12]

Rapid immigration and expansion had created urgent problems for the city government, whose physical and social services were continuously under pressure. The City Council was alarmed by the problems of infant mortality, domestic hygiene, and child care, and a great number of privately funded welfare agencies responded to perceived needs. The Methodist Church's All People's Mission, for example, was involved in an aggressive program of social and intellectual as well as religious welfare for immigrants, and other organizations, staffed mainly by women, offered help.[13]

News about women's activities was carried by the local newspapers, which employed many female journalists. Indeed, the national Canadian Women's Press Club was founded in Winnipeg in 1906, and its national headquarters remained there until the First World War.[14] Coverage was given at length, during McWilliams's first winter in Winnipeg, to the sensational statements of the Rev. Dr J.G. Shearer, general secretary of the national Moral and Social Reform Council. "They have the rottenest conditions of things in Winnipeg in connection with the

question of social vice to be found in any city in Canada"
reported the Toronto *Globe* after Shearer's return from the
West.[15] Practically every day during that year's civic election
campaign, the issue of a segregated area for prostitutes was
before the reading public.[16] The paper reported a mass meeting
of women who endorsed (in vain) the reform mayoral candidate.[17]

The *Free Press* reported problems facing female factory workers and gave continuing coverage to international news on
women's suffrage, including the report of a petition from Manitoba Icelandic women to the provincial legislature.[18] There
were columns on the need for immigrant domestic workers and
news about several local organizations seeking to promote a
dower law for women as well as protective legislation.[19] In the
quantity, sophistication, and presentation of journalism
respecting women, Winnipeg was clearly superior to Peterborough and comparable with both the Minneapolis and Detroit
of ten years before.

Some form of volunteer work was usual for the thousands
of adult women who retired from the labour market on marriage, if, indeed, they had earned their living at all.[20] As a
barrister's wife, McWilliams could choose from a wide spec-
trum of women's work described by the *Women's Paper*, a supplement to a *Winnipeg Telegram* of 1907.

The *Women's Paper*'s chief goal was to record the work of
Winnipeg club women from the onset of organized activity in
the 1880s up to 1907. The second aim was to raise funds for a
Young Women's Christian Association (YWCA) building to serve
the needs of wage-earning women.[21]

After pride of place was given to the work and future plans
of the YWCA, fourteen columns of the *Women's Paper* were
devoted to "The Wide, Wide World." This meant missionary
support work. Churches raised funds to sponsor women missionaries as well as nurses, physicians, and teachers, and they
supported institutions such as schools, orphanages, and kindergartens. They helped build and furnish ministers' houses,
and supported denominational newsletters and publications.[22]

The "Women's Work" section documented, in thirty-six columns, women's caring for the poor, the sick, and the needy.

Most of those organizations, like the YWCA, were Christian and Protestant. Some had funding originating from government as well as from voluntary subscription.

Such a service was the Margaret Scott Nursing Mission, named after "the city's missionary to our poor," elsewhere in the *Women's Paper* eulogized as "gold that needs no gilding ... an unwearied worker who hides from public praise." The mission provided trained nurses to visit home patients. Its purpose was "to minister spiritually and physically to the sick poor in our midst," especially to those unable to have a prolonged hospital stay because of poverty, responsibility for dependents, or because they did not need constant attention.[23]

The Margaret Scott Mission was unique to Winnipeg, founded by one determined woman with the administrative capacity to mobilize financial and human resources for a specific purpose. Other organizations drew on the experience of national societies, and the *Women's Paper's* section on "Woman's Work" listed several local chapters of what were in 1907 dominion-wide societies: the Red Cross, the groups that became the Victorian Order of Nurses, the Girls' Friendly Society, the Council of Women, and the Aberdeen Society.

Officers of these societies were drawn repeatedly from among the wives of the Winnipeg establishment. Wives of lieutenant-governors served as honorary and active presidents, and the same names appeared many times.[24] The societies' activities before 1907 were primarily directed towards fundraising. The Council of Women, founded by Lady Aberdeen in 1893, was an umbrella society with an international branch to elevate members to a high level of unity in applying the "Golden Rule to society, custom and law."[25] Members of these societies provided the money to pay others to do the work.

Somewhat more direct involvement in welfare work was required by the locally founded groups, like the Margaret Scott Mission. Their approach was expressed in the *Women's Paper's* account of the Children's Aid Society: "Wayward children are not necessarily children of vicious tendencies ... their surroundings do not afford sufficient outlet, and they make this outlet for themselves in wrong-doing. The evident remedy is to change the character of the surroundings."[26] This belief sustained the preachers and believers of the social gospel in Canada and the idealism of women who worked for the benefit of the poor and the needy. These women primarily worked on committees, determining the policy and objectives of the boards on which they sat, but they too were involved in fund-raising, and in this they solicited large donations from the businessmen of their acquaintance and raised money themselves. "Young girls have held flower shows for their [the children's] benefit; boys have had acrobatic performances in the barn, and donated the proceeds; artists and musicians have given their services freely to the cause; busy women have taken time from their many home duties to plan and work for them, and have gone back to their own little flocks, with more thankful hearts."[27]

The Winnipeg *Women's Paper* described the concerns of the socially aware, economically secure women of the generation up to 1907, but did not provide a complete account. It ignored their regular church-centred activity. St. Stephen's Presbyterian Church, for example, which the McWilliamses attended, supported local Bible study, Sunday school, and social meetings for quilting. It also maintained a missionary in India and a mission in Winnipeg, and operated its own building, Church House, as a "throbbing centre of religious, social and athletic activity."[28] And the paper made no more than perfunctory mention of volunteer work performed by non-Protestants or non-British women.

Nevertheless, it can be said that the *Women's Paper* did indicate the range of charitable welfare work barristers' wives and their neighbours expected to do. Some women went further – they analysed and criticized the system that gave rise to social problems. Winnipeg at the beginning of the twentieth century has been characterized as "an intensely political city" that manifested its vitality in newspaper articles, Sunday sermons, Canadian Club speeches for the well-to-do, and debates at the People's Forum for residents of the North End. Political reforms were advocated, and some, like compulsory education, women's suffrage, and prohibition, were acceptable within mainstream politics and were included in the platform of the opposition Liberal Party for the 1915 provincial election.[29]

In the fall of 1910 Margaret McWilliams took time to determine her future commitments. By the time the First World War

broke out four years later, she already had substantial achievements to her credit. Wary of identifying with the more radical
reformers, she nevertheless collaborated with them and at the
same time gave her attention to non-political work with children.

McWilliams from the start engaged in free-lance journalism,
but this took second place to her public service work.[30] Her
first Winnipeg ventures involved children: a babies' milk depot
and a free kindergarten. The babies' milk depot was associated
with the new Children's Hospital. Babies of poor families were
brought there for bottle feeding. By 1914 the Depot Board, of
which Margaret was the secretary, had persuaded the City to
assume responsibility. In August of that year, the depot was
feeding 111 babies every day.[31]

The Winnipeg Free Kindergarten Association was founded
in 1892 by M.S. Colby, sister-in-law to Sir James Aikins,
Roland's new law partner. Its object was "the establishment and
maintenance of free kindergartens in the city, to promote good
work among the needy and neglected children."[32] McWilliams
was familiar with the free kindergartens in Minneapolis, and
in Detroit she had gained two years of direct experience in the
education of children by editing the "Journal Junior." She joined
the association's board in 1910, and although she continued to
serve as an officer until 1915, she soon satisfied her desire to
help children.[33]

Within a year McWilliams identified three women's organizations closer to her interests: the University Women's Club,
the Women's Canadian Club, and the Local Council of Women.
Over the next forty years, the first of these was to absorb more
of her attention than any other club.

The founding of the University Women's Club was the result
of a meeting called by three university graduates for 5 May
1909. Twelve members were enrolled, and Dr Mary Crawford,
later a founder of the Political Equality League, was elected
president. Originally, charter members were to be limited to
thirty, but this number was increased to fifty, thereby allowing
McWilliams, who applied to join in May 1911, to qualify as a
charter member.[34] Her sponsors were Mary Crawford and Kennethe Haig, a journalist, two single professional women.
McWilliams was elected in September 1911 and immediately

had an opportunity to prove her mettle when she was appointed to a subcommittee charged with making full arrangements "to bring Mrs Pankhurst to Winnipeg."

The club, small as it was, was not of one mind concerning the visit of the most famous militant British suffragette. The December executive meeting resolved that Mrs Pankhurst not be given a reception by the club. At the club's regular meeting, McWilliams seconded Kennethe Haig's motion that there be no collection of funds for the Women's Suffrage Movement.[35] McWilliams was not an active worker for suffrage. Thirty years later she referred to the pre-suffrage time: "They [women] did not see any necessity for the suffrage – the world was theirs anyway."[36] She was not speaking for the entire club – many members, including her sponsor Mary Crawford, were suffragists.[37]

At the end of McWilliams's first year in the club, she was instrumental in effecting a change in its operation, and at the end of her second, she brought in plans for wide-ranging reform. At the May 1912 business meeting, she seconded a motion to concentrate the club's activities around outside speakers, as distinct from "friends" whose time and energy were taxed, and a year later she was elected as president.[38] In a series of moves, she transformed the University Women's Club into a vehicle for educational and social reform. She began by proposing the constitution be amended. This became her standard move in other organizations, too: after achieving a position of influence, she would then impose her view of constitutional power. In the case of the University Women's Club, McWilliams first established the framework of seven meetings, October to April, and instituted a membership drive. Office holding was limited to two consecutive years.[39]

At the outset of her term in 1913, she proposed that the club's activities be directed by four groups: a lecture committee; a social committee, with specific responsibility for bringing members into contact with undergraduates of the university; a music committee, "to arrange for several twilight organ recitals on Saturday afternoons"; and, her major proposal, a "civic or industrial committee." This latter would "undertake a thoroughgoing accurate investigation, with the purpose of publicising it, in regard to conditions of one branch of industrial labour in the city." More than this investigation marked McWilliams's term, however. Each member was asked to serve on a committee.[40]

The Political Equality League (PEL), formed in Manitoba in 1912 to work for women's suffrage, wrote to the University Women's Club in November 1913 asking for co-operation in the formation of a specifically women's civic organization that would promote women as candidates for school trustee. McWilliams was delegated to attend a PEL meeting. She reported back that the group agreed not to sponsor a woman trustee straightaway, but it would support one of her own interests – the securing of a better and cheaper milk supply. She also agreed with other secondary objectives of the PEL: the use of schools as social centres, the establishment of "comfort stations" in downtown districts, and the hiring of more women factory inspectors.[41]

The highlight of her first year in office was an enormously successful lecture given by Helen Keller, on which the club made a profit of $672. Not all her plans matured, however. The twilight organ recitals were abandoned, "as no co-operation from the organists could be secured."[42]

McWilliams's second year in office was marked by the outbreak of war, and the purpose of the club's first meeting that October was to consider "what course of action would be wise and patriotic in the present circumstances."[43] It was proposed that lectures and Civic Committee activities be suspended in a shift towards traditional women's work: sewing shirts for soldiers. From the floor of the meeting came an additional suggestion: that "food vigilance duty" be undertaken to prevent unnecessary rises in the price of food during the war. Sewing was instituted, twice a week, with about thirty members in attendance, but the food vigilance study was deferred as only one member besides the executive attended the meeting where it was to be considered. The season's major product was as follows: 20 dressing gowns, 36 shirts, 103 pairs of socks, 3 skull caps, 2 helmets, 5 scarves, and 39 dozen bandages.[44] The University Women's Club records contain no criticism of war of the sort generated by Winnipeg journalist Francis Marion Beynon in the *Grain Growers' Guide*.[45]

Just before McWilliams surrendered office, the club approved a motion supporting the mayor of Winnipeg's initiative concerning unemployment in the city. Members grandly spoke for "the women of the city" in expressing confidence that they "will heartily endorse every expenditure that may be necessary" to provide work, especially for married men, whose wives and families were sharing in their suffering.[46]

McWilliams's most notable achievement during her first four years in Winnipeg was the report she wrote based on the findings of the Civic Committee, "The Work of Women and Girls in the Department Stores of Winnipeg." The report summarized the working conditions of female sales clerks, and its model was explicitly American: Elizabeth Beardsley Butler's *Saleswomen in Mercantile Stores*, a study of the larger stores of Baltimore published in 1912. The object and methods of study paralleled investigations by the English Fabian Society and the Women's Co-operative Guild that had chronicled the terrain of working-class experience.[47] The report's first objective was the "dissemination of the facts." Its second aim was of a reforming and educational nature: that is, to determine what sort of education and "opportunity" ought to be made available to women working in department stores.[48]

In method, the committee showed a determination unswayed by its preliminary correspondence with social workers who had undertaken this sort of work elsewhere. These workers' unanimous opinion was that volunteers could not successfully elicit and analyse the information necessary for such a study. The committee, however, confidently welcomed the opportunity to train ten of its members, who were after all university graduates, in field work. Armed with Butler's book about Baltimore, these members set out to gather information about the working conditions, the number of occupations of employees, and their weekly wages, hours of work, and nationality.

Winnipeg's extraordinarily rapid expansion even within the previous ten years, together with an exceptional turnover of staff (women married early and also tended to migrate further west), prevented the fieldworkers from reproducing all features of the Baltimore model. They nevertheless recorded their impression that women employed in Winnipeg department stores exhibited a "general youthfulness."[49]

The committee confined its investigations to four department stores: the Winnipeg stores of the two Canadian chains, Eaton's and the Hudson's Bay Company, and two local department stores, Robinson's and Carsley's. Following Butler, the field-workers tried to elicit information from both management officials and employees, as well as make their own personal observations. They exercised considerable discretionary judgment concering "facts." Nevertheless, the report was thorough and painstaking.

Findings were organized within, first, a section relating to physical conditions, including "Store Construction" and "Arrangements for Comfort of Employees"; secondly, a section describing the organization of the work force, its hours of work, and its remuneration; and thirdly, a section explicitly describing "Hardships of the Occupation."

All four stores, having been recently enlarged, shared the problems associated with buildings not designed for their eventual purpose. Ventilation was poor and heating arrangements unsatisfactory. Many employees contracted severe colds and had to take unpaid time off. The committee also faulted the stores for not conforming to provincial legislation in the matter of seats for saleswomen. It thought more should have been done to provide a rest room containing a couch. Saleswomen were treated reasonably well with respect to their use of toilet facilities, but this was not so for cashiers. Cash registers could not be left unattended, so if a cashier wished to relieve herself, she first had to send a messenger to the office – "naturally this amounts almost to a prohibition." The committee approved the stores' practice of giving a full hour at noon and promoted the idea of a "well-regulated lunch-room, where nourishing meals could be procured at cost."

"Welfare work" was interpreted by the committee as pertaining to sickness, pensions, and social organizations. It praised the store that employed nurses to visit the homes of employees off sick and another store "where the old time paternal relation still exists." The committee reported, without editorial comment, on a pension scheme offered by one store. The pension "will be paid for life, so long as the pensioner does not marry, does not enter any employment similar to that which the company gives, and leads a moral life." The report strongly approved the promotion of athletic and social clubs, which, it contended, contributed to the happiness of the employees.[50]

The report's second major section concerned the labour force's structure, hours of work, and remuneration. It found no fault with the hours of work, which generally amounted to ten and a half hours per day, six days per week, with occasional half days off during the summer. Overall, "the hours in force compare favourably with those in force in any city on the continent."

Wages were considerably better than "they are popularly believed to be." There was general uniformity of wage levels among all stores, and the committee discovered some saleswomen earning "at least 9 dollars a week."[51] These wages can be compared with those of other occupations. Professor Carrie Derrick of McGill University examined statistics for wage-earning women throughout Canada in 1913 and concluded that "for every woman who earns $8.50 a week there are twelve who get only $5.00 a week." In 1913 in Winnipeg, J.S. Woodsworth, then superintendent of All People's Mission, noted that two years previously a committee investigated women working as store clerks and in factories. Only 20 percent received over $7 a week and over 10 percent received less than $3.[52] In 1917 the secretary of the Manitoba Bureau of Labour undertook a survey to discover "the accurate facts with reference to wages paid to females in the Province." The average weekly wage in the largest occupation category, women garment workers, was $10.47 a week. His observation was that, overall, wages were "hardly enough for subsistence," but in 1914 the University Women's Club committee came to no such dramatic conclusion.[53]

The committee went to considerable trouble to understand the structure of the work force and its employment opportunities. In three of the stores an incentive system for wages was in place. With respect to managerial staff, "one of the stores has a rigid rule that no woman can be a manager" and another store "has no woman manager." The manager was responsible to the general management and supervised his or her own department and the associated workroom. The heads of work-rooms, where some merchandise was made and alterations were carried out, were women. Beneath these managerial staff were sales personnel, below whom were messenger girls, wrappers, stock girls, and cashiers. Altogether, in February 1914, a month identified as the slackest in sales, the four department stores' labour force was 2,432.[54]

The report's third section identified "Hardships." Neither of the two most important working conditions, hours or wages, had been considered by the committee to be unfair, and consequently they were only cursorily mentioned in this part. The members of the University Women's Club showed their awareness of the concept of a practical minimum wage when they wrote that an adequate minimum wage should provide for "food, proper lodging, car fare, clothes, recreation and possible sickness." They quoted "social workers" in Winnipeg putting this figure at "eight to nine dollars," and reiterated that "the efficient adult saleswomen in Winnipeg" earned that minimum. The various categories of messenger, wrapper, cashier, and stock girl frequently did not carry this wage, but the committee vaguely justified this with the notion that "there must be an apprentice stage" and that the lower-paid workers "constitute only a fair and legitimate percentage of the whole."[55] (The committee, however, had no statistical information on the number earning each wage.)

The committee considered that the provincial legislation governing working conditions – specifically concerning the provision of seats to workers – was "excellent" and merely remained to be enforced. Ventilation was singled out as a hardship, as was nervous tension. This latter was ascribed to the pressure of working under an incentive system and to the multiplicity of sales slips and forms that had to be filled in. The committee pointed to a social problem not directly related to an employers' responsibility – the shortage of housing for women workers. Appalling stories about the difficulty of finding accommodation were common. One of the committee's two major recommendations was that "some body of women interested in community service" should provide an accommodation referral service for "business women." Its other recommendation was that "the school board" should provide training for women who were going to work in stores.[56]

This report throws light on life in Winnipeg department stores just before the First World War and, by extension, on life as a sales clerk elsewhere. The report was sent to the "employers and employees concerned, to the city council, city clergy, and those throughout the Province and Dominion interested in economic questions." A review of the report appeared in the *Labour Gazette*, and the report was sent out on request to various government and academic organizations in the United States and England.

The report additionally revealed the concerns, attitudes, and methods of the women who undertook the investigation. There was sympathy for women who had to stand up all day, in draughts and sometimes evil-smelling air, who had to dry their hands on unclean linen, who had to write a myriad of sales slips and receipts, who had to search for cheap living accommodation, and who were concerned about their moral reputation. These were practical and palpable aggravations the club women could readily understand, and they expressed their concern. The report is eloquent in its silence as well as in its observations. No mention of unions; no mention of extended protective legislation (except in the matter of seats for workers); no agitation for fewer hours or greater pay. Still, the information it presented and the publicity generated undoubtedly helped create the climate of opinion that would lead to the appointment of women factory inspectors and the passing in 1918 of a minimum wage law.[57]

By the time McWilliams relinquished the presidency of the University Women's Club, she had developed a certain method of operating. She liked to have something concrete to show for her efforts. Usually she became an officer of the organizations she worked in, frequently at the presidential level. There were few she did not dominate. She often persuaded the organization to sponsor and produce published reports. She demanded reciprocal aid from her expanding network. She called on contacts to provide help when she wanted it. Nurtured by the close circle of appreciative friends in the University Women's Club, she manifested increasing confidence in her own judgment. McWilliams always recognized that the support of other women was central to her own agenda, whose features became more obvious during her first decade in Winnipeg.

CHAPTER FOUR

The First Decade

McWilliams's first decade in Winnipeg gave her multiplying opportunities for women's work, and this experience served as an apprenticeship for feminism. The University Women's Club was the keystone of her public service, but she was never confined to it alone. Early in 1911 she applied for membership in the Women's Canadian Club, and at its fourth annual meeting that fall she became secretary, a post she retained for the next two years, overlapping with her University Women's Club presidency. She kept a close connection with the Women's Canadian Club thereafter. Secondly, she became a regular member of the newly formed Social Science Study Club. Thirdly, after relinquishing her office with the University Women's Club, she became secretary of the Local Council of Women, a position she kept until 1916, when she became the council's president for four years. She was also active in the National Council of Women, chairing a subcommittee to revise the council's constitution. Besides these regular major commitments, she found time for new interests: church work, the 1917 election, monitoring food prices for the Manitoba government, and a postwar organization of social welfare agencies.

One cause McWilliams did not take up was suffrage. She supported the Liberal Party, which included women's suffrage in its platform after 1914, but she was not a member of the Political Equality League. The reason is obscure. After women were enfranchised, she was one of the first to be actively involved in electoral campaigns, and by the early twenties she was urging women to become candidates. Yet before 1916 she was not an active suffragist. She later claimed there were too many other demands on her time: "pioneering in Western Canada ... we had to be in a hurry." Pioneers had brought with them standards of an older and more developed way of life. "We had to get things done; we had each of us to do two women's work according to our earlier standards."[1] McWilliams's engagement in other activities, however, suggests her increasing commitment to feminism.

By 1910 the Women's Canadian Club had become a large and flourishing organization with a patriotic purpose, promoting both educational and activist strategies.[2] Each month members heard an invited speaker. Topics were sometimes of personal interest, as when a local woman described her attendance at the coronation of George V or when Miss Mary Vaux of Philadelphia gave a travel talk, with slides, on the Canadian Rockies. This was not the rule, however.[3]

During the early years of McWilliams's membership, the club on the whole was concerned with the situation of women, and its agenda encompassed the need for selective activism. The executive in December 1911 decided, after an internal debate, to maintain its support for homesteads for women legislation, but when in October 1912 the new Political Equality League asked if the club was "in sympathy with the Equal Suffrage Movement," the secretary (McWilliams) "was directed to reply that the club did not willingly enter into any controversy nor commit itself to either side of a disputed question."[4]

Yet the program of speakers during 1911 and 1912 indicated a very real interest in women and politics. Dr Adam Shortt, head of the Civil Service Commission in Ottawa, spoke about "Women in National Life." As secretary, McWilliams entered a brief summary of his speech into the minutes, and his views of the franchise were consistent with what McWilliams later said were her own. The vote was "after all a small thing which could not yield the benefits hoped from it ... there was a vast body of work waiting to be done both in the way of making and enforcing law which could be done, he thought, as well without the franchise as with it."[5] The club invited a Winnipeg lawyer, known for "his interest in all matters of progress including legislation for the protection of women" to speak on the present state of laws concerning women in Manitoba. There

were 155 present to hear him.[6] The club also invited an Anglican clergyman to address "Some Aspects of the Women's Question," which he did, from the point of view of "one opposed
entirely to the granting of that franchise." Over three hundred
turned out for this "courageous and honest expression of his
opinions."[7]

The club furnished large audiences for Miss Elwood, head
of Evangelea House in Toronto, the "largest settlement house
in Canada"; Dr Wilfred Grenfell, who spoke of his Labrador
missionary work; and Dr J.W. Robertson, chairman of the Royal
Commission on Industrial Education and Technical Training,
who talked about Montessori's teaching methods.[8] The club's
political neutrality was temporarily dissolved when Nellie
McClung, following a talk by an American actress on Canadian
womanhood, delighted her audience with "breezy humour" –
after which the club approved support for the dower law,
whereby a wife was guaranteed inheritance of the family
home, then under consideration in the Manitoba legislature.[9]
McWilliams ceased to be secretary in 1914, and after the outbreak of war the club tended to emphasize patriotic issues. Still,
their largest audience – 925 members and guests – turned out
not for a war speaker but for an entertainer, actor Sir Johnston
Forbes-Robertson, in March 1915.[10]

McWilliams kept close connections with the Women's Canadian Club even while she was busy as secretary, then president,
of the Local Council of Women, and in early 1916 she was
appointed to chair a committee set up to revise the Women's
Canadian Club consititution – the second time she had this
duty. Her committee's draft was presented and approved in
November. In its section on qualifications for membership, the
constitution firmly identified the club with that body of public
opinion that was suspicious of the "foreign-born" in Canada.
"Any woman, at least 18 years of age, who is British born, a
British subject, or whose husband is a British subject, and is
in sympathy with the objects of the Club, shall be eligible for
membership."

McWilliams wrote into the constitution a disclaimer of the
kind of activism that had embarrassed some members in 1911
and 1912: "Action on religious or political issues may not be
taken by the Club." She also restated its purpose in terms that
could be used to describe her own personal mission: "It is the

purpose of the Club to foster patriotism; to create an intelligent public opinion on all matters relating to National life; to conserve the traditions of the past while building the greater future; and to unite Canadians for the welfare and progress of the Dominion."[11]

Much of the Women's Canadian Club business – correspondence relating to the speakers, reminders and fee solicitation to members – was performed by McWilliams as secretary up to 1914. Work of a more intellectually stimulating nature she found in the more intimate setting of a new club, the Social Science Study Club. This was founded in 1912 by a small group indignant at "the number of intelligent women who were spending their afternoons playing euchre." The club restricted membership to thirty and held meetings in private homes. The first president was Miss Eva Jones, headmistress of Havergal Ladies' College.[12] Each season members elected four officers and an advisory committee, and the topics for study, along with an occasional reading list, were set out on printed cards.

McWilliams was a founder-member of the Social Science Study Club and first appeared on its advisory committee in the 1913–14 season, when the club adopted a single theme, "The City and Its Health." The format for meetings that year included the presentation of a ten-minute paper ("a very brief summary of conditions in our own city, with suggestions for improvement, will be in order") followed by a general discussion. Over the year, seven meetings were held, and the topics suggest the intellectual orientation of educated and energetic women looking out for their own economic comfort as well as that of other women. First – in time and no doubt in terms of self-interest – was the topic "The Possibility of a Household Service Guild (to meet the ever-present servant problem)." The next month, November, dealt with the local condition of factory workers and shop girls and provided members with an informed opinion that they could use in the contemporaneous University Women's Club enquiry. In December the Social Science Study Club heard a paper on housing; in January, on recreation; in February, on the food and water supply; in March, on preventible diseases; and in April, on accidents.[13]

The following year, 1914–15, when McWilliams was still president of the University Women's Club, she held no office in the Study Club but did lead the discussion in one meeting.

The year's theme was "Education." After four meetings devoted to the general topic, primary and secondary education, and the preparation of the teacher, McWilliams's session dealt with "The Woman at the University." She prescribed three books for preliminary reading, of which one was the already famous *Women and Economics* by Charlotte Perkins Gilman. In 1915–16, her year as secretary of the Local Council of Women, McWilliams shared the topic "The War and Democracy" with two other women. In 1917–18, she gave a paper on "The State and Parenthood," a topic reflecting her developing interest in social work. The theme for 1918–19 was peculiarly apt in view of the Winnipeg General Strike of May 1919: "Modern Trade Unionism or Collective Bargaining." She was again on the Study Club's advisory committee in 1919–20, her last year of the Local Council of Women presidency. The theme that year was "Citizenship."[14]

In the Social Science Study Club, McWilliams joined with women eager to inform themselves of the important political, economic, and social problems of the time. Although the meetings were designed for self-education, there were practical effects when individual members applied their knowledge to the production of reports, recommendations, or policy resolutions in other forums, like the University Women's Club and the Local Council of Women, or directly for government. A founder-member, Mrs C.A. Mackenzie, claimed credit for social legislation (for example, the minimum wage legislation of 1919) that followed research performed by the club.[15]

McWilliams clearly benefited from her membership, which she kept up at least into the 1930s, and she regularly appeared on the program. Her topics reflected her wide interests; the League of Nations (1924), Canada and international relations (1928), industrial progress in Russia (1931), and, when she was elected an alderman, "A Woman's View of Civic Administration" (1933) and "A Year of Civic Responsibility" (1934).[16] Work performed for these meetings also bore fruit in McWilliams's other educational pursuits, especially the current events classes. She made it count. Her long commitment to this regular intellectual exercise provided a constant accompaniment to her more practical activities.

In 1915 McWilliams became secretary of the Local Council of Women. The Winnipeg council had been formed in 1894, one of the first of the seven local councils established after Lady Aberdeen established the National Council of Women in 1893. In 1894 the LCW of Winnipeg had twelve affiliated societies. By 1907 it had seventeen, and by 1912, twenty.[17] Its purpose was to be guided by the "Golden Rule" in working for improvements in "society, custom and the Law," and before McWilliams joined, the LCW had contributed to such good works as the appointment of a matron at the police station and fund-raising for a famine in India. Affiliated societies saw some advantage to association with a local umbrella group with formal links to a national, and international, political pressure group. In 1915 the Women's Christian Temperance Union was affiliated, as was the Canadian Women's Press Club.[18] The LCW's connection with the prestigious National Council and its ability to attract officers from prominent social and business families made it potentially influential.

In Winnipeg, the Local Council of Women, like the Women's Canadian Club, was reluctant to move away from welfare concerns into issues that provoked political controversy. When, at its 1911 annual meeting, a letter was read from the Women's Labour League asking for co-operation in a deputation urging the government to implement women's suffrage, the LCW resolved that the matter "be not re-opened" and that the Women's Labour League be notified to that effect.[19] Nellie McClung considered that the council contained too many women "afraid to be associated with any controversial subject." She put it down to their husbands' not letting them "'go active.' It might imperil their jobs."[20] Yet on many issues the LCW did take a stand and promoted reform "for the good of the community" as its members saw it. After McWilliams became secretary in 1915, the LCW intensified its lobbying of other women's groups for co-operation in demanding government agencies to institute reforms.

In the spring of 1915, the LCW was successful in convincing the University Women's Club to join in urging the mayor of Winnipeg to find work for unemployed men. The two groups demonstrated particular concern for the "wives and families sharing in their suffering." McWilliams neatly linked both clubs – the University Women's Club, whose president she still was, and the Local Council, whose secretary she was about to become.[21] Later that year, in October, the LCW successfully solicited support from the University Women's Club for a new by-law that required bread to be wrapped.[22] McWilliams was nominated by the University Women's Club for president of the LCW in March 1916, and as president she again sought the club's support, this time for widows and families of soldiers killed in the war.

In January 1917 the Local Council of Women presented a list of resolutions to the University Women's Club for its support. These had originated with the Political Equality League of Manitoba and concerned women's holding public office, but also safeguarded women's responsibilities in the home. A law was proposed to allow a wife a claim to the conjugal dwelling so that it could not be sold, leased, or otherwise disposed of without her permission; equal guardianship of both parents over children was proposed; and the interest of a widow and family in the estate of a deceased husband was to be protected. Other proposals concerned the state supervision and protection of the mentally handicapped, and the regulation of "moving pictures."[23]

For the rest of her term, McWilliams presided over a local council that considered an increasing volume of social welfare, economic, and political issues. Its various committees suggest the group's priorities: conservation, public health, immigration, the mentally handicapped, "equal moral standards," nursing, "better care for young women," "objectionable printed material," moving pictures, and agriculture for women. In these the Local Council was not alone: this sort of model was also followed by the National Council.[24] The LCW activism attracted, rather than deterred, support. By the end of McWilliams's term, there were over sixty affiliated groups.[25]

McWilliams's growing prominence at this local level gave her stature within the National Council, and in 1917 Winnipeg was host to the National Council of Women's annual meeting. The meeting resulted in a summary document, *Women's Platform, 1917*, which identified the National Council's concerns and policies. The National Council promoted an interventionist and managing role for the state in social and moral welfare, but it retained, for the most part, a laissez-faire approach to economic policy. McWilliams found the National Council too conservative for her developing taste.

The National Council of Women considered it was the "duty of the State to provide care and training for those who are either permanently or temporarily unfit for normal life." It wished to see a federal department of health with direct responsibility for controlling venereal diseases, for the custodial care of the mentally handicapped and for the provision and monitoring of many public health measures. The state should "demand" a certificate of health before marriage. With respect to women's employment, the National Council wanted local councils to concern themselves with adequate technical and vocational training for boys and girls, special mention being made of a problem close to its members' hearts, the need for trained domestic help. The National Council supported the professionalization of nurses and teachers by calling for government registration and in one clause promoted adequate factory inspection, the regulation of hours of work, and "a systematic enquiry into existing conditions." The National Council expressed support for a federal branch of child welfare and urged close state regulation of food production, distribution, and conservation.

In the section "Women as Citizens" in *Women's Platform, 1917*, the National Council condemned party factions and patronage and the secret dispensation of funds. Omitted from the *Platform* but unanimously approved by the meeting was a motion urging the dominion government to grant the federal franchise to all women immediately.[26] On the subject of education, the *Platform* saw the goal of the school system as being "to train the children as good citizens." Every community should provide supervised amusement for young people, and this extended to ensuring women's participation in boards of film censors. On the issues of immigration and settlement, the National Council had a long list of recommendations designed to facilitate the assimilation and integration of "immigrants" into national life.[27]

At the national convention, the national president described the future responsibility of the organization as being "to cleanse cosmopolitan Canadian morally, socially, and politically." She called upon women "to remove the social sins and the social inequality that are a reproach to any people," but among the women present there was no unanimity on the means to that end.

The *Platform* was a collection of resolutions approved by majority vote, but some delegates' proposals were not approved. A resolution from Halifax advocating a single tax, a levy on land values, was defeated. A resolution asking the governement to establish a minimum wage was ruled out of order. A resolution advocating the removal of all duty on foodstuffs was lost; an argument against it was that "this would be class legislation, and would leave the farming community open to competition while the manufacturer would be under the protection of the tariff." There was division, too, about women working in the labour force: a motion that asked the National Council to affix a union label to all its printed matter, which could assist working women, was defeated. A resolution calling for much greater state regulation of the food and fuel aspects of the economy was "referred," as was one calling for "conscription of wealth" along with conscription of manpower in the war effort.[28] These failed resolutions show the political limits of this particular group of women. They were limits that McWilliams was not willing to recognize for herself.

The annual meeting of June 1917 served to clarify for McWilliams her own political priorities. McWilliams's views on politics differed from those of the National Council of Women, and this ideological distinction was to be exacerbated by her growing identification with a western resentment of eastern domination.

In August 1917 the western Liberals held their convention in Winnipeg. This was immediately followed by meetings of Winnipeg Liberals in favour of Union government.[29] McWilliams attended several of these Liberal Party meetings, which considered such matters as the desirability of a Union government in which Liberals would reject the anti-conscription policy of their own leader, Sir Wilfrid Laurier, and join a coalition governement under the Conservative prime minister, Sir Robert Borden. She spoke up "for the women." McWilliams declared at one meeting "that there were two and only two points on which the women of Winnipeg should declare themselves, a non-partisan national government, and conscription of men, women, wealth, labour and resources." In a letter she noted she was supported by "Miss Houston of the garment

workers and Mrs Laird of the Labour League and Ida Bauslaugh" – Bauslaugh was a female factory inspector.[30]

Both in policy and political alliances, McWilliams differed
from majority opinion in the National Council of Women. She
wished to see a genuinely national government, and like the
moderate labour supporters, she wanted conscription of men
to come only in a package with conscription of other resources
– "conscription of wealth" was the undefined form used. During the election called later in the year, she was moderately
active and participated in an intriguing debate at Teulon, Manitoba, with a woman much further to the left than herself.

Helen Armstrong was president of the Women's Labour
League and the wife of George Armstrong, a radical socialist
carpenter and an "exponent of Marxian economics."[31] The Teulon meeting in December 1917 was addressed by the federal
minister of public works. The *Manitoba Free Press* reported that
Helen Armstrong "gave a rather violent tirade against the
Union government, and painted a dark picture of the life of a
Canadian soldier. She also spoke of the woes of the working
classes, and denounced capitalists of all kinds." By way of contrast, McWilliams's speech "was a splendid example of what
may be expected from the right type of modern woman. It was
a brilliant and forcible argument for Union government." The
reporter concluded that Armstrong's "violent and denuncia-
tory" arguments made a poor impression, while the meeting
vigorously cheered the pro-Union speeches.[32]

McWilliams's moderate views were tempered by strong patriotism and support of the war effort, but she was theoretically
sympathetic towards labour. At the time of the Winnipeg General Strike, she was not on the side of the strikers, deploring
the notion that one section of the community, labour, should
dictate to the others, but she was also impatient with the
dominion government: "A strike which involves one third of
the population is not to be settled by a wave of a cabinet minister's hand and the lordly admonition 'Now go back to work
all of you, or your job is gone.'" The Union government was "a
spineless aggregation."[33]

McWilliams did not voice a bold and comprehensive political
platform until 1931, when she and her husband collaborated

under the pseudonym Oliver Stowell in a blueprint for reform, *If I Were King of Canada*, but Roland in 1918 did go so far as to draft a proposal for discussion by the Winnipeg Liberal Party. In many ways it prefigured the 1931 book. Its political colours were indeed much less conservative than those of the National Council of Women.

Roland McWilliams thought western Liberals should take the lead in forming a new political party, and considered this a better alternative to remaining "tied to the heels of Eastern connections." Such a party would have a policy "so liberal and progressive that it will command the support of all Liberals, of the farmers, of the labour men and of all the new and independent voters to whom the call for the new and better day in Canada appeals." It would rally the support of "the two new elements in the electorate upon whom the result depends – the soldiers and the women ... For a name the best I can think of is the Radical party."

Roland's "Radical Policy for Canada" was to be based on the following:

1. The Tariff
    An immediate and substantial all round reduction except on luxuries.
    Free food, free raw materials, free implements.
    The increase of the British Preference.
    Reciprocity with the United States.
2. The Land
    The Land for the settler and first of all for the returned soldier.
    Expropriation of idle land at not more than cost.
3. Labour
    The maintenance of adequate standards of living and of minimum wages.
    The right of arbitration for public employees.
4. The Soldiers
    The retention of all soldiers from the fighting areas in the service at employments of productive value until they can find employment in civil life. Preference to returned soldiers in all Government appointments.
5. Public Utililties
    Government control of all national utilities and natural resources.
    The steady extension of Government ownership and operation.

6. Taxation
   Payment of the war charges by income and excess profits taxes
   and not by levies on consumption.[34]

Margaret McWilliams could recognize that this "Radical Policy" was incompatible with the politics of the National Council.
She was also irritated at the council's domination by women
from Ontario and Montreal. In 1918, when she agreed to chair
a committee on the constitution of the National Council of
Women, she was joining the Local Council in Winnipeg with
the councils of the other Prairie provinces in an effort to reduce
the influence of eastern Canada on the national structure.
McWilliams was disenchanted with the National Council and
saw the opportunity to revise its constitution as "a sort of last
stand ... for more progressive things and ... should we succeed,
we will really accomplish a good deal for the women of Canada."
She surveyed local councils to determine their views on twenty-
two questions. In correspondence with Violet McNaughton, the
committee member from Saskatchewan, she frankly declared
her hope was to "cut out some of the dead wood."[35] McNaughton
too thought "the N.C.W. is going to pieces."[36] By February 1919
McWilliams was not optimistic about the outcome. Question-
naires had been distributed to committee members, and in their
replies she found that "the conservatives vote in a solid phalanx
... while the radicals vary." She wanted McNaughton "to help
fight for a western view of things."[37]

McWilliams hoped to reduce the influence of the entrenched
eastern councils on the National Council by decentralizing oper-
ations. Her committee recommended biennial, rather than
annual, meetings and the elimination of proxy voting, but neither proposal was accepted by the National Council. Even before
the National Council meeting at Regina, McWilliams was thoroughly disaffected: "I am willing to make a good many sacrifices
to help put the NCW on its feet, but not to put my head in a
good tight noose."[38] Her proposals would allow the National
Council to adapt to conditions changed by the war, by the
growth of the West, by increased economic burdens for women,
and, above all, by the granting of the franchise, which, she now
recognized, "brings a revolutionary change in the relation of
women to their country, placing on them a responsibility in the

fulfilment of which they will pay the price of the new and greater opportunity which is theirs." At the Regina meeting, the old guard defeated her proposals. McWilliams was attacked for being "the embodiment of the materialism of the West."[39] She thereupon disaffiliated the Winnipeg council, a move followed by the Saskatchewan and Alberta councils as well.[40]

Towards the end of the war, McWilliams was adding to her activities through work with groups not exclusively composed of women. After 1916 she was one of the three women of twelve people serving on the executive of the Red Cross in Winnipeg. It was one of the few organizations she joined where she did not serve as president, although for many years she remained on the board.[41] There she gained a general perspective on social welfare work as a whole. In these days before a welfare state, the Red Cross generated or supervised welfare work in a wide-ranging way, and by the end of the war there were several signs that McWilliams was keen to be more involved in the newly professionalizing area of social work.

Her church provided one opportunity. The McWilliamses attended the Presbyterian St. Stephen's, Broadway, whose minister was the Rev. Charles W. Gordon. His fame was national in scope, and he was reputed to be a millionaire.[42] He was a popular novelist, writing as Ralph Connor, and a frequent speaker on political issues. The congregation of St. Stephen's was governed by a Deacon's Court of thirty-six laymen, along with the ministers and elected elders.[43] Roland was elected to the Deacon's Court for the first time in 1916.[44] Very soon the women of the congregation were pressing for their inclusion on subcommittees, and in 1918 Margaret McWilliams, along with a small number of other women, was elected to the Public Welfare Committee. This committee rapidly stirred up the Deacon's Court by requesting authorization to send a telegram to "the Government at Ottawa in support of total prohibition." The action was approved, but when it was delayed for a month, the committee chair was peremptorily directed to carry out his mandate. That same year, McWilliams urged members of the congregation to acquaint themselves with public welfare work and recommended a questionnaire be distributed to discover people's interests.[45]

McWilliams's interest in social work was mobilized by the provincial government when in 1919 it set in motion a policy to consolidate its supervision of existing social agencies and thus avoid duplication. As a delegate from the Local Council of Women, she attended an organizational meeting for the Central Council of Social Agencies along with representatives from twenty-four other groups.[46] This was not the first time she had been noticed by the Manitoba government. Her enthusiasm for monitoring wartime food prices and supplies had been evident in December 1916 when she addressed the University Women's Club on "the present situation in Winnipeg with regard to the prices of various foods, and gave some of the facts regarding apparently very great profits made by some firms supplying food."[47] She was appointed to the provincial government Food Board in 1917, and in May 1918 spoke concerning the board's work to the Women's Canadian Club.[48]

The year 1917 deepened her appetite for public service. We have already seen her involvement in both the Local Council and National Council of Women, the western Liberal Party, her church, the Food Board, and the 1917 election. That spring, McWilliams proved her ability to work with women with a variety of political commitments when she joined a war-memorial planning group that was organizing a "Women's Foundation Tribute Night" to raise funds in May 1917.[49] Also in 1917 she was appointed to the Council of the University of Manitoba. Her husband had been teaching in the Law School and was employed by the university to prepare its new constitutional structure of that year. McWilliams's appointment could be seen as a mark of indirect courtesy to Roland, but was also a measure of the community prominence she had achieved.[50]

By the end of the war, McWilliams was in her forty-fourth year. Her first nine years in Winnipeg had primarily been taken up with women's groups that identified women's problems and supported and promoted progress for women. She had received recognition. In 1914 she was featured in the *Canadian Courier* as "a woman whose sense of citizenship has made her a well-known figure in western life."[51] She had also met limits – she was unable to carry all before her in the National Council of Women. Her ideas on women, on women's place in society, and on their opportunities were still developing and were based on a wealth of knowledge and direct experience.

McWilliams had not been a suffragist. Once the vote was won, however, she was active in urging women to use it well, and she herself did much to educate women in public affairs.

By exhortation and example, she urged women to take their place in public office and on commissions and committees. Women should share with men the responsibility for government. With respect to women's rights as well as responsibilities in the family, she never hesitated. She supported the Dower and Homestead acts, whose purpose was to improve women's economic security, and legislation concerning child custody. While she was president of the Local Council of Women, the province passed mothers' allowance legislation, with the LCW's support. Protective factory legislation also attracted support from McWilliams's organizations. She welcomed the state as a vehicle for progress towards the provision of both equal rights for women and women's rights in the family and workplace.

In retrospect those years seem crammed with phenomenal activity. McWilliams was one of a small group of educated, economically secure women whose concerns distinguished them from others who had neither the time nor the inclination to stir beyond family concerns. Poor women had to work, both inside the home and, for wages, outside, and many women of the middle class, once they had completed their daily domestic tasks, with or without a servant's help, were content with a routine of caring for their families and visiting their friends. From such a group of indifferent women, complacent in their afternoon euchre, the feminists wished to distance themselves. The women (not all feminists) who went to the Women's Canadian Club wanted a minimum of serious entertainment; they joined the club to hear monthly speakers from a national and international circuit who brought them in touch with a wider world. Women who joined the University Women's Club were from a much more select group; they had a university degree and wanted to be actively involved, on a weekly basis, with other like-minded friends. The Local Council of Women was fed by other women's organizations. Women who accepted office with the LCW already had an organizational base, but once they were on the council executive, they became involved in activist research and lobbying.

Women who were officers in these organizations were to some extent socially, but neither intellectually nor politically, homogeneous. If they were university graduates, their parents had enjoyed both a certain economic standard of living and a progressive view of women's role in society. Some women's initial support came not from a father but from a husband's prosperity and permission. It was inconceivable for a woman to enter this cohort without the advantage of parental or marital support, usually both. To that extent, the women shared a common sympathetic background.

Beyond the common denominator of a comfortable household, there was considerable variety. The relatively few single professional women of the time gravitated towards such groups as the University Women's Club or the Canadian Women's Press Club, where they formed a larger proportion than in the population of women as a whole; they tended to have salaried professional jobs with employers unlikely to discriminate against feminist activity. The majority of the organizations' officers were married, and a married woman, either through affectionate consideration or mindful that her own social and economic position depended on her husband's earning power, prudently would not offend his susceptibilities. (Without surviving evidence, we do not know whether McWilliams's lack of support for suffrage was out of deference for what she saw as Roland's interest. Nevertheless, Nellie McClung was probably correct when she emphasized that husbands who did not want their wives to "go active" had considerable influence on the 1911 Local Council of Women. Some of those husbands were businessmen and professionals, sensitive to the approval of traditionally minded peers. McClung herself had a husband who was first a self-employed pharmacist and then an insurance agent, but her own success as a novelist – she sold 100,000 copies of her first book – brought her a certain economic independence within her household. Such economic self-sufficiency was extraordinary.) Married women tended at least not to defy, and at most to share, the political sympathies of their husbands. Insofar as politics was divided between Liberals and Conservatives, it was natural that the prominent women would also exhibit these differing allegiances.

Women in this pool of activists enjoyed economic security, family support, sometimes a university education, usually a Protestant religion, and almost invariably an Ontario or British background. In 1917 they joined in saying that they desired a non-partisan government in power. A few were pacifists. One almost universal feature was support for prohibition. McClung voiced a commonly held view when she explained "why we concentrated on the liquor traffic. It was corporeal and always present; it walked our streets; it threw its challenge in our faces ... We knew about the men who cashed their wheat tickets and spent most of it over the bar, forgetting to bring home the children's shoes ... Oh no, there was nothing fanciful about the evils of intemperance with its waste of money as well as its moral hazards ... We believed we could shape the world nearer to our heart's desire if we had a dry Canada."[52]

These were McWilliams's peers. They differed among themselves on the degree and direction of state involvement in economic and social life, but these feminists of the post-suffrage generation shared many views. They did not consider that motherhood was limiting, nor that homemaking was demeaning. They did not romanticize women's position in the labour force: they were aware of the low pay, lack of opportunities, and often deplorable working conditions of women in factory and sales work. They became aware of discrimination in the professions. They wanted equal rights as a minimum, they promoted women's rights within the family, and they supported protective legislation for women in the labour force.

McWilliams had become a feminist in the most comprehensive sense of the word. Her particular sense of mission was based on a recognition of her privileges, not of birth or wealth, but of education and opportunity, derived from luck as much as from merit. The *Canadian Courier* wrote in 1914 that Margaret McWilliams was "a shining example, not of the superiority of the university women, necessarily, but of the fine practical uses such women may make, if they will, of the specialised training which they have received."[53] McWilliams thought educated women could repay society for their good fortune through public service, working with, and on behalf of, women. Her feminism was liberating and helped to create the climate in which women were later able to imagine, and demand, more.

CHAPTER FIVE

"Education in All Its Phases"

In 1950 Margaret McWilliams wrote a brief account of her years as first president of the Canadian Federation of University Women. McWilliams summarized the CFUW's historical origins, its expanding membership, and its early aims and achievements. The club's priorities were her own. Of individual members, "almost half were giving their return to the state through leadership in voluntary organizations." Public service by educated women was, she considered, one of the major benefits the university women's clubs could provide. The declared first interest of the new federation was "education in all its phases."[1]

Education in at least three phases could be seen as McWilliams's personal theme in the next decade and beyond. Within the CFUW, she was mainly preoccupied with the university-educated woman, devoting much energy to the establishment of post-graduate scholarships for women. She was also concerned with employment prospects for women in universities and with their chances of being asked to serve on the universities' governing bodies. Working conditions and opportunities for women in teaching, a profession that employed "a little more than one-third" of the membership, was another early concern. Education could contribute to international understanding and peace, and a measure of her hopes for international co-operation was her work performed for the CFUW's International Relations Committee.

Secondly, and still partly under the aegis of the university women's clubs, McWilliams was herself concerned with the continuing education of the woman graduate. In Winnipeg she instituted current events classes at the club, and after she ceased to direct them personally, these classes continued with a momentum of their own. Her concern for civic education went beyond the narrow band of graduates. She wished to educate any lively-minded woman in political and international events, and her first current events classes were intended for interested women regardless of their educational background. From small beginnings these general classes evolved over thirty years into an extraordinary Winnipeg institution, and she did not give them up until she was seventy-two years old.

Thirdly, McWilliams was interested in education in the provincial university and in the public schools. She served on the University of Manitoba Council from 1917 to 1933. Immediately after the first war, she helped found the National Council on Character Education. In this organization she personified the "moral regenerators" of her university youth, those moral reformers who wished to see "the ethics of Jesus the controlling force of our national life."[2] One of the council's first concerns was the textbooks used in the schools, an interest that remained with McWilliams until her early seventies. In 1948 she published *This New Canada*, intended as a textbook, the culmination of her desire to help forge an educated citizenry of all ages.

In these three phases, McWilliams's approach to education – and to so much in her life – manifested the social philosophy encapsulated by John Watson, professor of philosophy at Queen's University from 1872 to 1922. In his *Outline of Philosophy*, published as a book in 1898, the year of McWilliams's graduation from the University of Toronto, he wrote, "the individual man ... must learn that, to set aside his individual inclinations and make himself an organ of the community is to be moral, and the only way to be moral." This has been described as "the most revealing and suggestive statement made by a Canadian philosopher in the nineteenth century."[3] Watson's ideas, strongly influenced by T.H. Green and other British idealists, were communicated from the 1870s onwards to his students over the next fifty years, who as clergymen, civil servants, and formulators of public opinion propagated the same basic views from the pulpit, in publications, and over the various lecture circuits across the country to groups like the

Women's Canadian Club as well as to the universities. These ideas provided the intellectual underpinning to the "social gospel."

The idealist approach preached "what was fundamentally a social ethic." Principal George Grant of Queen's, "the most influential clergyman in Canada in the second half of the Victorian era," rendered this explicit when he said that practical preaching "aims at establishing the Kingdom of God on earth" in a "gospel of active social service." Education was to produce a citizen who, in Watson's words, would "seek his freedom where alone it can be found – in the subordination of his own will to the good of others." The community had pre-eminence over the individual, whose service could be performed "in ascending forms: from the level of the church, the civil service, or the empire." A younger exponent of idealism, George John Blewett, a teacher at Wesley College in Winnipeg before McWilliams's arrival in 1910, declared "the citizenship to which we are called is a heavenly citizenship [which] ... must first be fulfilled upon the earth, in the life in which our duties are those of the good neighbour, the honest citizen, the devoted churchman ... The perfection of human life [for citizens] lies in being at one with God ... by flinging themselves into the labour and causes of the history in which God is realising His eternal purpose."[4]

McWilliams's personal philosophy was consonant with these views. Towards the end of her life, she rephrased Watson's gospel of active social service in her reminder that, despite two world wars, "every individual is a member of the democracy and shares in its responsibilities as well as in its privileges." She acknowledged in 1947 that "we are in danger of becoming masterless men and women." The true master for her was Jesus, "leading us into the true way of life, the end of which is the realisation of the Kingdom of God on Earth," but for those who preferred more secular terminology, she offered the concept of "excellence."[5]

Education had a critical role to play in the formation of the moral individual and the just society. It was the priority of the first CFUW, established largely at McWilliams's initiative. She put to good measure the lessons she had learned in both the Local Council and the National Council of Women. The first specific suggestion of a national organization came to the Winnipeg club in April 1917. Mrs Broadus of Edmonton in a letter "raised the question of a dominion-wide union of University Women's Clubs" but slightly muddied the water by calling attention to the practice of her own club, which admitted many members who were not graduates of any university. Such practice was anathema to the Winnipeg club, whose April meeting, while considering "the time ripe for preparatory measures," decided to confine its informal enquiries to those organizations that admitted only graduates. No action was taken until a year later, when in June 1918 "the report of the committee formed to draw up a provisional constitution for the proposed federation of University clubs of Canada" was adopted. By the next spring, plans were under way for a half dozen Canadian clubs to meet in Winnipeg, after McWilliams had visited Toronto "for their opinion."[6]

This sequence, culled from contemporary archives, suggests that there was plenty of internal interest in a Canadian federation, yet when McWilliams wrote her account in 1950, she identified "the effective impulse" as coming from Dr Winifred Cullis, a British university medical lecturer who had spent the war years at the University of Toronto.[7] Certainly Cullis's suggestion was timely, for the American Association of University Women was trying to organize an international federation, and if there were a Canadian federation, Canada could be a founder-member. The Canadians were not quite quick enough. The American and British organizations arranged to meet in London in July 1919, and although McWilliams had met the Toronto women in March, they did not plan to have a Canadian meeting in Winnipeg until August.[8]

Despite the "almost disastrous" effect of the Winnipeg General Strike during May and June 1919, thirteen delegates, representing McGill, Ottawa, Toronto, Winnipeg, Regina, Edmonton, and Victoria, attended the organizational meeting in Winnipeg in August 1919. McWilliams was unanimously elected president. "It was owing to the persistent effort of Mrs McWilliams that a proposed constitution was drawn up in the beginning and it was she who had threshed out difficulties of procedure with the Toronto Club in March 1919." As she was "an eastern graduate and resided in the west [she] was exactly the right President for our new Federation."[9] Subsequently the new International Federation of University Women elected her vice-president, a position she retained until after the 1922 Paris meeting. After she relinquished the Canadian presidency in 1923, she continued to be active in the Canadian Federation, particularly on the International Relations Committee, even when she was a municipal politician. She continued to attend and participate in triennial meetings of the International Federation all her life.

Constitutionally the new Canadian Federation avoided what McWilliams had seen as the autocracy of the National Council of Women. The constitutional reforms rejected in 1919 by the National Council now were enshrined in the new university federation. There was to be no proxy voting. Triennial, rather than annual meetings, were established; the intention was to reduce the influence of richer or more populated areas in order to allow democratization or at least to minimize the influence of eastern Canada (Toronto) over the rest of the country. On the issue of membership raised in 1917 by the Edmonton club, the constitution firmly declared that each member must hold a degree from a recognized university or its academic equivalent.[10]

The 1919 Winnipeg meeting discussed work to be undertaken by the federation. Out of several topics, priority was given, at McWilliams's initiative, to a travelling scholarship. This was intended to provide a women's equivalent of the Rhodes Scholarship for which only men were eligible. The motion was carried that delegates recommend to their home clubs "the establishment of a federation scholarship for women of the yearly value of one thousand dollars to be tenable in a British University." To help finance this, the CFUW would recommend national lecture tours. The Winnipeg club had shown the way: it brought Ian Hay and Frederick Palmer during the war and raised $1,500. Also, it was proposed that the federation should publish an annual newsletter (this became the CFUW *Chronicle*) and should encourage membership development and inter-club meetings. "Public work" among its members was to be encouraged, to "induce women of suitable gifts and endowments to stand for election as members of school boards and of the governing bodies of universities and colleges."[11]

With minor modifications, the 1919 plans were ratified at the CFUW's first triennial meeting in Toronto in August 1920. Almost every proposal, either on the constitution, by-laws, or drawn from recommendations of the committees on education, vocations, publications, and scholarships, met debate, and few motions were carried without some amendment. Yet discussion was not protacted. Delegates spent a "most delightful evening" seeing through Hart House, were treated to a "most delightful tea-party" at the Royal Canadian Yacht Club, and enjoyed "a very delicious dinner" at Sunnyside Pavilion followed by a tour of Canadian artists' works at the Exhibition Grounds. They did not convene until ten o'clock every morning and took two-hour luncheons. The scholarship was established, although the university at which the recipient was to study did not necessarily have to be British: it was left "to the Committee of Selection in consultation with the candidate." The annual newsletter was approved. Two reports with extensive recommendations were considered, on education and employment, and these give an interesting indication of the flavour of opinion of this first generation of university-educated women.

The education report was produced by Geneva Misener of the Classics Department at the University of Alberta and the Edmonton University Women's Club. She had attended the Winnipeg meeting in 1919, at which she had "made a plea for larger professional life for women, bemoaning the fact that so few made the professions a life work but were willing to forego great opportunities for that of marriage when there should really be no necessity for so doing. Marriage and a profession may go hand in hand for a woman as for a man." Misener's 1920 report recommended that more research be done on teaching as a profession for women and that there be greater high school opportunities "for each child," a "broader, cross-Canada" financing of secondary education. Misener was particularly concerned about the professional status and needs of school teachers. She suggested a minimum requirement of "a three years' course in High School and six months' of professional training"; the meeting modified this, expressing in a more general way support for "higher qualifications" for teachers.

Misener also wanted "an adequate salary schedule" based on a sophisticated appreciation of six variables: the cost of living, the cost of education, remuneration in other work, the value of a teacher to the community, a teacher's academic and professional standing, and, significantly, the principle of equal pay for equal work. In no province at the time did the latter apply, nor was it a demand from the early teachers' associations. The CFUW was persuaded to include this point by Jessie Dykes of Toronto, who described an exemplary scheme in Norway: "Men and women doing the same work must have the same qualifications and receive exactly the same salary." But still there was the assumption that a family's livelihood would be produced by the father and that the mother would be unemployed outside the household. "In order to meet the difficulty of maintaining a family a married man receives a special marriage allowance as an annual addition to his income. An additional annual allowance is then made for each child, the same child allowance is granted to a widow."

The assumption was maintained that only in the absence of a male breadwinner would a woman be working at all: she would be a spinster or a widow. Misener's 1919 declaration that marriage and employment "may" go hand in hand for a woman was not developed. Interwar feminists struggled continually to reconcile work and family in theory and in practice and were rarely able to reach consensus.

The second major report studied the job opportunities for university women in Canada. Its title, "Vocations," reveals an assumption that one was "called," paralleling the call of a priest to ordination. Invocation of a deity helped to justify the still unfamiliar phenomenon of a middle-class woman working for her living. The report was produced by Elsinore McPherson of Toronto, who had been awarded a research scholarship, and its recommendations were designed to broaden horizons for university women. Each club was asked to urge its local university to set up "a bureau of appointments" with a view to founding a "central university bureau for professional people." In the meantime, university graduates were encouraged to provide a support and information network for new graduates.[12]

This declaration of the second report, which expressed solidarity with new recruits to the privileged group of women graduates, echoed throughout the first triennial meeting. McWilliams's opening remarks as president noted "that we from our experiences travelling along the road away from our Universities wanted to make the way easier and broader for those coming after." The constitution's statement of purpose voiced concern for university women's intellectual welfare and public opportunities: "(a) To stimulate the interest of university women in public affairs, and to afford an opportunity for the expression of united opinion. (b) To promote the higher education of women, and especially to encourage research work. (c) To facilitate social intercourse and co-operation between the women of different universities."[13]

Throughout her life, McWilliams was one of a large number of idealists who considered that privilege should be paid for by public service. As "Alison Craig" (pen-name of McWilliams's old friend Kennethe Haig) noted in 1923, "the gift of a university education carries with it an obligation, to make return of service. Canadian democracy is committed in its very foundations to education – and this great experiment in human values demands ... the intelligent support of those who have enjoyed its benefits."[14] Graduates should not be satisfied by personal gain, but should contribute to community welfare.

The first three years of the CFUW life were important in ensuring its survival and its present and future effectiveness. There were sixteen branches with 1,300 members, holding degrees from seventy-five universities, "thus establishing the international character of the national body." In numbers the National Federation of University Women could not vie with the National Council of Women, but McWilliams was at pains to stress its quality.[15] The clubs were drawn together through common interests, presenting lectures by prominent personalities (the federation had invited Madame Curie in 1921 and Bliss Carman in 1922) and contributing to the international scholarship fund. This closeness was reinforced by McWilliams's own presidential visits to each of the clubs once and to several twice.[16]

It is not easy to judge how effective the federation was in its first three years. In some specific areas it met expectations. The opportunity to express a united opinion had been taken by the executive in 1921, when it supported the appointment of a woman senator.[17] Also, reports presented at both triennials (in 1920 on education and vocations, in 1923 on libraries and the employment of women in universities) had alerted the membership to some of the difficulties experienced by women working in professions. One such problem was set out for delegates by a guest from the American Association of University Women. The association had conducted a survey in universities to discover why so few university positions were held by women. Responses were blunt. "I think it is psychologically impossible for men entirely to ignore in their dealings with women the fact that they are dealing with persons that are not men," said one man. "This makes men find life simpler in its workaday aspects when one's colleagues and instructors are men." The CFUW distributed its investigative reports throughout Canada and even abroad, when requests were made, and thus contributed to a measure of public awareness.[18]

In one area, the scholarship, the federation was without doubt successful. Three had been awarded in the first three years. As a result, two women were studying in Paris and one in London. This annual scholarship was financed not through endowment but through current income derived from a levy based on membership size of each club and the lecture tours, where local clubs charged the general public admission.

In these first years, the CFUW had two direct involvements with the International Federation. First, there was a contribution to Crosby Hall, which was designed to be an international clubhouse in London for university women of all national clubs; and secondly, the Canadian Federation helped finance the travel expenses of its president to the first biennial in Paris in 1922, where McWilliams's work as international vice-president brought recognition to the CFUW. The national organization continued to defray costs incurred by officers who attended international meetings as delegates, a matter of considerable benefit to McWilliams and others.

After four years of demanding work with the Canadian Federation, McWilliams could feel pleased to have provided what her successor called "dynamic leadership" nationally and to have shown the flag internationally.[19] The triennial report of her presidential successors continued to follow the policy lines she had been instrumental in laying out; the provision of graduate scholarships and the identification of opportunities and problems for women in education remained the federation's major concerns. Her foresight and administrative skill established the CFUW on the course it was to take for over a generation, and in the long term this must have satisfied her at least as much as the "sheaf of pink roses" given her by the members of the 1923 triennial.[20] But the confusion over promoting awareness on the one hand and activism on the other was highlighted in the federation's new International Relations Committee, whose convenor McWilliams became in 1923. Activism could be measured; awareness was intangible.

As we have seen, McWilliams was no pacifist during the First World War. She nevertheless hoped that non-violent solutions could be found for political problems, and she can be described as one of the many "fairweather or peacetime pacifists."[21] She considered that the International Federation of University Women was justified in its aim to bring about "understanding and friendship between the university women of the nations of the world," and she also concurred with its further purpose, to "develop between their countries sympathy and mutual helpfulness."[22] However, she never went so far as the president of Bryn Mawr, who, at a reception given by the American Association of University Women for the visiting Madame Curie, declared: "We women can and must stop war. Unless we stop it, no one will stop it."[23] Still, when in 1922 McWilliams was asked in Regina what the IFUW's purpose was, she replied that it existed "primarily for aiding in promoting international unity and unbreakable peace." Her hope – "the thought trembled in my mind" – was that within the IFUW "Canada's great role might be interpreter among the nations."[24] The IFUW provided a means to the end of forming an "entente cordiale" among university women, which in turn was part of the process of strengthening the bonds of good will between nations. "To be internationally minded means to give a world scope to the terms liberty, equality, fraternity." College women had the responsibility "to work toward bringing about world peace."[25]

McWilliams chaired the discussion at the Paris IFUW meeting that led to the establishment of a framework designed to embody its purpose. This was to be accomplished by each national federation's forming its own Committee on International Relations. She heard Professor Cullis speak of the importance of living and working in a foreign country in order to encourage international co-operation. The particular ways the IFUW hoped to achieve this were by establishing scholarships (like the Canadian Federation's), by exchange lectureships, and by hospitality (it was hoped that members from one country would be able to stay in clubhouses set up in another). McWilliams herself closed the debate with a speech expressing her faith in the particular aptitude for peace of university women "and men," who "held within themselves the key to the friendship of the world."[26]

In the loftiest statement she was to make concerning the benefits and responsibilities associated with a university education, McWilliams identified

the understanding mind, the dispassionate, impersonal mind, the mind that while it did not give up convictions, because it knew the value of convictions, yet respected convictions differing from its own, could believe that they might be well based and was certain to believe that they were honest; the mind that knew it must not judge; the mind that was tolerant – in short, the mind that understood. There was nothing that the world required more today than the exercise of that understanding mind ... The members of the Federation would go back to their countries inspired to work for the creation of the state of peace, the mind to peace, which was another way of saying the understanding mind ... She had seen now so many signs of a world in which service to one's fellows was to be the mark of life and growth, that she had regained confidence in her vision that humanity was entering on a period that would be remembered as one of the great times in the history of the world, when the university men and women, standing on the threshold of a new world, had their great opportunity to take their own world and lift it up on to this other level, to take another step forward toward that time when we should have attained a state of happiness and perfection which was yet a long way off.[27]

When, a year later, McWilliams ceased to be the Canadian president, she chose the International Relations Committee as the forum for her continuing commitment to the organization.

Almost inevitably, this committee failed to match the expectations stated in 1922, but in many ways the Canadian Federation was to achieve many of the more down-to-earth objectives set out by Winifred Cullis. The committee report to the 1926 Montreal triennial was in fact McWilliams's account of the 1926 Amsterdam International Federation conference, highlighting three prominent issues: eligibility requirements demanded by national clubs, the role of married women in the professions, and the question of whether married women could retain their citizenship of birth.[28] The next year, McWilliams reported action in four areas. For the International Federation, the committee had identified a list of books "reflecting the life and thought of Canada." It had provided members of the Canadian Federation travelling in Europe and America with letters of introduction to other clubs. It had encouraged Canadian clubs to form groups for the study of international problems. It had provided an information exchange for scholarships. Together, these achievements fell short of the committee's noble aims, but they were nevertheless constructive and significant.[29]

At the annual executive meeting of 1936, held in Winnipeg, the Canadian Federation heard a full report from the International Relations Committee's convenor, Miss I. Brittain. The committee relayed information concerning the International Federation and its work on behalf of women, including the visit of a 120-strong deputation from women's organizations that presented a peace petition to the president of the League of Nations. Growing international political tension was reflected in the withdrawal of national German and Italian federations from the International Federation and the actual dissolution of the Italian federation by the Italian government.

At the meeting, McWilliams offered a spirited criticism of the committee's membership, which she considered to be dominated by eastern Canada. The committee was one of the "two most important committees of the Federation" and "the Federation was organised to make the International possible and existed for the purpose of disseminating knowledge of international affairs." As it was presently operating, said

McWilliams, according to a verbatim report of that meeting, "if you are going to have an International committee of Montreal, or Montreal and Toronto, then you simply leave us out." McWilliams noted she was ex-officio on the committee and severely criticized the convenor for not having kept her committee privy to important international developments. The meeting moved that members in future be "representative of the different parts of Canada."[30] By the time of the 1938 annual executive meeting, McWilliams was again serving as convenor and her report underlined its own wide-ranging membership – from Vancouver, Calgary, Regina, Winnipeg, and Moncton, with only one from Toronto and none from Montreal.[31]

There is little evidence to suggest the International Relations Committee did much to promote international peace and understanding. Indeed, it generated domestic discord. As originally conceived by the International Federation, the national international relations committees were to provide academic exchanges, both of graduate students and established scholars. Insofar as this goal was effected by the Canadian Federation, it was done by the Scholarship Committee rather than the International Relations Committee. It would seem that McWilliams's 1936 claim that the International Relations Committee was one of the two most important committees of the cfuw was inflated. This is not to suggest that the Canadian Federation was reluctant to fulfil commitments to scholarship, to promoting interest in current events, or to the propagation of peace, but its International Relations Committee does not appear to have taken leadership in any of these areas.

The education of public opinion about world events was one of McWilliams's passions from a very early stage. The International Relations Committee of the Canadian Federation of University Women had a disappointing record, but she could point to success in a remarkable institution that she created and developed over thirty years. This was her current events class.

McWilliams's objective was to "inspire and impart her own intellectual curiosity" in the study of the country's affairs and world events. This she did by conducting classes that avoided being "stilted or academic. They kept the intimate touch."[32] Her audiences thought she was successful. She brought the class to an end in the autumn of 1947, and in January 1948 women who had participated over the years joined to pay tribute to her. To show their appreciation for what she had given them, they commissioned a beautiful illuminated scroll for presentation: "your example of an informed mind untiring in pursuit of facts; your discernment and understanding of the clash of world forces; your wonder at the Great and the Good; your courage in Dark Days; your pride in our Canadian heritage and your Pilgrim Faith in the Future Welfare of Man." This was a highly significant testament. Echoing her own language, the scroll inscribed McWilliams's hopes for her own life, of which this particular work was its exemplary manifestation: "By giving of Yourself freely in Public Life you have set an example in Citizenship and social responsibility. There has been no savour of complacency or narrowness."[33] The class's view of McWilliams was as she herself must have wished to appear.

Year after year women considered it worth their while to attend these classes. McWilliams was good entertainment in the days before television or even, in the 1920s, radio, when going out to hear public speakers provided welcome punctuation to weeks, especially during the winter, that offered little diversion. There are signs that she provided more than a diversion. Men in government respected her and liked to know what was said in the classes. She was considered "quite influential" by members of successive governments, said C. Rhodes Smith, who worked with her in the Winnipeg City Council and who in the 1940s became a minister in the provincial government.[34] Douglas Campbell, premier in 1948, noted that his colleagues hesitated to cross her, aware that she was well informed and forthcoming with her opinions on public events.[35] Possibly by educating their wives, the current events classes raised the level of domestic discourse. In 1951 Winnipeg writer Kathleen Strange said that because of the classes "numbers of women have become world citizens in thought."[36] Certainly McWilliams took pride in them.

The classes' origins are not entirely clear. In 1920, by which time McWilliams was beginning to achieve national prominence, she informed an interviewer from *Saturday Night* that she had been conducting the classes "bi-weekly since the first year of the war."[37] The earliest formal notice is to be found in the Deacon's Court minutes of St. Stephen's, Broadway, Church in May 1920, when the minister, the Rev. C.W. Gordon, commended Mrs McWilliams on her Wednesday-morning "weekly meetings for discussion of current topics" that had taken place in the church since the previous fall.[38] Over the same season, at the University Women's Club, she "consented to give instruction in Current Events."[39] The immediate impetus, McWilliams later said, was that "fellow members of her church became confused by names of foreign countries during World War One." Her interpretations soon attracted outsiders, and "her lectures grew to be one of the important events of the Winnipeg winter season for women."[40]

The University Women's Club current events offshoot had an uncertain start, and developed as a variant of the main plant. In November 1919, McWilliams allotted topics to members in preparation for the first "current events" night. One person was to report on the result of the civic elections, another on the international situation in Europe, and two were to produce an outline of current events taking place. Two weeks later, in a classroom of the University Arts Buildings, reports were duly made, and McWilliams then commented on two important events: the peace treaty and a coal strike. Then more topics were allotted for the next meeting. Towards the end of January the club president bewailed "the lack of audience at the current events discussion meetings and urged a larger and more encouraging audience." No more took place until April, when "as this was 'Current Events' night, Mrs McWilliams took charge." Several reports were presented, on the peace treaty, local labour conditions (a year after the General Strike), and affairs in Germany. And at the final current events night of that year, an appreciative vote of thanks was given to Mrs McWilliams.[41]

McWilliams was not particularly pleased with this experiment. At a meeting of the executive in June, the University Women's Club president was directed specifically to "request her continuation of the Current Events meetings." However, the president, who was busy at the time working with McWilliams in connection with the new Canadian Federation, later reported that "in view of the St. Stephen's Church meetings Mrs McWilliams declined to continue the Current Events meetings with the University Club." Members were sufficiently stimulated to proceed without her. At the first business meeting of the 1920–21 year, a committee was established to organize current events classes for the year.[42] These meetings, alternating with "regular" meetings of the club, continued through the season. After the presentation of reports, members would vote on which events had been most important. Current events meetings, though less frequent, were maintained during the 1921–22 season as well.

McWilliams's main current events class had its life outside the University Women's Club. Although at least once role-playing was used in a mock election devised to illustrate proportional representation, these proper current events classes evolved into regular lectures rather than discussions.[43] McWilliams used blackboard and chalk. Women who used to go remember her as a fascinating speaker. She would review the events of the week before her presentation and bring in anecdotes from her own travels in Canada and abroad.

Indeed, one student recollects a clear connection between the classes and the trips. In the days before people did much travelling, McWilliams "liked to travel." Isobel Scurfield, who had just begun a teaching career in 1922, used to go with her sister to the University Arts Building every Monday evening at 7:30. "We did pay a fee, quite small, everybody paid a fee, and this went into what she called her travel fund ... She and her husband would go off every summer" on the proceeds.[44]

A letter circulated to the members of the class in April 1924 bore witness to the more modest financial contribution actually made. The secretary of the students' committee, Annie Fraser, pointed out that "Mrs McWilliams has carried on this work all these years without receiving *one cent* of remuneration. It has been the custom at Christmastime or at the end of the season to present her with flowers, and during the past two years, since the Class has grown to such large proportions, magazines, necessary for her to obtain the information which she presents so comprehensively to the Class, have been paid for out of the general funds. At the close of each season any surplus funds have been turned over to some charitable institution. Your committee feel that the time has come when Mrs McWilliams should receive something more than compliments and kind words." As a surprise, the committee proposed to consign that year's surplus funds to help finance McWilliams's planned trip to the IFUW conference at Christiania (Oslo), Norway. Members were solicited additionally for specific contributions: "The committee would suggest $1.00." The letter incidentally demonstrated Fraser's conviction of McWilliams's good standing: "It is a credit, not only to Winnipeg but to Canada, to have such a delegate represent our nation."[45]

Students included single working women. Many teachers used to go in the evening, and during daytime meetings "women who were civic minded attended."[46] One such student was Edith McColl, a Bryn Mawr graduate who had moved to Winnipeg in 1912 on her marriage to a civil engineer. In October 1924 she noted in a letter to her sister: "Current Events class – Mrs McWilliams started a morning class $5 – 1st & 3rd Tues. at 10.30. The evening one is $2 (one eve.) She wants question & discussion." McColl was primed to "help with discussion" and was flattered to be favoured by McWilliams's attention.[47] Numbers of students varied. Journalist Amy Roe wrote in 1952 that "at one point the total number attending evening and morning classes numbered 1200."[48]

One vivid account of her preparation and performance was written by McWilliams's niece Helen. "At 500 Stradbrooke Ave they had thrown together the parlor and living room so that over 100 people could be seated. Every Tuesday and Thursday morning the seats were filled – and every Wednesday evening she had a lecture in a hall down-town – holding 600 – entirely men! All this concerned current events – it was a relevation to me the way her mind worked – she read all the papers but pedantic Uncle Roly would read to her all the background information – the papers from all over the country – the encyclopaedia – she never took a note – listened but just kept on with her knitting or crocheting ... And the next morning I would sit in the back of the room and hear her give such a dramatic account of the news – not at all what Uncle Roly had read to her the night before!"[49]

This memory derives from the winter of 1929–30, which Helen spent with the McWilliamses after her mother's death. The reference to "entirely men" is nowhere corroborated. Other written and verbal accounts agree that McWilliams's audience was constituted by women. And McWilliams's preparation drew on years of formal and informal study. The papers presented to associations and other meetings provided her with background knowledge, as did the research she did before travelling and for writing her books. By 1930 she had travelled several times in Europe and had written, with Roland, *Russia in 1926,* and her own history book, *Manitoba Milestones.* She had become skilful in the organizing and presentation of material, and the current events classes afforded her a regular intellectual exercise. That she recognized their value and enjoyed the work is clear from her maintaining the classes through the 1930s, when her work as alderman gave her ample reason to retire, and even into the 1940s, when she held current events classes in the ballroom of Government House.

We cannot now tell, if we ever could, the extent to which some women in Winnipeg became better informed as a result of the McWilliams current events class. It is reasonable to note, however, her authority in an area traditionally associated with men, and the respect accorded her not only by successive years of students but by their husbands as well. McWilliams's own authority was founded upon her own educational credentials and her continuing interest in current events, as well as upon her skill in presentation. Her performances served to undercut the idea that men were the sole source of wisdom. Women as well could enrol as undergraduates at universities and could frequent public libraries to keep up with the literature. Formal education showed her how to study for the rest of her life. Education was the key to McWilliams's intellectual world.

She exhorted women in other cities to keep up with events. Regular reading of the newspaper was "a service to ourselves in that the imagination becomes stimulated and our own lives broadened by the contact with great events all over the world." A journalist herself, still writing occasional pieces, she knew some sections of a newspaper must be read with discretion, but on the whole newspapers were indispensable for keeping readers in touch with the "great world."[50]

In an interview with Hilda Ridley in 1920, McWilliams said that her "peculiar mission" was to be "an educational force."[51] By then she was involved in higher education too, having already served three years on the Council of the University of Manitoba.

In 1917 a new act organizing the university was passed by the Manitoba legislature. It was drafted by Roland and stipulated a nine-member board of governors and a council, six of whose twenty-eight members were appointed by the lieutenant-governor-in-council. One of these was Margaret McWilliams.

The council had "general charge of the academic work of the University" and McWilliams was the only woman member, in a war year when 3 of the teaching faculty of 48, and 38 of the 155 graduates, were women.[52] McWilliams regularly attended the monthly meetings, furthering her interest in continuing education by serving on the Extension Committee. She was disappointed that more women were not appointed to university government and resigned from the council on the issue in October 1933. Earlier that year a scandal associated with the defalcation by the bursar led to the resignation of all members of the board. The government made new appointments, of whom only one was a woman, McWilliams's friend and colleague from the University Women's Club, the Women's Canadian Club, and the Social Science Study Club, Mary Speechly.[53] McWilliams subsequently advised the council "that she had tendered her resignation to the Lieutenant-Governor-in-Council from the University Council as a protest against the ignoring of women in the appointments to the new Board of Governors."[54]

McWilliams was unable to dominate the University Council, and to that extent, her experience as a member was unusual. She was able nevertheless to gain some benefit. For many seasons she held her current events class in the University Arts Building on Broadway. But she became increasingly frustrated with the low numbers and slow careers of women on the faculty and was particularly chagrined when in 1923 the university president, James Maclean, refused to respond to her request, as president of the CFUW, for data on women at the university.[55] Despite her reverence for university education, she was critical of the university's reluctance to welcome women into university government, and she was always wary of pedantry and knowledge that seemed to her to have no practical application.[56]

Nevertheless, McWilliams believed in the power of the mind. In her concern with public school education, she insisted on "character" and on the desirability for education to raise the general moral and spiritual plane of "the nation." These concepts echoed the inspiration of T.H. Green. Green argued that democracy must be based on religion and that compulsory education was part of the state's obligation to promote morality.[57] When McWilliams described the establishment in 1919 of the National Council of Education – originally known as the National Council on Character Education – she said its origin lay in the hope that evangelical regeneration would make the nation strong: "By an equal ardent pursuit of the great ethical ideals of Jesus our country might become a great moral force."[58] McWilliams analysed the problems around this pursuit into a three-part agenda. The first was to ensure that textbooks inculcated the right ideals. The second was to train the teacher in order that she, or he, might properly educate the child. The third was to create support in the public at large.

The new National Council looked to social science for aid.[59] It wanted experts with learned credentials to survey existing Canadian textbooks in three areas: literature, history, and geography. Members wanted to see if the current books reflected and promoted not only nationalist but also Christian ideals. The council's second agenda item agreed with the CFUW's and National Council of Women's call for an improved teaching profession. The National Council on Education wished to raise standards for admission into the profession and to improve teachers' social status and scale of remuneration. In regard to the third agenda item, the council wanted to enlist "the press, the pulpit and ... the various community and welfare organisations" to contribute to "lay" support for a revitalization of education.[60] Considering themselves "modernist pilgrims," the council members were convinced that social action should be the central focus of Christianity.[61]

McWilliams was imbued with the idealism associated with T.H. Green and Professor Watson, scholar of Kant and Hegel. She was slower to learn about the liberal individualism of John

Stuart Mill, whose work was not in her university curriculum. She accepted the nineteenth-century notion of nationalism as a liberating force and saw society as a corporate whole rather than a stratified struggle of classes. She took for granted the Whig idea of history with its stepping stones to the present, superior, world of progress. She was also concerned to include awareness of values in the educational system – and to her this unquestionably meant the application of Christian (preferably Protestant) ethics to public life as well as to private. The idea that each citizen contributed to public service through the machinery of state democracy was welcome to her – and as we shall see, she was most critical of people who neglected to involve themselves in the new opportunities offered by liberal democracy. In her faith in the goodness of human nature and the beneficence of the state, she remained a product of nineteenth-century idealism, with confidence in the future. Neither the First nor the Second World War dampened her hope. McWilliams retained a conviction that human society could be improved, that the key to amelioration was in education, and that textbooks were a central element in the system.

In 1948 she published her own textbook, *This New Canada*, testimony to her own experience as an educator and to her still bright ideals for the future. Organized into sections, subsections, and further subdivisions, each with its own title, the book allows the reader to follow her line of thought. Her chauvinism was expressed carefully and without too much hyperbole. Canada was "a new, great country already exercising an influence in the councils of the world powers far beyond that to which the size of her population would entitle her ... Deep in the hearts of Canadian people is a desire to see their country play a worthy part by the side of other nations."[62] Canada's world influence was analysed as a product of its "chief" position in the new Commonwealth, its contribution to the Allied side during the Second World War, and its close relations with the United States. The second section considered "Canada's Path to Nationhood" with minimum reference to difficulties or disagreements over race, class, or region. Later she acknowledged that "mutual understanding" between English and French was difficult, but she briskly remarked that "any young citizen aspiring to public life should make a point of becoming fluent in both languages."[63] At all government levels the state was presented as rightfully omnipotent and beneficent.

The fourth and final section was hortatory, recapitulating the ideals that had inspired her youth and sustained her whole life. Canadians should "take their fair share" in "carrying on the life of the nation." Those who refused were "careless," "indifferent," "unthinking," "just lazy," or "just thoroughly self-ish." McWilliams's nationalism did not involve anti-American-ism. Her final sentence expressed the faith that Canada would become a country where "every citizen shall in truth have the 'right to life, liberty and the pursuit of happiness.'"[64] Uncritical and platitudinous, *This New Canada* advocated the subordina-tion of the individual in the service of the state, just as Profes-sor Watson and Principal Grant had preached two generations earlier. This was what McWilliams had attempted. She was asking of others no more than what she had demanded of herself: uncritical selflessness in the interests of the community.

CHAPTER SIX

Geography and History

"Geography and history are two of the greatest factors in moulding the character and the institutions of a people ... and the conditions of the present are the produce of the past."[1] McWilliams applied herself to understanding and explaining the present partly because she considered it her duty as a university-educated citizen with certain gifts. She also enjoyed it.

Learning about geography and history through foreign travel was one of her favourite pastimes. Beginning in 1922 McWilliams travelled abroad frequently, preparing for a trip by reading books and articles for months before. Some of her expenses were defrayed by organizations whose international conferences she attended. She was a Canadian delegate at International Federation of University Women conferences in Paris in 1922, Christiania (Oslo) in 1924, Amsterdam in 1926, and Paris again in 1937. She represented Canada at the International Labour Organization (ILO) conference in Geneva in 1930 and at a conference of the Institute of Pacific Relations in China in 1931. When she went to Paris in 1937, she attended a housing conference as a Winnipeg alderman. She usually managed to incorporate sightseeing into the visits, and afterwards she would make use of her observations and direct experience in the current events classes and in addresses and speeches to various organizations.

Ever on the alert for writing opportunities, McWilliams produced newspaper and magazine articles based on trips to Paris, Oslo, Russia, and China. One trip resulted in a book published with her husband, *Russia in 1926*.

McWilliams's first trip to Europe in 1922 was documented in a euphoric account published in the *Western Home Monthly*. She tried to describe "the spell the old world cast": "Why did no-one ever tell me it would be like this?"[2] Before she embarked, her friends joined in a ritual farewell. At the annual meeting of the Winnipeg University Women's Club in May 1922, while sixty-seven members enjoyed high tea, "Mrs McWilliams, President of the National Federation, and Vice-President of the International Federation, was presented with a silk umbrella and a slicker, previous to her departure for Paris."[3] McWilliams travelled first to London, where she gave a maple leaf pin to Princess Mary, King George V's daughter. This was a wedding gift from the Winnipeg branches of the University Women's Club and the Women's Canadian Club.[4] She was rewarded with an audience with Her Royal Highness, "a striking looking woman," in McWilliams's words, who "has to work exceptionally hard at her numerous duties."[5] Princess Mary "expressed much interest in the work of Canadian University women and was delighted to hear that a scholarship is being provided annually to send one of the graduates to Europe."[6]

McWilliams then arrived in Paris, where three hundred women representing fifteen nations met in Reid Hall.[7] This eighteenth-century building near the Luxembourg Gardens was the gift of Mrs Whitelaw Reid, wife of the American ambassador in Paris before the First World War. She had established it as a girls' club for young American women studying art and music in Paris. After the war, it was intended to serve as a residence for university women studying in Paris and as an international centre; it was officially opened for this latter purpose at the IFUW meeting. The building, modernized and decorated, provided sleeping accommodation as well as a large hall and smaller meeting rooms. In the garden and the courtyard "we could sit at morning coffee or afternoon tea between sessions and have those little private chats."[8]

From McWilliams's point of view, the major accomplishment of this Paris meeting was the setting up of machinery for promoting international good will, but she also valued the sight-seeing and new personal contacts. Tours organized for the delegates included excursions to various points of interest – a factory that made Sèvres porcelain, the Institute of Radium, museums, an observatory, and the city of Rheims ("for two hours we motored through the shattered streets of what had been a beautiful and pacific city. Of twelve thousand homes, ten thousand were utterly destroyed by bombardment").[9]

When McWilliams was interviewed two months after the meeting, she was asked to speak "about the delegates," who "are in a sense, representatives of this new day, the first in written history when womankind as such is being given an opportunity to investigate the storehouses of history." McWilliams was warm in her praise; she had discerned "underneath all differences of speech and type ... one mind. Was it the product of womanhood or of university education or both?" She was not sure, but "the important thing was that it was there, and in it I saw hope for civilization in the hope of tolerant internationalism." This sense of unity triumphed over the differences that had emerged over specific issues – whether or not married women should have a profession, the pace at which women were entering business and professional life in various countries, the issue of equal pay for equal work – issues that had already engaged the Canadians both in the National Federation and in the Winnipeg club.

McWilliams was left with an impression of being part of an international community of women, "not set apart" but dedicated to "the service especially of the women of their nation."[10] Through the example and conversation of these women – "leaders in French thought; college presidents from America, so numerous as to be no longer intellectual caviar; a doctor of philosophy, said to be the best known woman in Spain; a former chief of service in Brussels hospitals; from England, a novelist and literary critic, professor of physiology and a Ll.B. from the industrial world; the oculist of a Milan hospital; Scandinavian women of distinction" – McWilliams's eyes were opened to possibilities more extensive than those she knew from previous study or observation.[11] There is no reason to doubt her sincerity when she said the meeting "had been one of the happiest and most inspiring experiences she has ever had."[12] This meeting, moreover, marks the beginning of her firm and unequivocal commitment to the distinctively feminist goals of women's equality and solidarity.

Her favourable response to this new vista was at odds with the reaction of the Toronto-bred wife of the new principal of Emmanuel College, Saskatoon. Mrs W.T. Hallam was "deeply disappointed with the whole atmosphere of the conference" and returned "shocked." The English women especially offended her. "Their attitude appears to be, 'well, I've the same rights as a man, and if I want to smoke and put my feet on the table, I am entitled to do it.'" Hallam had expected the conference to discuss educational ideas in their broadest and highest sense. Instead, the women smoked continuously, "lighting one cigarette from another," and "they talked about the place of married women in the professions, and equal salaries for women and men." In the process, the English woman was "becoming unsexed. She has lost her feminine charm, and is virtually a neuter ... The English University woman ... is making a grave mistake in aping man."

Hallam's remarks, which were published in an Ottawa newspaper, led to an editorial in the *Manitoba Free Press:* "One swallow doesn't make a summer nor one puff a race of cigarette inhalers." Proceeding to put Mrs Hallam down, the newspaper of McWilliams's city noted "what Toronto thinks today Europe thought a generation ago." A fellow delegate, Mrs W.J. Sykes of Ottawa, was more forthright. "Where has Mrs W.T. Hallam been living?" she asked. She herself had observed no smoking at the meetings, nor did she think English women were any "coarser" than the Americans or Canadians.[13]

This first European trip left a profound impression on McWilliams, beyond enjoyment. It gave her a sense of participating in the building of important international contacts and in the confirmation of a more forthright feminism. She spoke of feeling the "sudden sense of the possession of the great things of the past." She had a new and vivid sense of the continuity of civilization, a dramatic realization for a "Western Canadian, living where anything that is fifty years old is just about old enough to be torn down to make way for something better." She described particular sites and her own reactions: "all the weeks held nothing more full of pure joy, more revealing, than an evening's walk along the royal mile" in Edinburgh. She felt "wonder" when contemplating memorials to religious martyrs, and recognized the "patient toil" displayed by the builders of walls and monuments that had taken years to construct. "And even more than the toil of the body could one tell of the labour of the mind and spirit which went into the making of the ordered system of government which is our pride."[14] McWilliams delighted in the company she found at IFUW meetings and never flagged in her expressions of pride and admiration.

In 1924 McWilliams was one of the fourteen Canadian delegates, five of them from Winnipeg, attending the IFUW biennial at Christiania, Norway, and she prepared meticulously. Expenses were partially covered by a collection from the current events class and by remuneration for articles she arranged to send to the *Winnipeg Tribune* (for $100) and the *Toronto Star*.[15] At the last minute she received an invitation to speak in London at Wembley Stadium during the Women's Week of the British Empire Exhibition. Initially she declined, as her intention was to spend a week in Norway with travelling companion Elsie Moore before the Christiania conference. On reflection and with additional information supplied by her friend Professor R.C. Wallace, in England at the time, she agreed to give up the week in Norway. He had discovered that she was supposed to "speak for Canada from the point of view of the Canadian woman on the outlook of Canada ... you would do so well that no one from Canada could do better."[16]

On the ship, Canadian Pacific's SS *Marloch*, she won first prize in a bridge tournament and made new friends among the passengers, many of whom were women professionals associated with the Overseas Education League. After touring in Scotland and York, McWilliams and Moore spent a hectic time in London, visiting IFUW friends, shopping, sightseeing, and going to the theatre. They attended sessions of the American and Canadian Bar associations and sat in on question period in the House of Commons. With the help of the Manitoba minister of labour, McWilliams met Margaret Bondfield, parliamentary secretary to the minister of labour in the first Labour government: "I liked her very much indeed."[17]

At the weekend McWilliams and Moore went to the seaside. On Brighton pier, McWilliams prepared her speech, "The Education of Women in Canada." She shared the Wembley platform with Canadian social worker Charlotte Whitton. One of her friends from the SS *Marloch* wrote: "You spoke awfully well, though of course the subject matter you all had to take was not *thrilling*. You were far the best."[18] McWilliams had a distinctly caustic opinion of the Wembley diversion. She had a dim view of the organizer, Lady McLaren Brown, wife of the Canadian Pacific Railway European general manager, who "did not ruin my speech though she nearly did, and 'hired minions' expresses her idea of us ... All that Wembley did for us was to get us five days longer in London." But, she admitted in a letter to Roland, "believe me, the five days were golden."[19]

At the IFUW conference, McWilliams thrilled to President Caroline Spurgeon's speech describing delegates in the "Baconian phrase" as "Merchants of Light," and she was especially impressed by the British delegates. "Lady Rhondda put up her case as well, I think, as it could have been done, and Mrs Corbett Ashby was brilliant." McWilliams was flattered by the attention she received. As vice-president, "I walked in the second place in the great procession and sat in the seats of the mighty at the dinners, and was generally very well treated. Of course I loved it – how could I help it, and they still seem to think that I am a wonder at presiding."[20]

This conference especially pleased her in its ceremony and side-trips. The opening events involved three hundred women, "wearing the academic dress to which their degrees entitled them," proceeding "down the centre of the great hall to the strains of Grieg music, played as none save the Scandinavians had ever heard it played before." McWilliams enjoyed the hospitality offered by the king and queen in the summer palace gardens, and she appreciated looking around the studio of Vigeland, a sculptor described as a modern Michelangelo. She relished a visit to the Viking ships, found preserved in peat. She told a romantic tale of love and death associated with them – the sort of story she incorporated four years later into her own history of Manitoba. She tried to imagine what had motivated the men to go out on the ocean in a tiny craft: "Standing there and looking out to sea beyond the island of the harbour far to the west, with a mist faintly tinged with blue softening every outline, and the sea as far as the eye could reach shining through the mist like molten gold, we could almost hear the call as it came to those old Vikings."[21]

After the Norwegian conference, McWilliams and Moore travelled in Denmark, Germany, Czechoslovakia, and Austria. McWilliams carried introductions from the Canadian Red Cross to their officers in each city, and she made contact with

IFUW friends and acquaintances. In Prague, President Masaryk, a close friend of McWilliams's IFUW colleague Dr Anna Bercofcova, "put his car, or one of them at our disposal. We had his chauffeur and for two days we have gone flying around in that car."[22] Under pressure, McWilliams managed to write her newspaper articles while "seething with stuff" and information.[23] Mindful that Roland was at home in Winnipeg in the quiet company of his mother and sister Millie, McWilliams looked forward to her return when she would have so much to tell him. Reassuring him with frequent letters, she kindly remarked, "You're a wizard at planning trips." She also noted that, after twenty-one years of marriage, "I even dream of you."[24]

In 1926 the McWilliamses travelled together to Europe. The IFUW biennial conference was in Amsterdam, and Roland, who chaired the Canadian national council of the YMCA, was to attend a conference in Helsinki. The McWilliamses therefore planned to go from Holland to Finland and thence as tourists to Russia. They would collaborate on a book in the form of "a woman's impressions of what she saw and heard, and a man's effort to estimate what is happening and what is likely to happen in this rapidly changing Russia." In the year before this trip, they deliberately set out to educate themselves, intending to test through actual experience the truth of what they read with the "open mind of the student."[25]

At the 1926 Amsterdam conference, delegates discussed reports on several issues, but the "keenest discussion" returned to a matter raised in previous years, both in international and national forums, "the question of the reconciliation of marriage with the following of a profession." In an astute observation McWilliams came nearer than before to approving the combination of motherhood and paid employment. "The education of women in the professions, in business and in motherhood, now having been made possible, the next thing is the education of men." She remained very conscious of the double burden of the working mother, or even the working wife, and her hint that men must be educated to share domestic responsibilities was significant.

McWilliams indicated that she was becoming aware that women's progress would not happen automatically. Formal obstacles were not the only barriers in the way. She expressed disappointment and even "chagrin" to discover "how far behind in business and professional life lag the English speaking women."[26] She thought the Europeans participated more in public life than the Canadians, Americans, and English. However, neither at this time nor later did she depart from her faith that personal efforts of women, supported informally by networks of women's organizations, would eventually make the difference. Encouragement must be given to individual women. Despite her belief in the power and goodness of the state, she also retained a respect for individual initiative.

Her ideas concerning the tensions between individual and collective responsibility, both at the informal level of clubs and at the more institutionalized level of government policy, were tested during the Russian trip. With respect to education, what she saw in Russia confirmed her existing convictions about its importance in inculcating moral and social values. Concerning the role of married women in the work force, she was impressed by the state-sponsored services designed to reduce the double burden the women carried. However, seeing first hand the intrusive nature of state policy in family matters caused her to question unlimited state power.

Both the McWilliamses made deliberate attempts to acquaint themselves with Russian policies and attitudes. So relaxed were they that twice they left behind precious papers and were saved from bureaucratic entanglements either by Russian efficiency or by luck. "We had travelled 1500 miles, visited three cities, whose population averaged over 1,000,000, gone wherever we pleased without escort or permission, crowded every hour of fifteen days full with observation and inquiries and searched for facts whatever they might be. We had not had one single objectionable experience, we had never been interfered with, we had had excellent accommodation at reasonable rates, we had found clean and well-conducted cities and railways, we had received courteous treatment everywhere."[27] Their "ingenuous air of surprise" contributed to the success of their eventual book.[28]

The first Russians the McWilliamses saw in 1926 were in Leningrad, which "must surely be the saddest city in all the world." Buildings and roads after the civil war were still in a state of disrepair, dirty and unkempt. Here and in Moscow, by their own choice, they had an English-speaking guide. With mild self-effacement, McWilliams said she was somewhat surprised to find "we are not brave pioneers venturing into one of the danger zones of the world" but merely one of many parties of tourists from several countries.

Attesting to her own interest in history, McWilliams spent her "happiest hours" in Leningrad's art galleries and museums. She enjoyed viewing the mundane articles displayed in the Revolutionary Museum. Initially, "in my own mind I had decided that this would be an effort to show up all the horrors and oppressions which had led to the revolution. It proved to be nothing of the sort. The idea behind it was rather to show the history of the revolutionary movement from that Dekabrist Revolution in 1825 down to the moment ... Infinite care had evidently been taken to get pictures of all the men and women who had sacrificed their lives for the movement." She noted the "faded photographs, tiny tintypes," pictures and accounts of incidents, and models of prisons, villages, and houses.[29]

Moscow was home to people who were "more alert, less sad, better dressed." Walking around the city on their own, the McWilliamses went into a cinema that happened to be showing Eisenstein's *Battleship Potemkin*. Much moved herself, McWilliams was astonished to see the laconic reaction of the audience: "They took it as calmly as though it had no relation to them at all." They had had more experience with both revolution and propaganda than she. The Lenin Mausoleum made a strong impression upon her, giving rise to feelings that became more insistent as the years passed. She noticed how "Leninism is being carefully built up into a cult in opposition to Christianity." She apprehended "a challenge which ought not to be lightly regarded."[30]

The McWilliamses devoted a chapter of *Russia in 1926* to the topic "Women." Margaret was particularly interested in divorce, for Russia was the one country she knew of with a secular and highly permissive law. She went straight to the top for her information, achieving "an interview with one of the leaders of the women's sections on the Communist party." This woman told her "probably as much as I shall be able to discover in the limited time available." As with the Revolutionary Museum, her prejudices were confounded. "Mme Boyakaskaja

... proved to be as much unlike my notion of a woman Communist as could well be. Nothing of the hawk-like eyes and hard mouth there." McWilliams reported some of Boyakaskaja's comments, and although she refrained from writing her own judgment, she managed to give the impression that Boyakaskaja had a valid opinion. "'You,' she said, 'are hypocrites and we are not ... if a man tires of his wife [in a bourgeois country] he in effect gets a new one. We simply make it possible for him to be honest in the matter.'"

McWilliams wrote about the divorce laws, which required one parent, usually the father, to support any children with up to half of his income. She discovered that Russian women, but not the men, supported it. She noted a discrepancy between declarations of political equality and the fact that politicians were universally male, a gap between promise and reality much like those to which she was becoming more sensitive in Western Europe and North America. She noted the information network that was generated by four women's journals circulating in different parts of the country. Most of all she was impressed with the child-care facilities provided by employers and also with maternity leave, but she saw "all these advantages which the married woman with children has gained" as bearing a more sinister aspect as well. "Slowly but surely ... the idea of the home as the unit of the state is being broken down ... the unit of the Soviet state is the child citizen ... to his care physically, his education, and his grounding in the principles of Leninism, the state is giving its most zealous effort."[31]

For information on education, McWilliams again went to the top and was granted an interview with a high official in the Commissariat of Education. "Crammed with information" given verbally and through English translations of descriptive brochures, she admired the Russian program to liquidate illiteracy. She was less enthusiastic about a system that effectively was "the chief weapon of communistic propaganda."[32] The Canadian Council on Character Education had similar aims and methods. This Russian trip had the effect of instilling some doubt into her enthusiasm for state control.

Roland's principal aim was to find out how successful the Bolsheviks were in challenging "the whole conception of personal advancement and profit making which has been the mainspring of the material progress of our race" and in the achievement of their desire to eliminate individual enterprise from economic life. Consequently, the McWilliamses toured factories and consulted leaders of the Trades Union Council. Roland was not convinced by what he saw. He thought there would be "grave economic difficulties ahead" due to a lack of capital and also because of what he identified as "the hard facts of selfish human nature." McWilliams concerned herself more with social issues – issues involving education and women – rather than with economics, but both she and Roland viewed with apprehension the parallels of a religious nature between Leninism and Christianity. The book they wrote, a hybrid travel guide, diary, and collection of prophecies, was a fascinating testimony to their own ideas, which unfolded in response to new information and situations. It validated their claim that they had approached the project with "the open mind of the student."[33] For McWilliams, this trip was an important step in her thought, marking as it does the beginning of a reconsideration of her previously unlimited acceptance of state beneficence. She was able to apply the experience to her work in journalism as well as to the book.[34]

McWilliams's next trip was to Geneva in 1930. She was to attend an International Labour Organization conference as a delegate of the Canadian government. She was immensely happy about this recognition from the dominion government – "fairy tales do sometimes still happen" – and also about the payment of expenses. Her return travel was covered, together with a per diem allowance of $15 for each day "necessarily occupied in connection with the mission in question including days on board ship."[35] Not an onerous responsibility, the commission came at a time when her niece Helen Stovel was already in Europe on an extended tour. McWilliams sent off a letter to Helen, hoping that they could find "three or four weeks in which to knock around" together. Excitement jumped off the page: "We might meet at the Italian lakes – and go over to Innsbruck and perhaps to Vienna – or else ... we should go up through Switzerland and to South Germany and then work towards the Rhine coming down it to Cologne and then through Belgium to England ... We can do anything we want to do."[36]

McWilliams had the pleasure of introducing her niece to European friends, and Helen preserved happy memories of this summer. At Geneva Helen walked into the conference building to find "Aunt Marg ... concluding a meeting in French ... I was very impressed." They toured Switzerland, Germany, and the Netherlands by train, steamer, and bus before flying ("my first flight," wrote Helen) to London. In England they stayed a short while in the country home of McWilliams's publisher, J.M. Dent.[37] "Mrs Dent sent me out to her garden to cut lavender which was later delivered to me on the ship home in sachets. Their chauffeur taught me how to drive on the left hand side of the road and Aunt Marg and I launched forth in a seven Austin for ten days in Cotswold [sic], Oxford, Cambridge, Stratford – unforgettable."

Helen loved their trip and so did McWilliams. Helen would later recall in a letter, "She had been abroad so many times and was pleased to show it all to me." A Buckingham Palace garden party to which they were invited proved memorable: "She knew we should go in by the back gate ... She was like a ship in full sail cutting thru the crowd until we suddenly ... came to a clearing – because there were the King (George) and Queen (Mary) – this was 1930 plus the Princess Royal and Edward, the Prince of Wales ... As we slowed up and backed away from the Royal Family we found ourselves standing next to many celebrities – on my right was Harry Lauder."[38]

So much of what we know of McWilliams's life is imbued with earnestness and duty. Rarely do we discover her bubbling over with pleasure, or so directly giving happiness to another person, as Helen clearly appreciated in the summer of 1930. A few photographs show McWilliams smiling or animated, but most show a strong, clear gaze imparting seriousness and assurance. In Helen's splendid evocation of "a ship in full sail," we see McWilliams's confidence but we also sense someone revelling in what she most enjoyed, showing her knowledge and power to an impressionable friend. In Helen's account of their joint holiday, no criticism clouds the memory.

By now a seasoned traveller in Europe and knowledgeable about Russia, McWilliams was glad of the chance to attend the 1931 conference organized by the Institute of Pacific Relations, scheduled to be held in Hangchow, China. The institute was founded in Honolulu in 1925, chiefly by YMCA officials. It was supported by two large organizations, the Rockefeller Foundation and the Carnegie Corporation, and by individuals. In Canada it was associated with the Institute of International Relations. ("No government people belong and they may not attend conferences.") Members were the United States, Canada, Great Britain, Japan, China, New Zealand, Australia, the Philippines, and Russia.[39] The single woman in a Canadian delegation of 13 out of a total attendance of 130 at the institute's third conference, McWilliams sent back a series of articles that were published in the *Manitoba Free Press* between 12 October and 5 December. She arrived back herself at the end of November. Her articles amount to some 14,000 words and reveal her own opinion about the Orient at that time, as well as some underlying assumptions that extended to political and social phenomena in general.[40]

The delegation set sail from Vancouver on 12 September. On 18 September the Japanese blew up the Southern Manchurian Railway and occupied Mukden. Worried about the feasibility of their conference, members of the Institute of Pacific Relations were relieved to learn that it would actually take place in Shanghai rather than on Chinese territory, where Japanese delegates would scarcely be welcome.[41] "There may be a real war before this reaches Winnipeg," she wrote on 26 September. Delegates spent twelve days in Japan before going on to the conference, and McWilliams reported that war feeling ran high: "Newspapers were showing military pictures, soldiers were coming and going, cadets were drilling in the parks."[42]

From the beginning of the conference, McWilliams was convinced it was worthwhile, mainly because the Chinese and Japanese were talking to each other. The arrangement was that each delegate was assigned to one of four round tables, each seating about thirty. Each table then discussed the same topic and reported through a chair to a meeting of the whole. Often the conference was briefed by visiting politicians, and delegates dwelt at length over a report prepared for the institute by Judge Feetham on the status of Shanghai. The conference hoped that some sort of permanent Chinese-Japanese board to settle differences would be established.[43]

Afterwards, the Chinese government invited delegates to visit various points in their country. Meeting Chiang Kai Shek, McWilliams admired his calm professionalism and "words of wisdom." He noted the importance of keeping an "ambitious, unruly minority" (meaning Communists) under control. In words that reverberated in McWilliams's own consciousness, he said, "Our work is not in the Pacific only. We work for the pacific development of the whole world."[44] Some of McWilliams's later China articles dealt with the economy and especially agriculture. Here she showed perspicuity and used to good effect R.H. Tawney's "Memorandum on Agriculture and Industry in China," published in 1932 as *Land and Labour in China*.[45] In her final article, she considered how far Japan was justified in invading Manchuria. She was sympathetic to Japan's point of view, which was that China was incapable of counteracting Soviet infiltration and could not resist a Russian annexation of Manchuria. Japan's invasion was therefore a pre-emptive strike against Russia. If China became closer to Russia, "no one who knows the situation seems to think that Russia's only gift to China will be arms and supplies. She will give also her political philosophy."[46] McWilliams's hostility towards communism was hardening.

The Institute of Pacific Relations' contacts were with "very highly placed Chinese politicians, diplomats and liberal intellectuals" who represented the opinions of the progressive elements of the Nationalist government. McWilliams took at face value Chiang Kai Shek's courtesy to visitors and his words of peace, but not so much as to be blinded to the real problems faced by Japan. She reported that the delegates were inspired by Chinese efforts to become a great nation, but she preserved impartiality at least to the extent of recognizing Russian threats.[47]

Another consequence of the China trip for McWilliams was a new respect for missionary activity. So many of the health and educational services in China had been initiated by Western-supported missionaries, funded by the typical women's work in which she had never involved herself and which indeed she had scorned. After she saw the good works in China and learned too of the institute's genesis in Honolulu, where "the people of great wealth ... are the children of missionaries" and had "an extraordinary sense of civic and social responsibility," she revised her view of Canadian women who supported local missionary society activities.[48] Helen Monk, a second cousin living in Winnipeg, recollected that before McWilliams went to China, she was dismissive of Monk's church work. After her return, McWilliams showed more respect.[49]

McWilliams's visit to China provided a "breathtaking opportunity to be at the crest of a tidal wave just before it breaks." She rode the wave in her inimitable way. On 16 December 1931, eleven days after the *Free Press* had published her last dispatch, the paper carried the headline "National Government in China Collapses." The same issue also carried a terse advertisement: "Mrs R.F. McWilliams Current Events Class. Theatre 'B,' Univeristy Bldg., TONIGHT, 8.15 pm. Subject: 'CHINA TODAY.' Class is open to men and women. Admission, 50¢."[50]

For almost twenty years McWilliams had been an observer and analyst of current events. In the 1930s she became an active participant, as an alderman of the City of Winnipeg, but she kept up both the current events classes and her travel interests. One of her municipal concerns was housing, and when she decided to visit the IFUW conference in Paris in 1937, she also arranged to attend a housing conference there at the same time. Her immediate impressions of this trip were rather different from those she would gain a few months later. When she was interviewed in Toronto on her return, she repeated a worry that had been noted in the early 1920s – that Canada lagged behind Europe in the integration of women in professional positions. She also noted that "everybody in Paris that I talked to was tense about the international situation." She even went so far as to express doubts about the relevance of the IFUW. She feared it was "becoming a little too academic, perhaps, too far away from life in general." She added, "I'm not academic."[51]

Later, she had a more mellow view. Writing in the CFUW *Chronicle*, she referred to her initial apprehension before the meeting. It was ten years since she had represented Canada at an IFUW gathering, and in the meantime she had been directly concerned as an alderman with acute problems of poverty and daily living during the Depression. That in itself was bound to lead to questions about the importance of such a conference and about her own sense of comfort in participating. But in retrospect, she was satisfied. She enjoyed meeting old friends.

"It was equally a delight to find that there were new friendships to be made … that there was … the same desire to understand, and by that understanding to weave still another strand in the bonds that international organizations create." She was glad to see "that the IFUW still appealed to distinguished women in many countries." She liked the setting, drinking tea in the garden and in the sidewalk cafés of Montparnasse. She was gratified to be treated as a famous person: being a woman alderman, she was invited to sign a special celebrity book by the City of Paris.[52] "Finally, and above all else, how good a thing it is to dwell in a safe and pleasant land like Canada."[53]

In 1937 a *Free Press* journalist referred to McWilliams as "the Winnipeg traveller."[54] She continued to travel abroad, and she was able to use this experience to develop her own ideas about world events. She liked meeting people, performing in conferences, rubbing shoulders with eminent people, and sightseeing. Roland was not totally at one with her in this. In a charming note he wrote to Helen on the eve of her European tour in 1930, he offered advice culled from his experience:

1. Go to bed when you lose sight of land and stay there till you approach Ireland.
2. Beware of the English breakfast.
3. Beware of the French taxis. If they run you down you will be fined for getting in the way.
4. Avoid museums and art galleries. They eat up time and you have none to spare.
5. Declare yourself a Canadian and so avoid being soaked. They have to get the loans out of America somehow.
6. Don't fall in love. There are better fish on this side.[55]

Travelling was one of the joint ventures of the McWilliamses. History was another interest they shared, but they had decidedly different approaches. Roland was analytical and sensitive to economic and constitutional issues, and he deliberately tried to discover clues to present politics in past trends. His book *Does History Repeat Itself?* was an interesting comparison of Europe after the French Revolution with Europe after the First World War, and his contribution to *Russia in 1926* ended with a question: Would a new Napoleon emerge? (He thought a "superman" would come forth).[56] Roland's *History* was forward-looking and relevant to the future. Margaret McWilliams's approach was more romantic. Like her husband, she was interested in finding examples of repeating trends, and towards the end of her life, she was much impressed by Toynbee.[57] She liked to imagine the emotions of individual persons and to re-create moments of drama. She was excited by stories of adventure, but she also liked to evoke daily life. Aware of the importance of economics, she nevertheless considered that spiritual forces were most important in motivating behaviour.

McWilliams's first historical project was *Women of Red River.* In February 1922 she was elected president of the Women's Canadian Club, the only person before 1932 to serve as president of both the wcc and the University Women's Club. She immediately revived a suggestion made fifteen years before by the first president, Mrs Sanford Evans, to collect and preserve data on the lives of Manitoba women.[58] Working with the secretary-treasurer, Edna Nash, McWilliams consulted with the editor of the *Free Press*, J.W. Dafoe, two professors at the university, Chester Martin and R.C. Wallace, and the provincial librarian, W.J. Healy. Healy agreed to write the book.[59] Members of the club would do the interviewing. Each month McWilliams reported progress in the collection of data and in the arrangements for illustrating and publishing the book. In September 1923, 1,800 copies of the first printing of 2,500 had already been sold through advance subscriptions. A celebratory luncheon was held, with the pioneer women as guests of honour. Two further editions were printed. By the end of 1923 the profit on the enterprise was $687.53.[60]

The subtitle describes the book as "written from the recollections of women surviving from the Red River era." Twenty-one line drawings by Charles Comfort illustrate houses, churches, furniture, agricultural and household implements, and the faces of many of the women interviewed. The oldest was Mrs William Cowan, ninety-one years of age. The chapter based on her recollections is indicative of the rest of the book. Direct quotes suggest immediacy. There are no direct references in footnotes, but occasionally the text notes a manuscript or printed source. Mrs Cowan, for instance, smiled at the memory of the first bishop of Rupert's Land, who, she said, wore

"lavender kid gloves when he preached." She then, according
to Healy, said, "In my husband's diary, which is now in the
Dominion archives at Ottawa, there is an entry recording that
Bishop Anderson preached for an hour and a half." She later
alluded to the Methodist missionary in Norway House in the
1850s and 1860s: "The letters he wrote to Toronto ... were published afterwards and made a very interesting book."[61] Anecdotes about a single person or topic flowed from Mrs Cowan's
lips, and talk of family weddings and funerals was punctuated
by lists of supplies needed for a journey to Moose Factory or
York Factory, by remarks on the kindness of Indians, by memories of distinguished visitors, and by news of her grandsons.
She herself disclaimed "earnestly any place of importance for
herself among the women of Red River." Conscious that she
was "one of the sheltered women," she thought others who
had suffered privations would have more valuable tales to tell.
The chapter ended on a symbolic note, speaking of the "sun-
sets that faded from the western sky long years ago" still shining in her memory.[62]

The chapters represent no chronological narrative, nor a per-
ceivable thematic arrangement. The vivid language and the
detailed observation render the subject matter, scattered and
unfocused as it is, very much alive. The book provides a mine
of information for the modern historian, especially on social
and economic matters, and is also valuable for studies of education, the church, morality, and politics. Mrs Cowan, for
example, described her family's escape from Fort Garry during
the Riel Rebellion of 1869–70, and later a whole chapter is
devoted to the way some women experienced those years.[63]

Contemporary reviews were all congratulatory. The *Regina
Morning Leader* called the book "a splendid work" of "romantic
history." The *New York Evening Post* praised the Women's Canadian Club for "adding to the scanty struggles and achievements
of perilous times." The *Times* of Victoria was glad to see a
"delightful narrative." The Toronto *Globe* noted "the Muse was
in happy frame of mind" in recording "romance, adventure,
chivalry, courage, and thrilling episodes." The magazine *Saturday Night* called it "this entrancing history." A crowning acco-
lade came from the *Canadian Historical Review*, in which
Professor Chester Martin of the University of Manitoba used

fulsome language with only modest, masked reservations: "No better book of its kind perhaps has appeared in Canada ... the wealth of material thus saved from oblivion is astonishing ... the historical value of this book is altogether exceptional."[64] McWilliams was happy to consult Martin when she came to write *Manitoba Milestones* five years later.

The main value of *Women of Red River* from our perspective, two generations later, is twofold. First, we can appreciate, along with McWilliams's contemporaries, the retrieval of information that might otherwise be lost. Secondly, we can now see how extraordinary it was for women to be thought worthy of contributing both to the raw material of history and to its interpretation. The women of the Women's Canadian Club were more adventurous than perhaps they realized in their recognition of women as repositories and conduits of happenings that could be considered historical. Moreover, much of the interviewing was done by the club's members. It is true that the final draft was produced by the provincial librarian, but he seems to have been treated literally as a hired hand, as he himself was ready to acknowledge. Thanking McWilliams as club president for his fee of $300, he noted, "Not only was the idea of the book of your origination, but the energy and power of carrying the thing through to success came from you and Mrs Nash and the other members of the Club actively associated with you in this work."[65] Women therefore were both the historical subjects and the historians, and successfully so. The reviews were favourable, the first printing was sold out within a couple of months, and there were two further printings within twelve months.

Women of Red River was a collective project. *Manitoba Milestones* was personal. Published in 1928, it was an accessible, readable account of how Manitoba came to be the way McWilliams saw the province in the 1920s. There were three colour pictures, fifty-five photographs, one map, and twenty-three figures. There were no footnotes, and only a brief bibliography supplemented by obscure references in the text and a handful of acknowledgments in the preface. Perhaps McWilliams considered such attributes to be off-putting academic paraphernalia, and she did not want to be considered "academic."

McWilliams's explicit aim was to write "the story of the growth" of Manitoba.[66] In 222 pages of prose, she devoted approximately equal space to explorers, fur traders, settlers, the period 1826–60, the Riel Rebellion, Manitoba's first decade as a Canadian province, early jurisdictional disputes, new immigrants, prewar economic booms and recessions, and the First World War, with a summary of the economic conditions of Winnipeg in 1922. A final chapter was devoted to miscellaneous compilations of facts she thought could speak for themselves, including lists of premiers of Manitoba, lists of military units that served in the Great War (with the names of their commanding officers), charts documenting the expansion of population, agricultural production, and hydro, and a "summary of events" that made note of a charity payment made in 1710 to Pierre Radisson's widow as well as the 1874 date of the first meeting of the Winnipeg City Council.

Apart from the chapter on immigration, "Homes on the Prairie," there was little information about women, social issues (except for education), or native people. *Women of Red River* was cited in the "select bibliography," but little of its content was integrated into *Manitoba Milestones*. However, McWilliams had read the secondary sources. The major texts of Ross (1856), Gunn (1880), Hill (1890), Begg (1894), Bryce (1900), and Martin (1916) were listed in the bibliography, and in addition, archival and newspaper sources, probably copied out of secondary works without precise identification, furnished verbatim quotations.[67] She acknowledged Agnes Laut and Lawrence Burpee, popular historians, for their work in the Chronicles of Canada series published during and after the First World War. McWilliams's *Manitoba Milestones* was a combination of the occasionally dry scholarship of nineteenth-century authors and the readable and romantic tone characterized by the Chronicles, whose general editor was George Wrong, her old University of Toronto history professor.[68]

Certainly McWilliams used her journalist's skill in keeping the reader's attention, and she was not above describing an imaginary landscape with birdsong and blossom to heighten an atmosphere she wished to re-create. Her occasionally flowery style, however, did not deflect the reader from judging the book fairly. One reviewer said the subject matter was "splendidly organised" and contained "many racy and vivid descriptions of scenes once familiar to the western plains." It appealed to the "general reader."[69] Historian W.L. Morton called *Manitoba Milestones* "first among its kind." It "achieved a fair balance between the 'romantic' story of the fur trade and the more realistic and more significant story of settlement."[70] Gerald Friesen, while omitting mention of McWilliams and her work from his *Canadian Prairies: A History*, elsewhere recognized her balanced judgment and clear exposition of most issues except in relation to the Winnipeg General Strike. "The sweep and balance of *Manitoba Milestones* were measures of the sophistication of Manitoba society in the 1920s."[71]

McWilliams also wrote a "little story book." *All Along the River*, which originated as brief address she gave to the Ladies of the British Medical Association at their meeting in Winnipeg in the summer of 1930, was later published in the form of a Christmas greeting. Nine pages long, it romanticized the Red River as "a subject to intrigue the mind" and emphasized the British connection. One recipient called it a delight and a "public benefaction."[72]

McWilliams was no intellectual pioneer. The traditional narrative story was her framework, but she analysed issues and presented them to the reader from the point of view of conflicting participants, not always a simple task, especially when, for example, the French and the English were struggling over education at the end of the nineteenth century. Her idea of what was important to study was basically traditional, but *Women of Red River* showed that her intellectual curiosity extended to women and women's perceptions. In that she remained singular. Even the more professional historians of later generations, like Morton and Friesen, remained deaf to the experience of women in Manitoba history.

McWilliams's main skill was in synthesis and presentation. She imagined her reader to be disinclined to undertake a serious course of study.[73] *Manitoba Milestones*, lacking the didacticism of *This New Canada* (published twenty years later), was more refreshing to read, and it reinforced her own notion of progress, both material and spiritual. The book, intended for a popular audience, was a selective summary of what was already known.

McWilliams determined to continue writing. "Today I began the actual writing of the wheat book," she recorded on 2 May 1930.[74] It was to be "the story of the rise and development of the farmers' institutions for selling wheat." J.M. Dent, publisher of *Russia in 1926* and *Manitoba Milestones*, "are going to publish it as soon as I am satisfied to let it out of my hands," which she expected to be in December 1930. She described the project in a letter to Violet McNaughton:

[It is a book] for the benefit of the man and woman on the street ... I am not writing an economic treatise – that would be presumption. But there is a human story which I think has never been gotten across to the public, and which would interest that public very much if it could be set down. I know that I myself am quite thrilled by it ... If I can get that thrill into black and white ... I feel it a worth while thing to do.

The book is not to be one of advocacy of the wheat pool. Its object is just to tell the story, but of course the wheat pool being the latest and least understood effort, about half the book, or more will concern itself with that organisation. I have read and read and read, and I have talked to Manitoba people and to some from the other provinces ... My own natural sympathies are all with the pool of course, but I ... want to be as fair and impartial as I can be.[75]

McWilliams wished to consult people in Saskatchewan, and McNaughton arranged meetings for her at the end of September.[76]

The typescript of "The Battle of Wheat" or "The Battle of the Giants" remained unfinished and can be found in the Manitoba Legislative Library. Only five chapters, out of a projected ten, were completed. Why it was left in limbo is unclear. It was uncharacteristic of McWilliams not to finish what she had begun. She signed a contract with Dent in January 1930, promising to deliver the manuscript by 1 July 1930.[77] The likeliest explanation is that she was diverted by what seemed to be the more pressing demand of writing the polemical *If I Were King of Canada* with her husband in response to the deepening Depression. Then in the fall of 1931 came her China trip and her newspaper assignments. Her life remained busy, and in 1933 she was elected as alderman. Any lingering aspirations for the life of a writer were firmly brought to earth by her new life in politics.

Neither *Manitoba Milestones, This New Canada,* nor "The Battle for Wheat" integrated women's experience into fairly traditional organizational frameworks. McWilliams's involvement with *Women of Red River* had not shown her how women's work could be considered as a major economic contribution to social development. Of course, she was not alone in this inability to incorporate women's work into mainstream history. In 1936 however, she was able to use women's testimony for a sociological study, first published in 1938 and significant enough to be reissued in 1970.[78]

H.F. Angus, professor of economics at the University of British Columbia, was preparing one volume in a series of studies on the relations between Canada and the United States for the Carnegie Endowment for International Peace. His intention was to reveal Canadian "popular opinion and attitudes" about the United States. For his project he chose a "special investigator" for each of six geographical areas, someone with "an open mind, and who had the requisite training and experience to deal with the difficult problems of research in public opinion." All the investigators were professional academics except for "Mrs R.F. McWilliams, author of revealing books on social life in the Canadian West."[79]

McWilliams analysed motion pictures, radio broadcasting, and press comment, and made a survey of opinion in rural Manitoba. She contacted fifty-one women, "leaders in their respective districts," and the same number of newspaper editors and publishers from "the smaller towns" of the province. Additionally, she made a detailed study in two small towns, one in central Manitoba and the other near the US border, "each in its way a typical community." She was surprised to discover a deep distrust of Americans in rural Manitoba.[80] Altogether she was credited directly with 81 out of 450 pages of text.

This enterprise demonstrated McWilliams's national reputation as a social commentator; her work was considered on a par with that of university academics. She was able to display skills of analysis, judgment, and presentation honed over the years in club activities and the current events classes. The project offered her the opportunity to learn about the ostensible subject of the study, Canadian public opinion of the United States, as well as the opportunity to learn more about the community that gave rise to such opinions. She accorded women in rural areas sufficient respect to make them, along with newspaper editors, her main informants. She was able to interpret "public opinion" more comprehensively than her colleagues, none of whom identified women as a resource. McWilliams's increased knowledge about contemporary Manitoba would prove helpful five years later when she and her husband made a deliberate attempt to meet people from the whole province, not just Winnipeg, after they moved into Government House. The thirties for McWilliams, however, were primarily years of immersion in urban affairs.

CHAPTER SEVEN

Politics

In 1933 Margaret McWilliams "felt herself part of a world wide movement that is forcing women to assume the duties of active citizenship."[1] As a candidate for alderman in the city of Winnipeg, she was continuing her involvement in active citizenship, represented not least by her current events classes, which sought to further the education of an informed electorate. However, she had not previously sought elected office outside women's organizations.

Although her participation in electoral politics dated from 1917, McWilliams seems not to have seriously considered becoming a candidate herself until 1933. *Saturday Night* asked her about this obvious point in an interview in May 1920. "It has been hoped that Mrs McWilliams might be induced to stand for election to the Manitoba Legislature, but, although of a valiant modern quality, the woman in her shrinks from the rough and tumble of politics and she is not yet opening that kind of account with the public." She was "possessed of no strong party passion and preferred the middle of the road." The interview concluded: "A large following of women believe in her, look to her for direction. This may seem a bigger work to her hand than a seat in legislative halls. She has earned the right to work in her own way."[2]

McWilliams was never a completely partisan Liberal. She was in favour of a Union government in 1917, and in 1931 advocated many issues that were not party policy. She was not as hopeful as some suffragists had been that women would be able to purify politics from the sidelines. Her old history professor,

George M. Wrong, had argued in 1917 that it would be "unwise" for women to become adherents of any party, on the grounds that their "detachment" made both "Liberals and Conservatives fear their power and accept their demands." He thought it was "foolish" for women "to attach themselves to a discredited system ... Women have the right to demand the purging of parties before they join either of them."[3]

Whether McWilliams ever had any sympathy with this point of view is debatable, but in the 1920s she confirmed her belief that women had to work within the existing political structure. In the 1921 federal election, she campaigned for Liberal candidate A.B. Hudson, speaking at a meeting where "the entire attendance was made up of women." She paid tribute to the suffragists – "that valiant band of women" – and divulged some "inner party history." In 1914 the Manitoba Liberal Party had discussed the inclusion of women's suffrage in its platform. "No agreement appearing possible, the vote of the committee was polled and resulted in a tie. The casting vote, which committed the party to the cause of women, was given by the chairman: Hudson." Here was a retroactive endorsement by McWilliams of women's suffrage. In her speech she did not confine herself to Hudson's admirable personal qualities but launched into an attack on the tariff and on the exploitative policies of manufacturers who "pile up profits." She appealed to women as consumers and housewives. "It was the duty of the woman, by wise spending, to make money go as far as possible."[4]

While McWilliams believed that it was important to be committed to existing political parties, she also favoured women's organizations within the parties. Speaking at the second annual meeting of the non-partisan League of Women Voters of Toronto in April 1926, she urged women to "show more courage in accepting office." She reflected that "with a system of government built on party lines," she did not see how anything could be accomplished "without going into parties and working through them."[5] In November of that year, McWilliams followed part of her own advice, joining with other Liberal women to found a women's Liberal association, initially based in the Winnipeg South Centre constituency, but by the end of

November organized to include women from all over Winnipeg.[6]

As already noted, with respect to seeking election herself, she did not solicit nomination in these early years of political involvement. Few women were successful in electoral politics in Manitoba or, indeed, in Canada. In 1920 Edith Rogers, also a Liberal, was elected to the Manitoba legislature. She was the sole woman member for several years, although other women ran both in 1920 and 1922. One other woman candidate, Harriet Dick, came very close to election in 1920, but the others all polled less than 1 percent of the vote. In the provincial election of 1927, only Rogers ran, and she was again re-elected.

Then in 1932 there was another election. Jessie Maclennan, a popular Winnipeg school trustee, and Beatrice Brigden, a veteran Independent Labour Party worker, were both candidates in a field of twenty-nine competing for ten Winnipeg seats.[7] This was possibly McWilliams's opportunity. Rogers was expected to run a fourth time, but "at the last moment Mrs Rogers withdrew," wrote McWilliams to McNaughton. "I could have run and it is generally thought I would have been elected. But the deputation came to see me at 2:30 in the afternoon and the nominating committee was meeting at 5, the convention at 8. I could not make over my life on that much notice. Besides I am not at all convinced that as a private member in a provincial house I could have done any more, or better, public service than I am now doing ... Anyway being in doubt I stayed in my own line. Had Mrs Rogers made known her decision a week early I think it is quite likely I should have been in the cabinet."[8]

A year later McWilliams agreed to be an aldermanic candidate in the civic election of November 1933. Again she did not seek the nomination but was in the happy position of being drafted by an efficient and effective organization. In the spring of 1933, the Professional and Business Women's Club considered organizing women candidates for school trustee and alderman, but rather than proceed, the club decided to offer its co-operation to the large umbrella organization, the Local Council of Women, with its fifty-six member groups.[9] In charge that year was Mrs W.T. Allison, a former student friend of

McWilliams's at the University of Toronto. Her husband's friendship with McWilliams went back even further, as he had served on the Harbord Collegiate Institute's literary executive.[10]

The Local Council canvassed member groups about the idea in principle of nominating two women as alderman and two as trustee. Receiving support, the council then began "a quest" for the "right women." In the event, only two women aldermanic candidates were named, Dr Ellen Douglass, the president of the Business and Professional Women's Club and a Winnipeg physician, and McWilliams. The council did not sponsor trustees but said "members should be left free to vote for" two sitting women trustees who were seeking re-election, independents Jessie Maclennan and Mary Dyma.[11] When two further women entered the contest for trustee, independent Jessie Kirk and socialist Gloria Queen-Hughes, Allison made no official comment. The council confined its support to Douglass and McWilliams.

The two aldermanic candidates shared the platform at meetings organized by the Local Council and had the benefit of an array of committees in charge of publicity, finance, and meetings. McWilliams's conviction that women should be part of the existing political structure led to her expression of regret that "women were put on the outside as a separate party ... It was long ago established that women are persons but it seems we are not yet 'citizens.'" Both women urged the creation of jobs for the unemployed and talked about the "fundamental problems in which women's interests were most closely concerned, namely welfare, housing, health, and civic economics." They both explicitly referred to the responsibility of women to contribute special skills to public life. Ellen Douglass just missed being elected. McWilliams was successful.[12]

McWilliams now had the opportunity to put into practice at least some of her ideas on politics. She seldom rushed to declare her political opinions, professing always to examine the context of a question and the arguments on several sides before coming to a conclusion. Such had been her method for issues in the University Women's Club and Local Council of Women, as well as for the articles she dispatched from China in 1931. This striving for fairness did not mean she could not make up her mind, nor that she could not act once she had done so. At the Toronto triennial meeting of the International Federation of University Women in 1947, McWilliams "told the members it was time they came down from their ivory tower and buckled down to work in a world of reality. There are many fields in which trained minds are needed."[13] Although her caution might provoke impatience in the more partisan, her opinions were respected as judicious. Moreover, she was able to keep the respect of colleagues who disagreed with her particular conclusions.[14]

The distillation of her political opinions on contemporary Canada is to be found in the book she and her husband wrote in 1931 under the joint pseudonym of Oliver Stowell, *If I Were King of Canada*. Its authorship was kept secret for a year. In June 1932 McWilliams gave a speech for the women graduates at the Alumni Federation dinner for the retiring president of the University of Toronto, Sir Robert Falconer. About 1,500 were in attendance, and at this dinner "the announcement was made that Roll and I were the authors."[15] They accepted common responsibility, although the contract with Dent stipulated Margaret as sole author.[16] By the time McWilliams accepted the aldermanic nomination, she was proud to acknowledge her co-authorship of a book that "created a stir because of its pertinent comments on business."[17]

If I Were King of Canada was published two years before the League for Social Reconstruction produced its manifesto and just before the Co-operative Commonwealth Federation was founded.[18] In January 1933 McWilliams expressed reservations concerning the latter: "I cannot myself feel that it is the group for which we are waiting and yet I sometimes wonder if I am myself holding back because I cannot always go full length with my radical friends."[19] In private McWilliams claimed that Roland was more inclined to be radical than she. In 1923 she had written to McNaughton, "I am not and never was afraid of having 'red' friends" but "my husband is much pinker than I am and also more understanding."[20]

Despite Margaret McWilliams's reluctance to identify with radicals, there was a remarkable similarity between McWilliams and those further to the left, both in their analysis of the current Canadian discontents and in the general remedies they proposed. *If I Were King of Canada* and the CCF's

Regina Manifesto of 1933 were both in the mainstream of Canadian thought in that they ascribed societal problems to a set of economic, rather than moral, factors.[21] The McWilliamses advocated state intervention, government planning, and some nationalization, and emphasized the need to cut through the constitutional red tape produced in the existing federal-provincial system. At the same time, they stressed the moral agency of the individual and, while severely criticizing the failures of parliamentary government, saw social revolution on a Russian model as a bogey to be feared and avoided. The McWilliamses hoped for a temporary suspension of Parliament while economic experts did a thorough economic and political renovation under a single benevolent dictator – a king of Canada – and at the end of this interval, power would return to a reformed and more efficient parliamentary system.

The title page quoted Milton: "The power of Kings and Magistrates is nothing else, but what is only derivative, transferred and committed to them in trust from the people, to the common good of them all ... from hence Aristotle and the best of political writers have defined a king, him who governs to the good and profit of his people, and not for his own ends." The book's theme was that the king, selected by the people, was the personification of a general will. The people were sovereign, keeping a watchful eye on the person so selected who even during his term might be recalled. Because the mechanics for the guardianship of the guardian were not specified, this kingship could theoretically degenerate into a fascist dictatorship, and a reference to a "too tender care for the rights of the individual" suggests a lack of concern for civil rights. However, the king's power was never absolute, never extended to the control of opinion, and was never admired as an end in itself. Rather the king was like a physician – "Canada is like a young man in the prime of manhood ... And yet he is sick."[22] Short-term remedies were to be accompanied with a fundamental and voluntary change in lifestyle.

The book began with prophetic imagery: "On the 30th of February the people of Canada rose up in rebellion. The cry of protest, raised first in Saskatchewan, was echoed in every part of the country." A surrealist scenario was anchored by plausible developments resulting in the gathering of "a mighty host" who, by airplane, train, automobile, and on foot, advanced on the capital: "To Ottawa to choose a king!" In sympathy with the crowd of 100,000 on Parliament Hill, members of Parliament in session declared in favour of a king who, for a period of three years, would have power over all institutions of government. The king was chosen by lots cast by seven men, the chief justice of Canada, the speakers of the Commons and Senate, the prime minister, the leader of the opposition, the president of the Bankers' Association, and the president of the United Farmers. Oliver Stowell, his name evoking Oliver Cromwell's, became the new king.[23]

Sixteen chapters followed. An emergency employment fund was established; the causes of the Depression were analysed; an economic general staff and public service corporations were appointed; money and credit were controlled and speculation was denounced; trade and tariffs were regulated; agriculture and education were examined; social services were overhauled; government was reformed; Canadian culture and a high moral fibre were promoted; and on the international scene, Canada was ready to take its place as the link between the old and the new world. In a mixture of analysis, prescription, and exhortation, the McWilliams political vision was presented.

According to the book, "The primary problems are economic." The institutions, like Parliament, that evolved in order to deal with political problems were no longer able to cope. The Depression demanded new measures: co-ordination and planning were required in order to reduce suffering and create the foundations of a new society. Immediate relief was the first priority. On top of the existing graduated income tax, a further "employment fund" tax was to be levied on those who received income, up to a maximum of 25 percent of one's monthly income. The fund so generated would then be applied mainly to the alleviation of suffering, but also to keeping productive industries going.[24]

The McWilliamses next envisioned the formation of an economic general staff. This body would have representation from each province, from different economic interests (manufacturing, shipping, and so on), and from labour and consumer groups; it would also include both men and women. The general staff would not be selected in a partisan, political way, but solely on grounds of "fitness." Twenty-four voluntary advisers would be serviced by six qualified, paid economists. A central bank would be established, as well as several centralized public service corporations to manage power utilities, transportation, and some important industries. Centralized planning would also guide agriculture. The McWilliamses were not full-fledged protectionists with respect to trade, and in this area they allowed a modified form of free trade.[25]

Education was crucial to the McWilliams vision. "We should desire for Canada an aristocracy, not of birth or of wealth, but of brains." "The ability to think, and the knowledge of interesting things to think about, must be cultivated in all our people." Moreover, thinkers must be free. "It is never desirable to interfere with academic freedom."[26] Social services also should be more plentiful and centralized: good health, economic comfort, and security should be basic. To this end, it was essential that medical services, including hospitals, be controlled by the state and there should be pensions for retired people. Employment and retirement insurance should be contributory. The state should encourage home-ownership through low-interest loans.[27]

The McWilliamses were more alert to the political problems created by this centralizing vision than to its financial cost. In a sweeping dismissal of sacred cows, they called for the reorganization of the House of Commons on a system of committees and pronounced that "as for the Senate, it might as well be abolished at once."[28] Provincial legislatures also should be reorganized, and higher posts in government reserved not for party servers but for people with specific training. Voters must be actively involved, and non-voters would be "placed on a black list" and deprived of the right to vote for the following five years.[29]

"No community should be left to grow as it will." The haphazard efforts and greed of individuals should be replaced by central planning. People weak in moral fibre must be protected from their base desires: gambling would be "rationalised," drinking liquor will be discouraged, financial speculation must be regulated.[30]

The McWilliams vision displayed a tension between freedom and control: they wanted freedom in thought, enquiry, and criticism, and a modified freedom in world trade. At the same time, they believed the state should centralize and control the development of communities, industries, and social services on a much wider and deeper scale than any Western nation of the time. They had seen communism in action in Russia and regretted its erosion of the moral responsibility of the individual; yet they did not trust the Canadian individual to withstand "the fever called get-rich-quick."[31] They had no conception of the financial costs of the increased social services and the centralized state management of resources. An attachment to intellectual freedom kept the McWilliamses from a thoroughgoing totalitarianism; a predilection for efficient planning and centralized management alienated them from classical liberalism; and their distaste for drinking and gambling led them to deplore an unrestricted personal liberty. *If I Were King of Canada* was the bloom of modernized "social uplifters" whose roots were firmly planted in a Presbyterian social gospel and whose stem had received a robust graft from secular economics.[32]

Margaret McWilliams recognized the book's affinity with many Independent Labour Party ideas, and lent a copy to J.S. Woodsworth, Labour MP for Winnipeg North Centre. He read it on a train journey to Ottawa. "There is much with which I am in hearty agreement," he wrote. He thought that the author was "one of the first to really question the slogans and beliefs which so far have been considered basic in our Canadian life." Woodsworth would have preferred more central control of national resources, but he was glad to see that financial speculators were "given a great wallop." He thought the proclamation idea was good but "should be followed up by a series of clear-cut emergency proclamations." Otherwise, the book was "a series of arguments convincing because of their sweet reasonableness," which, he implied, was politically insufficient.[33]

Frank Underhill, a leader of the League for Social Reconstruction and a major author of the Regina Manifesto, reviewed the book in the *Canadian Forum*. At that time, he considered it "sound and sensible both in its analysis and in its proposals for reforms. Its main conclusions are those to which most thinking Canadians are coming."[34] *Saturday Night* also judged "nothing startling" in the McWilliamses' ideas, which, it stated, "could be applied immediately with profit to the community." However, the reviewer thought that this was a forlorn hope. Present leaders, including the eponymous Mackenzie King, "are only concerned with hanging on until the crisis passes."[35]

In their book, the McWilliamses looked forward to the end of the king's reign, when he could become "one of thousands of Canadians eager to serve their country if they can but find the way."[36] Margaret McWilliams found her own way two years after the book's publication, in the context of Winnipeg city politics in 1933. The political arena of a municipality was vastly different from that of an apocalyptic kingdom.

Politics in Winnipeg in the interwar years were defined to a large extend by the 1919 Winnipeg General Strike. During the strike the Citizens' Committee of One Thousand was formed in opposition to the Central Strike Committee. Neither group was entirely homogeneous in class or ideology, but for over a generation thereafter "the politics of class had come to stay."[37] Most municipal candidates expressed loyalty either to Labour or to "non-Labour" – that is, the Citizens.[38] McWilliams enjoyed Citizen support when she stood for later re-election.

Winnipeg experienced geographical as well as ideological division. Before 1920 there were seven wards, but this number was reduced to three in 1920 in a "gerrymander by Winnipeg's establishment directed against labour."[39] Each ward returned six aldermen, half being elected each year. South Winnipeg, Ward I, was "the rightist stronghold," never sending more than one Labour alderman to City Council. Ward II was in the north-central parts of Winnipeg and was "politically the middle of the road ward." Sometimes it elected two Labour and one non-Labour member, sometimes the reverse. Ward III was the northern and northwestern part of the city, "council's extreme left," which by the 1930s "usually elect(ed) one Communist, one Independent Labour Party [ILP], and one non-Labour alderman." "Ward III is predominantly red and pink; ward I the arch-conservative blue and white; ward II, neither one thing nor another."[40] McWilliams was returned for Ward I.

Both geography and ideology reflected the class and ethnic structure of Winnipeg. "The further into the 'North End' (and hence out of the physical sight of the city's 'best' citizens) the more radical became the reputation of the community, and more un-'Canadian' the individuals within it."[41] None of the three wards had regularly returned women to office, but McWilliams was not a total pioneer. Before 1933, there had been one woman alderman, Jessie Kirk, elected in Ward II in 1920, and eight unsuccessful candidacies. There had been more women school trustees: seven had each been elected once, and Jessie Maclennan, elected for Ward II in 1925, had been re-elected every two years since.[42]

The issue in all mayoralty campaigns during the 1930s was fiscal responsibility in the face of unprecedented demand for services. Most Citizen aldermanic candidates agreed with Mayor R.H. Webb when he said in 1933, "We have to live within our means ... and see that our city lives within its means." On the other side, John Queen, Independent Labour Party candidate for mayor, reminded the electorate that "in July 1933, there were 25,000 more people on relief in Manitoba than in July, 1932" and that somehow the city government had to respond to their needs.[43] McWilliams's seven years as alderman saw three mayors: "Citizen" Webb was mayor in 1933–35; a Citizen dentist, F.E. Warriner, served as mayor in 1936–37; and Queen was mayor in 1935–36 and 1937–40. The McWilliams Janus-like regard for both centralized efficiency and the provision of a fairly high level of social services was about to be tested.

In the event, McWilliams balanced both. Never a time-server, she took several policy initiatives and also discharged the day-to-day responsibilities, attending standing committees, special committees, and subcommittees. During her first year she became known as "'Winnipeg's live-wire alderman': the sight of her at the wheel of her little roadster was a familiar one in every part of the city. She was content, as good reporters are, only with first-hand information on the problems she had been appointed to solve."[44] Chair of the Standing Committee on Health in 1937 and 1938, she also chaired several special committees, most notably Unemployment Relief in 1939, Centralized Purchasing, and the committee to consider the administration of public assistance.[45]

During the civic election campaign of 1937, McWilliams summarized her main areas of interest, which neatly fell into Stowell's twin categories. She was interested in the notion of a city manager and had already initiated a process of centralized purchasing. During the next two years she was to effect the amalgamation of the Unemployment Relief and Social Welfare departments. Along the same lines, she also believed "in a well kept city, with tidy streets and garbage trucks kept covered as they're going through the streets." She added to municipal amenities through her personal support of libraries, parks, and, particularly, low-cost housing. McWilliams also displayed Stowell's concern for social services, especially for the unemployed. In 1937 she singled out her long-time interest in the provision of affordable milk as an example.[46] There were also three other areas that over the years attracted her energy: the application of adult universal suffrage to city politics, the working conditions of city employees, and the role of women in public life.

Long after McWilliams's death, one of her friends, Lila Honeyman, reminisced about Margaret's early work as an alderman: "My husband had already held the same office for several years. As a novice, Margaret was eager to profit from his experience and to glean all the background information she could, and she showed great appreciation of his knowledge and assistance."[47] Egbert D. Honeyman stood by McWilliams. They acted as substitutes for one another on the standing committees, and in July 1934, when she precipitately tried to restore to school teachers some of their reduced wages without directing her motion through the Finance Committee first, he was the one alderman who supported her in council.[48]

McWilliams learnt the rules quickly, and although she was normally inclined to vote with the Citizen aldermen, there were times when she did not. In such polarized councils, when the voting was frequently 9 to 9 and the mayor had the casting vote, every vote counted. She ran counter to the phalanx of Citizens in 1935 and "saved the day for the leftists" when she suggested that the idea of the extended franchise "be submitted to a plebiscite."[49] In 1936 she maintained this commitment to a wider representation when she moved to have more seats for the city of Winnipeg in the provincial legislature.[50]

Most work of council was done in committee, and as each committee was carefully composed of both labour and citizen aldermen, a report would usually have the solid support of all members, thus attracting both labour and citizen support from the rest of council. McWilliams was a stern believer in committee unity and criticized those, like Jake Penner, a member of the Communist Party elected under the Workers' Unity League label, who would not always abide by previous consensus.[51]

After an apprentice year, McWilliams, at the first working council meeting of 1935, moved to introduce the idea of a central purchasing agent. Gasoline, for example, was purchased by several city departments, often at different prices. "Some paid 25.1 cents a gallon, others paid a little over 27 cents."[52] Her move to set up an investigatory committee resulted in the establishment of an ongoing system which by 1938 operated under its own momentum.[53] Along the same lines, she urged the appointment of a city manager. She was successful in getting two departments joined and a single director of public welfare appointed. Only two years passed from the time she made these suggestions, in May 1938, to the time the merging took place and a director was appointed. Considering the inbuilt inertia of any large bureaucracy, this was a considerable achievement and in line with her desire to reduce duplication and bring "good housekeeping principles" to city hall.[54]

As noted, McWilliams wanted to improve the city's amenities. Working with her old ally, the Local Council of Women, she advocated in 1935 the establishment of a library board composed of both aldermen and lay people. After two years she reported two major initiatives, a book drive to acquire "the largest increase in any one year since 1916" and the establishment of library branches in schools.[55] In her first year as an alderman, she involved herself in a gardening project for unemployed people. The city distributed free seed to those participating – "4,200 had received free seed and 3,794 were now registered." The chair of the Relief Committee, Alderman Andrew, "complimented Alderman McWilliams in her activity in connection with the organization of the gardening work."[56] McWilliams regarded this project as a "self-help scheme," holding firmly to the notion that people should contribute towards their own welfare.[57] Labour Council members repeatedly criticized the policy of compulsory work for relief qualification, and the Workers' Unity League members, Jake Penner and Joe

Forkin, condemned it, but McWilliams never wavered. In 1937 "we put 500 to 600 men cleaning the streets this summer, they earned their relief, were beholden to nobody, and they got a fair wage."[58] She was sensitive to what she saw as the psychology of those receiving relief: "To raise the morale of the unemployed by a process of rehabilitation will mean educating the public.[59]

McWilliams considered that one of the "hurdles" she had to overcome as a new alderman was an idea that "her attitude on all relief matters would be one of sentimentalism."[60] She did not automatically give credence to stories of hardship, and towards the end of the thirties, she did not hesitate to use "visitors" as inspectors, investigating charges of fraud among relief recipients. Nor did she refrain from prosecuting those who had been in wrongful receipt of relief, in contravention of the policy guidelines.[61]

She was fair-minded. On 3 July 1936 she was appointed to a four-member subcommittee to examine the relief problems of unemployed single men. Alderman Rhodes Smith was the chair. From then until 11 July, when the report was written, the members of the subcommittee met daily from 8:30 a.m. to 6:30 p.m. They acquired statistics, conducted interviews, and made many visits to groups and individuals. They saw rooming houses that were verminous and dining halls where loaves of bread were mouldy on one side.[62] "She [McWilliams] wanted to be sure they [the unemployed] got all they were entitled to."[63] While dispensing with some of the unverifiable complaints, the majority agreed that some improvements could be made. McWilliams here demonstrated a desire to work with the system and to achieve practical results.

Another committee member, Alderman Forkin of the Workers' Unity League, had a different agenda. He dismissed the system of "mass feeding, housing and clothing" as "demoralising, degrading, and inhuman." The men needed "work at decent wages, and until this can be secured for them, should be given three meals a day on a restaurant voucher, the right to choose their own doctors, vouchers to provide adequate and varied clothing, proper housing and a cash voucher for incidentals such as razor blades, hair cuts, tooth paste etc. ... I am well aware of the additional expense involved, but I believe there are adequate compensations to the City of Winnipeg also."[64] Forkin was one of the few officials in public life who wished to bring about an entirely new social system. McWilliams did not consider the existing establishment satisfactory, but she preferred to do what she could to alleviate suffering and improve the situation without making exorbitant demands on those who were still economically secure. She would learn from Forkin's ideas, nevertheless, and in 1940 "her last appeal as an alderman was for a concerted effort to get away from the present meal-ticket basis of relief."[65]

In other ways as well, McWilliams worked to bring understanding and efficiency to the administration of relief. She ensured that there were more women than men social workers in relief work, believing that women were better able to solve problems concerning children and young girls while visiting homes and less likely to exploit their clients.[66] She had the Women's Unemployment Relief Department reorganized under a woman supervisor.[67] Later, when the numbers on relief were being reduced, she encouraged the City to take over responsibility for a girls domestic training scheme from the Winnipeg Junior League, which had paid the salary of a teacher in "domestic training." In 1937 she reported to council that "in the past six months 58 girls entered the school of whom 38 are now off relief."[68]

McWilliams's concern for civic employees was demonstrated in her ill-fated motion to restore school teachers' salaries to their level before cuts, but she did not let her embarrassment over conciliar red tape staunch her interest. She worked to include teachers in a pension scheme, and her Health Committee introduced regulations on half-day closings for retail stores.[69] The bread-and-butter issues before the Health Committee brought her in close contact with civic housekeeping on a minute scale. All in a month's work were matters connected with the purchase of automobiles for the food division of the Health Department; the awarding of contracts for supplying prescriptions and medicine for "indigent patients"; applications for licensing billiard rooms, dance halls, pin-ball machines;[70] and the purchase of oats "for feeding of City owned horses in the street cleaning and scavenging division of the Health Department."[71]

This acquaintance with the daily management of a city made her intimately aware of the problems of poverty and overcrowding, and she developed an early interest in housing. In May 1935 she had the Health Department produce a statistical report on "certain social conditions in Winnipeg." Using an assorted list of indices, the study showed that two contiguous areas of the city, immediately north of Portage Avenue and west of Main Street, experienced much worse conditions than the rest of the city. In these two areas, infant mortality was higher; the incidence of scarlet fever and tuberculosis was higher; there was twice the number of admissions into the public wards of hospitals; there was much more – up to triple – the number of Children's Aid cases per 1,000 population; and there was between two and eight times the rate of the rest of the city's venereal disease cases, and between three and eight times the rate of the rest of the city's arrests per 1,000 population.[72] McWilliams used this report in a special committee on housing conditions, on which she sat from 1935. In October 1937 she addressed the Local Council of Women on the subject of "Homes at Moderate Prices." A prototype house had been built as an example of an affordable home for the "low-salaried man."[73]

The Housing Committee produced a report in May 1938. It proposed to meet two objectives at once: to employ "a very large number of relief recipients" and to build approximately five hundred rental dwellings that would be "available to the low-income group only." Financing would be shared with the dominion government. The report clearly demonstrated the need for affordable housing.[74] The proposed remedy, as described, would contribute in only a minor way to solving an enormous problem. Still, the City built a model house for $4,000 and "set off a minor housing boom."[75] McWilliams's efforts in having the problem analysed and presented in a graphic and accessible way helped to create a sympathetic atmosphere in a council whose Citizen members were disinclined to expand social services.[76]

Throughout her tenure as alderman, McWilliams laboured on two fronts with respect to the issue of women in public life. On the one hand, she had to prove her own credentials with her colleagues, and on the other, she continually strove to persuade more women to join the ranks. The first led her into some difficulties of etiquette. "When she first went to Council meeting, last January, the mode of address was, 'Lady and Gentlemen.' The whole eighteen recognised the awkwardness of it, and at last a brave one ventured: 'Do you mind if I just say, "Gentlemen"?' Mrs McWilliams was quick to reply, 'I'd much rather you would.'"[77] With a degree of self-knowledge, she recognized that another "hurdle" she had to face was "the foregone conclusion that she was a 'highbrow and a managing female.'"[78]

McWilliams understood there was a wide reluctance on the part of women to be exposed to these situations. She patiently tried to learn how to work with men.[79] She realized that other people might have difficulty working with a woman in authority. When she became chair of the Unemployment Relief Committee in 1939, she said, "Perhaps my most difficult task will be in making the citizens with whom I have to deal forget I am a woman."[80] She sometimes resented what she saw as a lack of support from women. In 1934 she was "keenly disappointed" that the Local Council of Women was not repeating its sponsorship of women candidates, that it "is not sending me a colleague at the city hall."[81] Her disappointment was expressed again in 1937: "The reason more women were not in public life ... was that 'women haven't stood behind them; they haven't believed women could do it.'"[82] McWilliams was apt to criticize "the meal-ticket woman ... the women who marry to escape the labour of a job ... We are a reproach to those women and they are antagonistic." She confessed she did not know how to win such women away from their indifference or opposition to, or suspicion of, women in public life. Until women felt comfortable supporting other women, progress would be painfully slow.[83]

McWilliams never fully analysed what "thinking of ourselves as women" meant. She knew women's support was the source of what authority she had, and she was sorry that few women were prepared to join her in the front lines. Yet her example of involvement in so many activities was enough to deter all but the very bold and energetic. And she was not particularly helpful when journalists and others asked her how she kept up with all her activities. "I just do it" was her response.[84]

CHAPTER EIGHT

Government House

At the age of sixty-six Margaret McWilliams experienced a third momentous change in the rhythm of her life. When she was twenty-eight, she had left employment in a large American city to become a full-time married woman in a small town in Ontario. Seven years later she moved to a large Canadian city and quickly established herself as a woman in the public sphere. Now life again altered abruptly when in October 1940 her husband was appointed lieutenant-governor of Manitoba.

Prime Minister Mackenzie King, an old college friend of both McWilliamses, was able to offer Roland this honour as a reward for loyal service to the Liberal Party. Personal wealth was normally expected in a lieutenant-governor, and it was commonly known that the McWilliamses lived in modest circumstances.[1] But Roland's legal and political interests were not so constrained. While managing his legal practice, he had lectured on constitutional law for the Manitoba Law Society and published several articles on the constitution. He had written a book, *Does History Repeat Itself?*, as well as the two books with his wife.[2] In his education, experience, understanding, and diplomatic personality, he was eminently qualified for the position, and two re-appointments, in 1945 and 1950, were proof that he performed well.

For a week Margaret hesitated over whether she would remain as alderman: her term would not expire for fourteen months. However, deciding that the position of lieutenant-governor "must be kept clear of all controversial or party issues," she resigned, expressing the hope that a woman would be elected to succeed her, and indeed, Hilda Hesson, a businesswoman, was elected in her place.[3] Now in 1940 she applied herself to being "the wife of my husband."[4]

In the event, McWilliams remained in Government House until her death in April 1952. She continued to direct the current events classes and to participate in many organizations, particularly the University Women's Club and the Canadian Federation of University Women. She served on two federal government bodies: one produced a report on the postwar problems of women, which developed her theories about women in society, and the other provided her with the "most intense conference I ever attended."[5] She made new initiatives, revitalizing the dormant Manitoba Historical Society and starting a women's chapter of the Canadian Institute of International Affairs. She wrote a new book. She remained very busy. To the business of Government House chatelaine she devoted her administrative skill and her own ideas about what should be done.

Ceremony and hospitality were the two major contributions of the lieutenant-governor to provincial life. The pageantry of the British parliamentary system was interpreted by McWilliams to her relatives. "This silly title of Lieut.-governor," she wrote to Helen, did not endow authority, "though nothing the government does, or the legislature, can become law until Roll signs it. Of course if he did not sign it, it would be a case of 'off with his head.' Which is about as logical as the British governing system ever is ... What Roly really is is the representative of the king, and he does the same thing in Manitoba that the King does in England."[6]

At the time of the visit of Princess Elizabeth in October 1951, the Manitoba Legislative Assembly was in brief session. Photographs were published whose pageantry perplexed McWilliams's brother Russell, and she offered this explanation: "Roll accompanied by the Princess was met at the door of the chamber by the Sergeant at Arms carrying the mace, and they were led by him to the dais which the Princess mounted. Roll would take the speakers chair which she did not [sic]. When he has done so the Sergeant makes three deep bows, and then stands to one side still holding the mace. When Roll has finished, the sergeant leads him out with the mace, takes him to the door, and then returns to lay the mace on the table as a sign that parliament is in session ... I have not seen the picture you saw, but quite evidently it is one of the sergeant making one of his three bows." McWilliams added, "You will find a setting out of these customs and the reason for them in a book called *This New Canada,*" whose second edition she was just finishing.[7]

Roland had a clear idea of his own dignity. When a reporter asked to see him, he refused, saying, "You do not interview the king."[8] His brother-in-law Hodder, never sympathetic to the McWilliamses, thought that "his position has gone to his head and he has a false sense of his own importance."[9] But Douglas Campbell, premier of the province after 1948, considered him "a gentleman among gentlemen, while he had lots of iron in his character, too. He was much more diplomatic, much less assertive than Margaret was."[10] Margaret McWilliams too could be dignified. Those who knew her remarked on her regal bearing.[11]

Ever mindful of her new circumstances, McWilliams wanted to ensure that Roland was accorded proper respect. "She always deferred to him – he was the lieutenant-governor!"[12] "She liked to make sure that Roly got his due."[13] "She wouldn't do anything to bring any criticism on herself that would reflect on Roly." Even though she was a heavy smoker, when she used the official car, with its chauffeur and flag, she would refrain from smoking.[14] However, she tempered this respect for the trappings of power with a comprehension of what Oliver Stowell as king of Canada had recognized as the sovereignty of the people. This she demonstrated in a practical way by opening up Government House to more ordinary people than it had seen through the sojourns of previous lieutenant-governors. Her new residence was not merely to be the venue for private parties or receptions for important people.

"Mostly before," wrote McWilliams to her niece Helen, "the people who have come to G.H. have been those who were either the personal friends of the lieutenant-governor or the so-called social set. This has been very marked in the last two – even the last three regimes, so that there had come two or three years ago a good deal of talk about abolishing G.H. as they have done in a couple of the provinces. There won't be any more talk while we stay. Roll by going about everywhere – among all kinds of people – has made the office real in a way it was not before, and even I who thought it was rather footless at first can see that it can be and is being made a force for steadiness and loyalty in a time of stress."[15]

After their first year, the McWilliamses found they had entertained five thousand people. "That included one large reception for men for Roly which comes on New Years day – one large one for me."[16] In 1946 they estimated they entertained "approximately 6,000 for a full year."[17] Big events alternated with more mundane occurrences. For instance, they provided hospitality for the governor general on his trips to and from the West Coast.[18]

McWilliams followed the traditional New Year levee, when "most leading citizens and the military" paid their respects to the king's representatives on New Year's Day, with a parallel levee for women in February, when "none of the ladies present could remember such a large attendance for any single event at the official residence."[19] She invited women's groups to hold their annual general meetings at Government House, and would hold a tea after the meetings.[20] There were special receptions to honour distinguished visitors or to commemorate important occasions. In January 1943 she had a reception for five hundred people for Mrs Garson, wife of the incoming premier. At that time Emily Garson asked McWilliams how she managed to remember people's names. "I put the names on a list on the bedpost overnight," replied McWilliams.[21]

Margaret and Roland invited more people to their house than had their predecessors. They attended Sunday service at churches of different denominations within a wide radius of the city, consciously identifying with their roles as royal emblems of imperial unity. With uncharacteristic self-importance, McWilliams noted to an interviewer: "Remembering that we are the personal representatives of His Majesty the King, such attendance seems only natural."[22] They also accepted many more invitations to visit all parts of the province in a purposeful program. In May 1941, for instance, Roland's office issued a schedule of Manitoba visits for the following six weeks. They were to go to Dauphin, Beausejour, Killarney, and Brandon. While Roland was addressing the Canadian Club and

a Canadian Legion meeting, Margaret was to speak to graduating nurses and high school students.[23]

The following year the McWilliamses took a trip to Swan
River near the Saskatchewan border. At each stop, Margaret
addressed meetings while Roland met local officials and occasionally made speeches himself. For instance, Roland noted
that on 28 May "Margaret addressed a woman's meeting on
Price Control while I wrote a couple of business letters and
had a sleep," but after the seven o'clock dinner, "I spoke for
one hour on the problems with which this country is faced
now during the war and at the conclusion of the war." Two days
later, while the lieutenant-governor spent the evening in the
officers' mess at Brandon, McWilliams drove to Souris and
addressed a convention of the Women's Institutes of South-
Western Manitoba on the topic of Russia. The following day
she gave a speech at Virden in the early afternoon and another
at Kenton, returning to her hotel in Brandon at 11 p.m. Roland
"cleared up some work then went for a walk and visited the
YMCA."[24] Both McWilliamses were gratified at the "evident
pleasure of the people whom we visited ... we were told that
it was the first time a Lieutenant-Governor had ever visited
their district officially."[25] McWilliams believed her husband had
"come out into a bright light of popularity that he did not have
before ... He is of course a new type of lieutenant-governor.
Very democratic – believing that he is lieut.-gov. for all the
people of the city and province and doing many things to show
it."[26]

As noted, the hospitality of Government House was to be
extended to visiting dignitaries as well. Two visits that caused
a considerable flutter were royal: the Duke of Kent in August
1941 and Princess Elizabeth with Prince Philip ten years later.

The news of the Duke of Kent's visit reached the
McWilliamses while they were on their holiday at Stony Lake,
outside Peterborough. With only six days to return to Winnipeg and make arrangements, they arrived with forty-eight
hours in hand, "only to discover that the basement where the
kitchen and all its works are, was flooded with a foot of water
and sewage ... That left Margaret one day in which to provide
for the visit of His Royal Highness." The disaster was com-
pounded. "Just to add to the troubles, I became a partial casu-

alty ... my hand had been bitten by a spider ... Sunday morning it was badly swollen and kept getting worse all day. One ankle was in the same condition. Monday morning before the Duke left, one eye was badly swollen." Nevertheless, "the visit was delightful."[27]

The duke had come to Canada to inspect Empire Air Training developments.[28] Arriving in Winnipeg on a Sunday, he was entertained to a supper for sixteen at Government House. Crowds of about four thousand lined the route from the airport, and outside Government House another crowd of "2,500, most of them women," waited to see him. Guests at the supper included military, naval, and air force commanders, the mayor, and the premier. The duke and an aide spent the night at Government House while the rest of his party stayed at the Royal Alexandra Hotel.[29] As always, there was speculation as to how he would cope with the abstinence of Government House.[30]

"There was never any liquor served at Government House."[31] This was due to a coincidence of principle and economy. In 1923 McWilliams wrote to Violet McNaughton, "Now I am working overtime speaking in the interests of prohibition. I have never been a teetotaller myself, but I can't help but feel strongly that having gained prohibition, it is too bad to go backward."[32] As private citizens, the McWilliamses had not served liquor or wine, and they were not averse to giving the impression that their lack of wealth obliged them to offer non-alcoholic punch at receptions or hot tomato juice at the levees. Although they kept a cook and a chauffeur, and employed a gardener and other occasional household help, the McWilliamses were not big spenders. Roland felt constrained to keep up his legal practice even when lieutenant-governor, and until 1949 he continued to work at his profession in the afternoons.[33]

After six years in the position, Roland prepared a memorandum on his expenses for the provincial government. In 1940 "I had taken the view ... that the day should be over when the proper discharge of public duties should depend on the largesse of the rich. I expected to spend in the discharge of my duties everything I received and probably a little more at my own option." As he had been unable to persuade the dominion government to assume the costs of operating his car, "I have gone into the hole at the rate of about $1,130 a year." He expected that costs, both in wages and in food, would increase. Roland emphasized their thrift. He gave very little to charity, "with the consequence that, so far as the public knows, I give nothing," and he stressed two important economies: "(a) We do not serve liquor which is customary and a very expensive form of entertainment; (b) We do not have a housekeeper or house manager and the work which such a person would do is done by Mrs McWilliams working excessively hard." He was glad when the provincial government paid for a new kitchen: "We shall now be able to move in this respect from medieval to modern conditions."[34]

Margaret McWilliams wrote for money as well as for her own satisfaction. When she completed a new edition of *This New Canada* in 1952, she said, "This book was urgent and it is important to me." She immediately elaborated: "It means for this year an addition to my income of about $1,400 and will mean a smaller income for several years." The same letter to her brother Russell contained more information about the McWilliamses' income: "We have recently had some good news. Lieutenant Governors in this country have been getting the same salaries they got in 1876. For people of wealth this does not matter so much but even they are restive under it. The government has always seemed to be afraid of raising the salaries though they have raised every other class of civil servants including themselves and the members of parliament. Now they are going to give us expense accounts and they are making them liberal ... the minimum for us is $5,000 a year. I can't believe it – nor could I ever tell anyone so they could understand, what a load will roll off my shoulders if and when we get it which apparently will be the first of September next."[35]

The second royal visit organized by the McWilliamses, with thrift and without wine, was that of Princess Elizabeth and the Duke of Edinburgh on 16 October 1951. The royal party was not staying overnight, but the McWilliamses were to escort them about the city, entertain them to dinner at Government House, then accompany them to the ballet in the evening. By early September, McWilliams had "the decorators inside and outside the house for a month and the end is not yet."[36] She borrowed a lot of dishes, which all had to be packed and returned after the visit.[37] The day was very busy for McWilliams, as she described it to her brother Russell:

[The day was] cold with a bad wind, but bright. The crowds were tremendous and very happy. Everywhere we went streets were crowded even to the last trip to the station to take the train for the western journey ... The fact that we were always in attendance, Roll walking with the Princess and I with the Duke does not show in these pictures. We were always watching to keep out of the way.

From the very beginning we were always late ... We had been told that the driving would be at the rate of 8–10 miles per hour, and everything was most carefully timed almost from corner to corner for this speed. However, citizens prepare, and Princes dispose. The Duke had a radio telephone to the pilot car, and he controlled the pace reducing it to 3–5 miles ... they were 25 minutes late arriving for dinner ... Hence I had 55 minutes from the time the Princess entered the room until she had to leave it to allow the other guests to leave and be seated at the ballet before she arrived ... Just how I was able to smile and chatter to keep things going at the head table I do not know, but I can tell you truthfully that I did, even to making the Duke laugh at one or two of the small mistakes. We were on time. As the Princess was going out the door, I said to her, "Well, ma'am, we've made it." She looked at me with a small smile and replied, "You're the only person who has been able to make me do it."[38]

McWilliams's pride in her accomplishment was tempered by her disappointment that "my delicious food over which we had spent endless hours" could not be fully appreciated and her regret that "all the fun and informality of a buffet was lost." She also had to contend with a disagreement with Roland over getting the royal party to the ballet on time. "He thought the lateness should have been shared with the Ballet."[39] McWilliams rested for two days after the visit and contemplated with horror the planned visit of the queen of Holland to Canada in April 1952. "I am praying that she will not come west ... Two queens in six months would be more of queens than I want to have."[40]

The death of King George VI in 1952 "brought a change in our lives which will be helpful. The mourning period lasts until

June first. Until then we cannot attend social functions – or big public dinners, and we cannot have any party at G.H. ... I am much relieved because Roll is getting tired much more easily, and is recovering slowly." She felt more involved with the institution of the Crown, since "the recent visit of the new Queen to this house made it all more real to us," but at the age of seventy-seven she was glad to curtail some activity.[41]

At the beginning of the McWilliamses' tenure, they were both still energetic. During the war, they tried to be "a force for steadiness in a time of stress." Margaret McWilliams gave radio talks and inspected troops.[42] To her niece in December 1941 she wrote that there would shortly be compulsory selective service "of everyone, man and woman, who isn't either too old or too young. I rather expect to be swearing falsely about my age."[43] But ten years later, at the time of the 1950 Red River floods, "the most catastrophic ever seen in Canada," McWilliams became "so tired."[44] Roland was an honorary chairman of the Manitoba Flood Relief Fund, and McWilliams was kept busy providing hospitality to visitors like the governor general, who inspected the dikes, and the United Kingdom high commissioner to Canada, who brought relief supplies.[45]

McWilliams was happy to commit substantial resources of time and energy to the continuing current events class, after 1940 idiosyncratically located in the ballroom. Each season, from October to March, the class met twice a month. In her class notes she chronicled the progress of the war. These notes were locked into the diary intended to be "a journal of happenings," and indeed, for a person devoted to public life, these events were the most significant happenings during the McWilliams tenure at Government House.[46]

Each class began with a review of intervening events and then went on to analyse selected topics. Always McWilliams strove to see the "sum total," which could be "missed as we take it day by day," and usually she isolated the few most important happenings of the period.[47] Some classes were confined to the study of Canadian events or the domestic or military policy of a single country, and occasionally she examined one particular idea from a historical perspective as well as in the light of recent events. For example, in January 1942 she looked at "the progress that has been made towards world organization for war and for the peace to follow." It was "not correct to say that the League [of Nations] was a failure. It ... showed it was possible to work together for the betterment of conditions in various fields." She then identified four main reasons why the league had not fulfilled its main purpose of preventing war. First, "peace cannot be maintained without police." Secondly, the requirement to have unanimity in decision making was unworkable. Thirdly, it was impossible for nations built on different ideologies to respect each other. Fourthly, the presence of the United States would have made "a vital difference." McWilliams still believed that "some form of world government is essential for the settlement of international problems without resort to war."[48]

After the publication in Britain of the Beveridge report on social security she took the opportunity to consider a topic which she had already covered theoretically in the 1931 *King of Canada* book and had experienced in a practical way during her work as an alderman. "The whole British world was stirred" by the "marvellous work of Beveridge." She lauded the idea of "one insurance policy covering needs from cradle to the grave for the whole population."[49]

McWilliams soon had the chance to support the implementation of a more widespread social security scheme in Canada when she was appointed to chair a subcommittee of the Federal Advisory Committee on Reconstruction. The Reconstruction Committee had been established in March 1941, and the following month Margaret Wherry, vice-president of the Federation of Business and Professional Women's Clubs, expressed her concern to the prime minister that no woman had been selected.[50] The consequence of Wherry's, and other women's, lobbying was the appointment of McWilliams and four other women in January 1943, and of five more women by April, to the Subcommittee on the Post-War Problems of Women. Its terms of reference were "to examine the problems relating to the re-establishment of women after the war and to make recommendations to the Committee on Reconstruction as to the procedure to deal with the problems and other matters relating to the welfare of women in the period of reconstruction."[51]

Subcommittee members were "overwhelmingly well-educated, of British origin, Protestant and middle-aged." In addition to McWilliams, who had become well acquainted with the problems of poor and unemployed women through her experience as an alderman, there were three other members who had direct knowledge about working women. The subcommittee had to work under awkward and severe restraints. Scattered from Vancouver to Fredericton, its members were asked to make a preliminary report by May on the issue of social security in relation to women, with particular reference to the Marsh Report, which was issued before the subcommittee's first meeting in March. Moreover, the original time frame for its wider mandate was reduced from eighteen to eight months. Added to these time restrictions was an insistence from Dr Cyril James, chairman of the Reconstruction Committee, that publicity be avoided.[52] The subcommittee collected data as well as it could and met only four times. Under such circumstances, it was extraordinary that two reports were produced at all. More remarkable was the feminism permeating the subcommittee's work.

It is true that the members of the subcommittee were "from the servant employing class, not from the class that would supply the domestic servants." Postwar planners to some extent took for granted "the old hope that domestic service would provide the needed jobs" for women in peacetime.[53] Certainly the subcommittee included a recommendation on household employment, but it is a mistake to focus exclusively on this aspect of its work. The declared assumptions of the subcommittee were three: that full employment would be an objective of postwar economic policy, that postwar problems of women could not be considered apart from postwar problems of society in general, and that women were right to hope to be "full members of a free community."[54] These premises led the subcommittee to make twelve major recommendations, many of which were still timely a generation later.[55]

The subcommittee reported at a time when agriculture employed the largest total of male workers and domestic work was the largest single occupation of females. The subcommittee, while expecting this to continue, made forceful recommendations for the improvement of wages, working conditions, and the status of household work. It also foresaw the economic dislocation of those women who were working in wartime occupations, and recommended that government provide retraining and training in technical and professional work. The subcommittee clearly promoted the idea that women should be competitive in the postwar labour market, even in sectors where they had not been numerous before.

Members were also concerned to integrate women into the newly developing plans for social security involving children's allowances, health insurance, nursery schools, unemployment insurance, workers' compensation, and minimum wage legislation. Both as producers in the labour force and as reproducers in the home, women were to be supported by state legislation and welfare programs. Moreover, there was to be no insistence that married women refrain from earning an income. On this last point the subcommittee was consistent with its own assumptions but not synchronized with public opinion. Members recognized from their wide sampling of public opinion the prevalence of the notion that "married women should not be allowed to work if their husbands have a good position and can keep the family and home comfortable,"[56] but the subcommittee firmly went out on a feminist limb:

1. To women in each group (married, single, farm) the right to choose what occupation she will follow must be conceded as a right to which every citizen is entitled. She must also have the right to equality of remuneration, working conditions, and opportunity for advancement.
2. We believe that the right to choose is not going to operate to make every woman, or even much larger groups of women want to leave their homes for the labour market. It is the right to choose which is demanded. Happier homes, and therefore, a happier democracy, will result from the recognition that women choose or do not choose marriage as their vocation. It must be remembered that for many single women marriage will be an impossibility because of the casualties of the war.
3. Many women in all three groups will find their situations changed in the post-war years. A large proportion of the women now working, both married and single, have been earning money for the first time, or the first time since marriage. They have gained an entirely new realisation of their skills and capacities. Many will return gladly to home life. Others will feel a sense of frustration

if they have not the opportunity to exercise these abilities. For some public activities will serve, others will wish to be gainfully employed.[57]

Canadian historian Gail Cuthbert Brandt concluded that the report "suffered from a lack of public support" and its recommendations remained to be repeated by the Royal Commission on the Status of Women in 1970.[58] As a measure of McWilliams's thinking about women, it showed considerable development. She wanted the individual woman to choose how to spend her life. She recognized that women were individuals, as well as members of families; hence they should be integrated into a large-scale welfare state as individuals and their continuing responsibilities as mothers and homemakers should be acknowledged. At no point did she denigrate the woman who chose homemaking exclusively. Indeed, she praised the home as the "foundation" of a "true democracy" and consequently believed that governments should "create conditions under which such homes can be successfully maintained."[59] The individual woman should have the right to choose the option of combining employment with motherhood. It was the responsibility of government to undertake or encourage measures that would allow women this choice. Given the brief time the subcommittee had, it is scarcely surprising there was little description of the contours of this new society. The subcommittee had, however, fulfilled its mandate in stating that the "welfare of women" should be viewed in terms of individual rights within the context of a society whose social programs permitted the well-being of both the individual and the family.

The subcommittee's outlook seems all the more unusual when it is compared with other committees charged with postwar planning. The Manitoba government named a committee on rehabilitation training in April 1944, to advise the minister of education. One of its five subcommittees was to consider the type of postwar training necessary for women then in the armed services. This subcommittee's recommendations conform to a pattern that could be discerned in the Women's Division of the National Selective Service.[60] The Manitoba subcommittee repeated McWilliams's "general considerations" about an individual woman's right to choose but interpreted the field of choice much more traditionally. The Manitoba sub-committee named "fields where many might be employed" and, in contrast to the approach taken by the McWilliams sub-committee, identified occupations in sectors and at levels long stereotyped by gender: personal, hospitality, and nursing services; salesmanship; the "needle trade" and "furriers" in the manufacturing sector; and "clerical and stenographic" work in the business sector. "Homemaking" was emphasized above all, but the Manitoba subcommittee ignored the elaborate suggestions the McWilliams subcommittee made for upgrading the training, pay, working conditions, and benefits for household workers.

About the only innovative idea the provincial subcommittee was prepared to recommend concerned university training. It stated that "there will be a need of qualified professional people," and it recommended more than one annual intake of students, "the expansion of post-graduate courses," and the establishment of new faculties "in physical education, dentistry, journalism, drama, radio and others." The Manitoba subcommittee made no effort to collect data beyond consultation with members of the Subcommittee on Women's Services "and many others" and brought no statistics or reasoning to support its conclusions.[61] Both in method and imagination this was a pedestrian undertaking, looking backwards to prewar days. The McWilliams report looked, with vision, into the future. This was doubtless one of reasons its recommendations were, in Brandt's description, "pigeon-holed and forgotten" by government. At the time, the report "quickly ran through its first edition because it came to be in such demand as study-group material for many women's organisations."[62]

The following year, McWilliams received another dominion appointment. She was Canada's only woman delegate to the United Nations Relief and Rehabilitation Administration's (UNRRA) conference held in Montreal, 15–27 September 1944.[63] UNRRA was first formed under a November 1943 agreement to effect relief for the "victims of war" in any area under the control of the "United Nations" – the allies of the United States – "through the provision of food, fuel, clothing, shelter and other basic necessities, medical and other essential services." The agreement was notable as a model for possible future international agencies.

UNRRA's second council meeting was to be held at the Montreal conference, and there policies would be decided upon. The Canadian representative on the UNRRA Council was Lester B. Pearson, then serving in the Canadian Embassy in Washington, whom McWilliams later persuaded to come to talk to one of her groups in Winnipeg. McWilliams was a member of UNRRA's Technical Advisory Committee on Displaced Persons and an alternate on the Welfare Committee. In the broad view, although these committees contributed to the planning process, they played "a minor role" in the development of UNRRA's work.[64] From the perspective of a delegate, McWilliams was "thrilled at the opportunity to be at the centre of things. Nobody was interested in anything but getting the most accomplished in the shortest time."[65] It "was the most intense conference she had ever attended."[66]

A reporter noted that McWilliams "returned full of enthusiasm for the work done there." She used New Testament terminology to explain the organization's work. "UNRRA is not a great overpowering Santa Claus. She is the good Samaritan sitting by the roadside, meting out the things that are needed," she told the Winnipeg Women's Liberal Association. The onset of peace made her optimistic. "We are definitely going to make a better world. It will not come overnight, but come it will."[67] Part of her enthusiasm was channelled into a new international affairs group.

One of McWilliams's great strengths was her ability to establish an organization on a sufficiently firm footing for it to survive and prosper long beyond its original impetus.[68] This knack was given early recognition by a group of women who wanted to set up a Winnipeg Junior League. An initial gathering, at which "we soon discovered we were not capable of forming any sort of club ... none of us knew anything of parliamentary procedure or how to elect a President and Directors," was "a complete fiasco." Then "someone had a brain-wave ... and phoned ... Mrs McWilliams and asked her what we should do." McWilliams herself was not a member, but her advice was enough to get the group going in 1926.[69] She also helped start the Community Players of Winnipeg in 1921, a group that encouraged the writing and production of Canadian plays.[70] Twenty-three years later she used the same skill to establish a new group in which she was personally very interested: a Winnipeg women's chapter of the Canadian Institute of International Affairs (CIIA).

The CIIA was a men's group and resisted the idea of women as members. McWilliams envisioned a new group of women who would give serious study to aspects of international politics after the war. She therefore selected a small number of women who shared her concern, drawn mainly but not exclusively from the international relations group of the University Women's Club, from her current events class, and also from among some recent young university graduates. Numbering about thirty-five, they included old friends like journalist Kennethe Haig, history teacher Elsie Moore, former colleagues in city government like ILP school trustee Gloria Queen Hughes, and younger women like Mrs W.L. Morton.[71] "Marcella Dafoe was called upon to telephone Mr Tarr of the CIIA to ask if they would permit a second chapter in Winnipeg. Marcie then wrote the required letter and permission was granted."[72]

Straightaway members chose to do research papers on specified topics. One paper was titled "European union," and another, with a Winnipeg twist, "Colonial Break-up," a direct reference to the annual catharsis when the winter ice in Winnipeg's two rivers thawed and break-up occurred. The organization of each meeting was similar to that which had been followed for years in the Social Science Study Club, but there were some differences. There was no nominating committee for the selection of officers; instead, a ballot was circulated with the name of every woman in the club on it. Each member had seven votes. The seven names attracting the highest number of votes were the nucleus of the executive. Members could co-opt up to four more, but the chair and vice-chair had to be from among the top seven. The group found that under this system, no one ever refused to serve.[73]

Another distinction was found in the group's external contacts. First, the CIIA network of speakers was available. A diplomat or politician would travel to Winnipeg, speak to the women in the late afternoon (the members who were high school teachers or civil servants could attend at this time), then transfer to the hospitality of the men's group and deliver an after-dinner speech to the men. The story was told that these visiting speakers came to regard the women's group as more serious and discreet than the men's: "We had Mike Pearson, who told us why Canada should recognize China, but he never opened his mouth to say this to the men."[74] Secondly, liaison was established with a similar group in Minneapolis drawn from the University of Minnesota Faculty Wives Association, the League of Women Voters, and a foreign policy club. There would be "annual joint meetings where papers would be given on subjects that both groups had studied. They met alternately in the two cities for several years."[75] As late as 1970 the two groups were co-ordinating their study topics.[76]

Interested women in other cities kept a careful watch on Winnipeg. "The Canadian Institute of International Affairs has been brought to state a policy of welcoming the formation of women's branches, which we accept as a halfway measure until we reach the ideal goal of mixed branches. One women's group has been set up in Winnipeg on the initiative of our club. Two other towns are likely to organise at once."[77] In Winnipeg the women's branch of the CIIA remained a going concern until, at the men's suggestion, the two branches merged in the early 1970s.[78]

Another of McWilliams's undertakings in 1944 involved the rejuvenation of the Manitoba Historical Society. McWilliams had already served as vice-president, in 1929, after the publication of *Manitoba Milestones*.[79] In the interwar years the society had been primarily "an agency for historical education," whose activities included the placement of plaques to commemorate important events in the province's history. However, "regular meetings ceased around 1936."[80] At an informal meeting in February 1944, McWilliams joined with Professor W.L. Morton from the University of Manitoba, provincial librarian Leslie Johnston, and five others to reconstitute the society.[81]

McWilliams became president, and during her four-year tenure she transformed the society into a highly active research-sponsoring agency. Membership increased to 101 in 1947. The society's receipts in the year ending May 1945 totalled $114 but were immediately multiplied by a grant of $3,700.[82] With the efficacious support of the minister of health, Ivan Schultz, government money allowed the society to fund research and publish a series of works on provincial ethnic groups and archaeology. The society's annual publication, *Transactions*, of the Historical and Scientific Society of Manitoba was resumed. The provincial government was persuaded to appoint an archivist by the society. McWilliams gave her name to an essay contest for high school students around the province.[83] The society never again had the resources to generate so much scholarship as well as public awareness.

In her seventies McWilliams was most gratified to receive substantial public recognition for her achievements. In 1945 the National Council of Women made her a life member.[84] She was also honoured by the universities of Manitoba and Toronto. In 1946, a year after her husband received an LL.D. from the University of Manitoba, McWilliams was awarded the same degree. The other recipient with her was Wesley McCurdy, publisher of the *Winnipeg Tribune*.[85] Two weeks later, the University Women's Club, whose interests were so bound up with her own, conferred upon McWilliams its first honorary membership. The president in 1946 was her close friend Avis Clark, and Doris Saunders, recipient of the 1925 CFUW scholarship, made the presentation to McWilliams.[86]

Her doctorate from the University of Toronto two years later, 1948, was a direct result of the concerted effort by colleagues in the Canadian Federation of University Women. Mrs R.B. Crummy, president of the federation in 1948, wrote to the chancellor of the University of Toronto, Vincent Massey, in February, noting that the convocation of 1948 would be the fiftieth anniversary of McWilliams's graduation:

In the intervening fifty years, as you are no doubt aware, Mrs McWilliams has done much to further the economic, cultural and spiritual betterment of Canada through her service in civic, provincial, and national bodies. As a member of the Winnipeg City Council, as a writer and a lecturer on current events, and as Chairman of the Subcommittee on Post-War Problems of Women (of the Advisory Committee on Reconstruction, James Commission), 1943, Mrs McWilliams contributed to Canadian information and public affairs.

Internationally, too, Mrs McWilliams's inspiration has been felt, notably as a Vice-President of the International Federation of University Women; as a delegate to the Pacific Relations Conference in Hanchow, 1931; as advisor to the Federal government's delegation to the labour conference of the League of Nations; and more recently as a Canadian delegate to UNRRA.

In 1919, Mrs McWilliams was one of the organisers and became the first President of the Canadian Federation of University Women, which now has branches in all major Canadian cities. This co-ordination of wide-spread efforts toward the encouragement of higher education, informed public opinion, Christian ideals of citizenship, and international understanding is now bearing fruit in many fields.[87]

So it happened that, in the company of the director emeritus of the Royal Ontario Museum and three religious dignitaries – a Roman Catholic cardinal, the United Church moderator, and the Anglican primate – Margaret McWilliams was awarded her second honorary degree, in June 1948. She was described as "representing the women of Canada" by the Toronto *Telegram*.[88]

McWilliams learned of the degree in April and wrote to Mrs Crummy to thank her and let her know her labours had borne a harvest:

For me it is very happy fruit. I cannot think of any honour which would mean more to me than this recognition by my own University. I think every graduate must feel so. I shall value it all the more because my public work has not been in that part of the country which the University of Toronto serves.

I am very grateful to those who have sought this recognition for me. I shall never know them all – but there are a few key people – among them yourself – and I want them to know that I am very happy over this. I find that as well as being happy I have a deep inward feeling of satisfaction. I'm not sure that this is entirely worthy – but I think you will understand. My warmest thanks go to you for your efforts on my behalf.[89]

Crummy's reference to "Christian ideals of citizenship" was no empty platitude. For most of her life, McWilliams had rarely spoken about religion. Her references to Jesus in public education had been exceptional. But after the Second World War she frequently interspersed her addresses with spiritual allusions. Speaking on "This Moment" to the Local Council of Women in September 1945, she combined a passion for international awareness and a confidence in women's capacity for equal responsibility with an explicit Christian conscience. "As war has ended we are saying, 'Whither now?' A great day has come for women. With the accepting of the United Nations charter, men and women are on an equal footing." Now there was the "possibility of peace, not peace as the absence of war, but peace positive, based on active co-operation by means of spiritual and mental forces ... We must first create peace within," that is, in the home, and in the community, then raise international co-operation to a level where "to think of the atomic bomb as an instrument of war is impossible ... Understanding of problems in our country is indispensable." She agreed with President Truman that "it must be through the spirit if we are to save the flesh." She finished on an inspirational note: "Realising that we stand as equals, let us accept our responsibilities, renew our spirits, renew our vows to God, and trust in His Divine Will."[90]

A vision of a Christian democrary increasingly permeated her public utterances. In 1947 she wrote the first of a series of articles designed to focus attention on the triennial meeting in Toronto of the International Federation of University Women. In this first article, entitled, "A Constructive Philosophy for Our Time: What Must I Do?", she considered that "for those who are strong enough to accept it, there is one clear way of life taught by Jesus." In secular terms, this meant the pursuit of excellence, and in McWilliams's opinion, this would require tolerance, the expression of opinion based on facts, and the promotion of peace. "We must work unceasingly, patiently and tolerantly to remove want and disease and, above all, fear, from all our people."[91]

Two years later McWilliams lectured on "The Way to Greatness" at University College of the University of Toronto. She emphasized the need to return to the moral standards of "our forefathers."[92] In September 1950 she was more forthcoming when addressing the United Church of Canada's "two great women's organisations," the Women's Association and the Women's Missionary Society – two organizations to which she herself had not belonged. Women were equal partners with men "in the great enterprise of making the Western democracies, or Canada, Christian ... I believe it is a great thing to be a Christian, but we are an inarticulate people. We have an idea that religion is our own business. I ask you: is it? Is it because we feel it is not fashionable to believe in good? I believe the time has come when our individual attitude must be made plain to all if we are to confront our challenge."[93] After her death, a columnist for the Toronto *Globe and Mail* noted that this was an occasion when women, "gathered from far and wide," learned "what they hadn't known before about the deep spiritual concerns of her life."[94]

In the last talk McWilliams gave before her death, she returned to this theme. The real danger from Russia in 1952 came not from the Cold War, but from the fact that "Russia holds a faith with fanatic enthusiasm, one which discards God entirely." The West had made few preparations to arm itself against the ideas of communism. "Our resources in such a battle should be our belief in God and His relevations, our faith in the Holy Spirit."[95] She combined her religious faith with a sense of how it could be put to practical political purpose.

Over her years in Government House, McWilliams had developed new interests and continued old ones. The increased hospitality and outreach of the lieutenant-governor might have been considered a full-time occupation in itself, but she had augmented that with her work on the postwar problems of women, the CIIA women's branch, the Manitoba Historical Society, and *This New Canada*. She could scarcely be described as retired. She helped inaugurate a contributory health insurance scheme, the Blue Cross, and persuaded a nineteen-year-old future Conservative premier of the province, Duff Roblin, to sell policies for it.[96] She brought the current events class to an end, but she continued to read and study widely, and give talks on public affairs.

One woman's recollection of a postwar lecture gives an insight into the resentment, as well as respect, that McWilliams could inspire. Jean Carson was sitting in the front row of a University Women's Club gathering and heard McWilliams refer to the Dumbarton Oaks negotiations between China, the Soviet Union, the United States, and the United Kingdom, which formulated proposals for a new international organization to succeed the League of Nations. Carson whispered to her neighbour, "What are Dumbarton Oaks?" McWilliams heard. She indignantly told Carson to go home and find out. Carson never forgot the episode.[97]

McWilliams became more friendly with her brothers. Niece Helen, Russell's child, called by Roland "the daughter long wished for," had an astringent recollection of family gatherings. "Her brothers hated her! Jealousy, jealousy!! Dad and she would fight whenever she visited us and Uncle Hod would hardly speak to her because he felt she was belittling his wife and his children and his three boys were brought up to ridicule her. Oh, so sad!!"[98] However, in 1950 Hodder had the McWilliamses to visit at his Maitland, Ontario, home and at about the same time Margaret developed a frequent correspondence with Russell. In the letters they exchanged news about stamps and the books they were reading, often at the recommendation of the other.[99] Anxieties concerning health were focused on Roland, not herself.

McWilliams was never to receive new royalties from *This New Canada*, nor did she benefit from the liberal expense allowance awarded to lieutenant-governors. She died, suddenly, on the afternoon of 12 April 1952, having signed her will only hours earlier. "Many people learned of her death through announcements from the pulpits at Easter Sunday services, and the shock could be felt," declared the leading editorial in Monday's *Winnipeg Tribune*.[100] "When our turn comes may we go with as little trouble as she did," wrote her brother Hodder.[101] Her death was more thoroughly documented than her life ever was. Tributes poured in. Her death was reported throughout Canada and in the United States.

"Margaret died about 5:45 in the afternoon of Saturday, April 12th."[102] Hodder described the cause of death as "an extreme case of hardening of the arteries."[103] Roland concluded that "Margaret died of exhaustion. For nearly sixty years she had been driving herself at a gallop, doing double or treble duty and it was amazing that she lived to be seventy-seven years of age and still full of mental vigour and spirit." She had been looking forward to a holiday they were to take on Vancouver Island. "She was out every one of the first four nights of the week ... On Saturday morning, she went down town ... Avis saw she was far from well" and had the doctor visit. He prescribed medication, which Margaret was unable to take, and after the doctor visited a second time, "she was unable to speak. Gradually and without any struggle or pain, the heart and the pulse and the breathing slowed down until the end came."[104]

There were over five hundred telegrams of condolence,[105] "and every flag in the city was at half mast." At the funeral were representatives from the governor general, the federal government, and other state bodies; "not a seat was empty and many people stood both inside and outside."[106] In addition to these signs of obvious respect, several of her women colleagues, at Roland's request, were honorary pallbearers. The local newspapers printed tributes from prominent women who had worked with her and, besides publishing their own encomiums in editorials, covered the funeral with extensive pictures and gave detailed accounts of her accomplishments.[107]

Hodder, who would never visit his sister at Government House when she was alive, found himself there at her death, and was irritated by the "protocol – protocol – protocol," not so much, however, as to restrain him and his son from taking an early-morning walk, "leaving Govt H. door unlatched (not protocol)" in search of coffee. The immense regard in which he could see that she was held had a profound effect on him. "I grieve that I did not do her due honour in her lifetime … No woman in Canada made such an impact on Canadian life in our time," he wrote.[108]

CHAPTER NINE

Margaret McWilliams, Women, and Feminists

In 1932 Margaret McWilliams addressed the Canadian Federation of University Women with the topic "When East Meets West," a theme used more than once to describe her own career. Born and educated in eastern Canada, she had chosen to live and work in the West. This address raised the theme to an international stage as she presented observations on China. She recalled a speech by "a very brilliant French woman lawyer" who began with the words "Now what you are going to see tonight is the mind of a French woman operating."[1]

In this biography we have searched for the mind of Margaret McWilliams. McWilliams's view of herself was inscribed in the scroll presented to her by the students of her current events classes. A public testimonial was entirely appropriate for a woman who had chosen public service as her career. Inevitably, her sincere belief in the objectives of the University Women's Club, the Women's Canadian Club, and the National Council of Education led to a certain solemnity of demeanour. There is a sense in which she personified the importance of being earnest. Yet with members of her family she was warm, friendly, and relaxed.[2] Close friends noted her sense of humour, and she herself urged other women not to be too tense.[3] "You warp your own judgment. You irritate other people. Those of you who have a sense of humour should always thank God that you have it, and those who haven't it should pray that in some way you may be able to get it."[4]

Public recognition was precious to her, and she honestly acknowledged its sweetness when thanking Mrs Crummy of the CFUW for instigating the process by which the University of Toronto awarded her an honorary degree.[5] Through public service McWilliams felt she could repay society for the gifts she had received: her wits, her character, her opportunities. Through public service she could also demonstrate those endowments. Imbued with the notion that the highest good was to serve the community, she shared the attitude of her teachers at the University of Toronto, contemporary clergy, and her fellow believers in the regeneration of society. This was a norm of service "that involved the Christian duty to help others" and invoked concepts of "self-help and community-building."[6]

McWilliams demanded of others what she had exacted from herself. In this she was setting herself to be a modern pilgrim: "pilgrims of peace abroad and pilgrims of understanding at home" was how she wished to see women with a university degree.[7] Unlike the men of her class and education in that she did not have to earn a living, she was also unlike the women in that she had no children to absorb her energy and emotional commitment. McWilliams more than most had time and attention for public service. Her marriage gave her love, security, and respectability. She enjoyed the company of nieces and nephews and their children.[8] The lack of children permitted her to indulge an appetite for citizenship on a scale that would otherwise have been most difficult.

The idea of public duty appealed widely to educated Protestant anglophone Canadians born before the First World War, nourished as they were on the philosophy of T.H. Green and the precepts of Professor Watson and Principal Grant.[9] McWilliams's colleagues in the women's organizations and her current events students found their entirely voluntary involvement worthwhile.

With respect to involvement in politics or in the labour force, McWilliams firmly held that a woman's primary responsibility was to her family, as a housekeeper and mother, but she saw this as no barrier. "A married woman's first job is to run her house and family, and not until she has learned to do that so smoothly that her absence for a meal does not upset the comfort of the home, should she take an outside job."[10] In the early twenties, her eyes were opened by friends in both the Canadian and the International federations of University Women to the possibilities of combining marriage with a career. Geneva Misener from Edmonton repeatedly urged the Canadian Federation to facilitate opportunities for married professional women. The issue was the main topic of discussion at Amsterdam.[11] In 1934 the CFUW president, Mrs Thom of Regina, strongly argued against marriage bars in public life: "Women, as individuals, should decide the question for themselves ... Those who choose to remain in their homes should not lose sight of their responsibility to society ... Women should 'face up,' take their places on school boards, on municipal councils, and with the experience thus gained, go on to larger spheres."[12]

Far from being a disadvantage, women's domestic experience was a positive benefit for public life, thought McWilliams. "My work is much like housework," she stated in 1939. She found "practical parallels to household management in the various problems" she faced in "running the city."[13] Running a household was good training for administrative work. By 1943 McWilliams was unequivocally stating that women, married or single, had the right to determine for themselves whether or not they should work for pay. "Speaking of rights of women, she pointed out that married men work, yet in Manitoba there are many rulings against married women working. 'They have an equal right to work' she said."[14] This statement of equal rights was thoroughly developed in her postwar problems report of 1943.

To McWilliams, equality was not to be interpreted as a denial of difference. "She contends that women are the equal of, though different from men in their various capabilities, and that each needs the other."[15] "Women's gifts and men's gifts are very different. We have a great gift for detail; we have been tidying things up for so long, we have a fine eye to see when they are not tidy." To a women's audience, she celebrated women's culture. Over the generations, "all you have learned, all your grandmother knew, [and] all your great-grandmother knew" have helped women to organize things – "a first-class gift for public service."[16] Women brought identifiable qualities to the service of the state, and the state should recognize the particular needs of women as mothers. The Post-War Problems Subcommittee recommended that maternity grants be paid by the state not only to employed women but also to farm women, in recognition of their largely unpaid economic contribution. McWilliams's feminism thus sought to have women benefit from both their sexual differences from men and their similarities to them.

By the late thirties McWilliams was aware that women in public life, in the labour force, in politics, or in volunteer public service could not rely on their own individual merits in order to be successful. Unlike some first-generation women professionals, who were attempting to assimilate into existing power structures without calling attention to gender, she considered that women needed to retain and develop women's sense of solidarity in order to achieve equality.[17] She delivered an address, "Opportunities for Women in Public Service," at the closing banquet of the nineteenth annual convention of the Quota Club International, held at Banff in the summer of 1938. Here she emphasized the importance of women supporting women. "I draw much strength from such relationships."

Unambiguously, in her Banff address, she said that women should run for elective office. "That is where we have to go … Don't think that I am too strong a feminist, but the men don't quite know what it is we are talking about when we are speaking about the thing that is fundamental to us, and we have got to be there to express our own views." In electoral politics, "you cannot march unless you have women behind you." McWilliams's reputation in provincial and federal life was based on her participation and leadership in women's organizations. She derived her initial municipal election success from the Local Council of Women. Whereas in 1933 she was not altogether happy with the idea of drafting women for public office, now, five years later, she recognized it as a positive step.

McWilliams thought that married women, especially middle-class women without the burden of earning their own livelihoods, should become readier to participate in public service. "We have got to learn to take marriage in our stride, children in our stride; our grandmothers did it … they didn't sit down and say to themselves that to bring up one or two children was the be-all and the end-all and took a woman's whole time." She understood the importance of economic independence but discounted the significance of women's economic dependence on husbands.

While appreciating the political value of women's organizations and women's solidarity, McWilliams at the same time thought it was important to work with men. Both separate and collaborative work were needed. "It took Adam and Eve to lose us our first Eden ... it will take the modern Adams and Eves to win us back our Eden."[18]

In her emphasis on the married woman's duty to participate more in public life, McWilliams differed from another prominent Canadian woman in public life, Charlotte Whitton. Whitton was a professional in child welfare work, "one of the ablest women in Canada," according to McWilliams.[19] Whitton disapproved of married women working outside the home. Whereas McWilliams claimed that a married woman "is a better worker than the single woman in the sense that she has greater steadiness, resourcefulness and more sense of responsibility," Whitton considered that single professional women should have the field for themselves.[20] Married women were intruders. Female participation in paid work, and leadership in volunteer organizations, should be reserved for the single women like herself whom she called the "secular unmarried."[21] McWilliams, however, wished to see extended to all women the opportunities and choices enjoyed by men.

Each was a feminist, and each was concerned primarily with the interest of the group with which she identified: educated married women or single professional women. Each claimed that her vision extended to other women, too. Neither McWilliams nor Whitton fully integrated the demands of reproduction into her view of society. McWilliams tried: she knew that someone had to look after the children and the housekeeping, and she hoped to raise the status of household work by incorporating it into an expanded labour code. Whitton's solution to that problem was to insist that mothers regard motherhood as a full-time occupation. In retrospect, McWilliams's vision of a society and state, which permitted individual choice, seems more realistic than Whitton's insistence that a woman's future life was determined forever at the time she decided to marry.

Whitton was bound by the notion that the model person was a male.[22] McWilliams, on the other hand, was struggling to imagine a vision of personhood that incorporated both equality and difference. Perhaps she was able to do this the more readily because of a model suggested by one other passion in her life: her religion.

If feminism was one guiding and growing beacon in McWilliams's life journey, Christianity was the other. "Margaret and I shared deep religious convictions, even though not always orthodox," wrote Roland when his wife died. "We had supreme confidence in a future life, the character of which will depend upon the life lived in this existence."[23] A woman who knew McWilliams in her seventies remarked, "Margaret McWilliams's background was Protestant, not Anglican, and I think she had been brought up to believe that one should do good in this world."[24] There was a potent evangelical strand in her faith. She felt all concerned citizens had a duty to pursue "the great ethical ideals of Jesus" and this fuelled her conviction that Christianity should be demonstrated in the service of the state. The visit to Russia gave rise to her belief that Leninism was being promoted as a religion challenging the values of Christianity, and the China visit opened her eyes further to the practical benefits, particularly in health care, that Christian missionaries had brought to people she viewed as pagans.

When General Evangeline Booth of the Salvation Army visited Winnipeg in 1937, McWilliams shared her platform with the lieutenant-governor, the attorney general, the president and chancellor of the University of Manitoba, and a senator, and she seconded the vote of thanks to Booth on behalf of an audience of four thousand, "spellbound by magnificent imagery, spiritual fire and brilliant oratory."[25] The Booth visit convinced McWilliams that she should declare her religious beliefs publicly. "It is only by example and testimony," she said in 1951, "that others can be truly helped."[26] During and after the Second World War, her invocation of Christianity became more insistent.

The gospel could provide McWilliams with a model of equality in diversity. Souls were equal in the sight of God, and individuals had different gifts to use in his service. The image of the Church as a corporate body, with each part contributing its own necessary and particular function, similarly supported the idea of a society with different groups, divided by class, ethnicity, and gender, working for the common good. She accepted the responsibility of being her brother's keeper. She had literally cared for her own brothers in their youth but not to the extent of self-sacrifice. Recognizing her own aptitudes, she could see herself as a Mary, not a Martha.

For her, the one exalted master was Jesus. McWilliams was never so strict as to shun non-believers. "Some are not willing, or not able, to accept this master. So we must seek to define our master in other terms." McWilliams used the term "excellence." For her, this did not mean obedience to dogma. It meant using all her God-given faculties, which included her capacities for thought, analysis, judgment, and criticism. A commitment to excellence would make each individual ask, "What is it that I can best do?"[27]

McWilliams's unwavering belief in the importance of an individual's moral agency was a balance to her faith in a beneficent state. At the University of Toronto she had studied the work of T.H. Green, who insisted not only on the importance of freedom *from* legal restraint, but also on the freedom *to* do good, and on the power of the state to identify the common good. The state should create an environment in which responsible citizens could act morally, and this was a pervasive assumption of late-nineteenth-century intellectuals.[28] Theorists of the social gospel, like the interwar feminists, believed in the state as a power for good. McWilliams welcomed the planned extension of state services into social policy at the end of the Second World War. Not against private charity, she nevertheless considered the state to be more efficient and even-handed. Her experience at city hall led her to remain optimistic in dealing with abuses of administration.

McWilliams was a Christian who believed in her duty to help in the moral regeneration of this present world. She was a feminist who believed that women should have equal rights and equal opportunities with men, and at the same time she believed that women had particular responsibilities associated with nurturing children and homes, duties that should also be acknowledged by commensurate rights. She believed in the beneficence of a state whose function was to create the environment in which individuals could pursue the objectives of a Christian democracy. Some historians have alleged that such objectives were reactionary, the wistful agenda of an oligarchy that was losing its power.[29] On the contrary, the social gospel was the expression of a generation of educated Canadians who sincerely wished to improve living and working conditions for all members of the population.

McWilliams welcomed new technology and took pride in identifying and analysing modern problems. Intensely patriotic, she saw herself also as a cosmopolitan creature. She recognized that the introduction and integration of women into the work force and politics would transform public life. She wanted the public good to be determined, and public services to be provided, by a democratic state. Volunteer organizations, too, should be democratic. When in 1919 the National Council of Women refused to slacken its autocratic grip over the local councils, McWilliams dissociated herself from it. McWilliams's faith in a benevolent state was never fascist idolatry. The Kingdom of Canada that Stowell ruled was intended to be temporary. It was legitimated and guarded by critical individuals who were always free to voice opposition. Overarching her religion and her feminism was an optimistic faith in democracy. Consequently, the education of the future citizen was crucially important.

"During her early days in public life ... she dreamed of a book which would fire the imagination of Canadian school children – a book with drama and action woven into the pages of fact and history."[30] *This New Canada*, a distillation of the notes of a lifetime, was the result. Intended to inspire children, the book condemned "those who take little or no interest in the affairs of their country and care little or nothing for the welfare of its citizens."[31] For McWilliams, *This New Canada* served as self-justification: like the current events scroll, it portrayed and promoted civic-mindedness. In a sense, the text stands as McWilliams's autobiography. It was her way of validating her concerns for a future generation.

The only version of her life that survives is the public version. We shall never know the full dimensions of her life's journey. One could argue that if McWilliams had wanted to reveal more of herself to posterity, she would have found a way to do so.[32] Possibly she deliberately chose to draw a thick veil of discretion over thoughts, feelings, and events that she considered out of the public domain.

The lack of a legacy of correspondence, diary, and memoirs may partially be due to the absence of an appropriate model. "Well into the twentieth century, it continued to be impossible for women to admit into their autobiographical narratives the claim of achievement, the admission of ambition, the recognition that accomplishment was neither luck nor the result of the efforts or generosity of others ... the only script for women's life insisted that work discover and pursue them, like the conventional romantic lover." Society and literature in the late 1940s were unable to provide a conceptual apparatus for describing a public woman's life in its totality.[33] McWilliams was not an inventor. Since she could not, by herself, imagine a new way of writing an honest life, perhaps she was wise to refrain.

There is a more practical explanation for the lack of an autobiography. Since the publication of *Women of Red River* in 1923, McWilliams had been sensitive to the need to preserve historical data, and after she became president of the Manitoba Historical Society in 1944, she repeatedly urged groups and individuals to conserve their archives. She made no systematic collection of her own, but this was most likely because all her energy went into activities that often appeared quite frenzied to friends and colleagues. She was not by nature an introvert, nor given to retrospection. For her this had benefits: "The insufferable loads of self-distrust and of perplexity as to whether some job was worth while, I think she never had to bear."[34] Her gain was historians' loss. As a "living dynamo" she existed in the present, which made too many demands on her time for her to reflect personally on her own life.[35] But its public aspect remains for us to see.

McWilliams felt herself part of a worldwide movement and was glad to work with other women for goals she was proud to share after her momentous visit to Europe in 1922. She was happy to know feminists from other countries and found their experience instructive. She was one of the few women constantly successful in elected politics, but she kept a sense of perspective. "The rung on which I belong is the lowest rung on the ladder" was how she described the "humble" work of alderman.[36] She never lost sight of her power base – women's organizations. In Canada her impact was mainly through her example, her work in the Canadian Federation of University Women, and her writings – her books and the report on the post war problems of women.

Before we can assess Margaret McWilliams's influence properly, we need to retrieve the experience of the women like her, in the cities and the countryside, across Canada. We need to know why some women found these feminists frightening. We need more community case studies. We need to dissect more meticulously a society that offered public opportunities to women while requiring them to maintain their traditional role in the family. We need to use modern scholarship to throw a lifeline to the women who could not write of their own lives.[37]

Meanwhile, we can use the reconstruction of one of those lives to tell us about the horizons, and the limits, of one interwar feminist. By 1943 McWilliams's feminism was full-fledged. Her developing experience and growing conviction led her to statements concerning equal rights, opportunities, and responsibilities, and at the same time to a recognition of women's particular contributions to society. Her acknowledgment of the dual nature of women's service was a reconciliation of the two major hallmarks of interwar feminism: concern for women as wives and mothers and, simultaneously, concern for them as workers and citizens. Margaret McWilliams's life story is a contribution towards the comprehension of the complexity of feminism, its definition, application, and meaning, not only in the past, but also in the present.

Notes

ABBREVIATIONS

CIIA   Canadian Institute of International Affairs
CFUW   Canadian Federation of University Women
CW   City of Winnipeg
IFUW   International Federation of University Women
JSP   Jack Stovel Papers
LCW   Local Council of Women
MSP   Margaret Stovel Papers
NAC   National Archives of Canada
PAM   Provincial Archives of Manitoba
PWPW   *Final Report of the Subcommittee on the Post-War Problems of Women,* 1943
SAB   Saskatchewan Archives Board
UMA   University of Manitoba Archives
UTA   University of Toronto Archives
UWC   University Women's Club
VMP   Velma McWilliams Papers
WCC   Women's Canadian Club
WP   *Winnipeg Telegram,* "Women's Paper," 8 May 1907
WWG   *The Work of Women and Girls in the Department Stores of Winnipeg,* Winnipeg, 1914

CHAPTER ONE: MARGARET
MCWILLIAMS

1 Wylie, "Margaret McWilliams," 279–98.
2 Cleverdon, *Woman Suffrage Movement*, 54.
3 *Minneapolis Journal*, 29 April 1924.
4 PAM, UWC, clippings, *Winnipeg Free Press*, 18 April 1936.
5 University Women's Club, Westgate, Winnipeg, Current Events Scroll presented to Dr Margaret McWilliams, 1948.
6 *Saturday Night*, 29 May 1920.
7 SAB, McNaughton Papers, Margaret McWilliams to Violet McNaughton, 4 June 1923.
8 JSP, Margaret McWilliams, "Eve, Where Art Thou?" November 1938, 3.
9 PAM, LCW, Annual Report, 1933; *Winnipeg Free Press*, 28 October 1933, 3, 28 November 1933.
10 NAC, CFUW, *History of the CFUW 1919–1949*, 5.
11 NAC, CFUW, Triennial, Minutes, 30 August 1921, 37.
12 *Winnipeg Tribune*, 8 September 1934.
13 Government of Canada, Advisory Committee on Reconstruction, *Final Report of the Subcommittee on the Post-War Problems of Women* (hereafter PWPW), November 1943, 13–14.
14 Pierson, "Home Aide," 89, 95; see also Brandt, "Pigeon-Holed."
15 PWPW, 11–12.
16 For example, *Winnipeg Tribune*, 8 November 1934, 20 November 1935, 16 November 1937; *Winnipeg Free Press*, 10 January 1939.
17 PAM, LCW, Margaret McWilliams to Premier Rodmond Roblin, 16 March 1915; Strong-Boag, "'Wages for Housework,'" 24–34.
18 McWilliams and McWilliams (Stowell, pseud.), *If I Were King of Canada*, 109–18.
19 *Winnipeg Tribune*, 8 November 1934, 18 November 1935.
20 PWPW, 10.
21 McWilliams and McWilliams, *Russia in 1926*, 65, 67, 73.
22 Underhill, Review of "If I Were King of Canada," 12, 154; Horn, *League for Social Reconstruction*, 219–20; Sangster, *Dreams of Equality*, 91–123.
23 PWPW, 13, 14, 19, 22.
24 PAM, WCC, Executive Minutes, 16 May 1923.
25 *Manitoba Free Press*, 20 September 1922.

26 VMP, Travel Scrapbook, League of Nations Association receipt, 21 July 1924.

27 VMP, Margaret McWilliams, "Opportunities for women in public service," *Quotarian* 16, no. 8 (1938): 14.

28 VMP, Red Journal, World Events, 21 January 1942.

29 Margaret McWilliams, "A Constructive Philosophy for Our Time: What Must I Do?" *Saturday Night*, 28 June 1947.

30 *Peterborough Examiner*, 5 May 1925.

31 VMP, Margaret McWilliams, "Opportunities for women," 14.

32 NAC, CFUW, Ursilla MacDonnell, "A Way to Greatness," CFUW *Chronicle*, 1952, 12.

33 Offen, "Defining Feminism," 119–57; Offen, "Use and Abuse of History"; Cott, *Grounding of Modern Feminism*; Lerner, *Creation of Patriarchy*, 231–43.

34 Cott, *Grounding of Modern Feminism*, 4–5.

35 Richards, *Sceptical Feminist*, 13–14.

36 Offen, "Defining Feminism," 135, 147, 151–2. See also Cott, "Comment," 203–5; Dubois, "Comment," 195–7; Cott, "Limits of 'Social Feminism,'" 809–29; and Black, *Social Feminism*, 53.

37 Lerner, *Creation of Patriarchy*, 236–7; Dubois, *Feminism and Suffrage*, 15–20.

38 Cott, *Grounding of Modern Feminism*, 126–42.

39 Ibid., 127, 128, 136, 138.

40 Harrison, *Prudent Revolutionaries*, 104; Alberti, *Beyond Suffrage*, 164–90.

41 Mabel Atkinson, "The Economic Foundations of the Women's Movement," quoted in Dyhouse, *Feminism and the Family*, 188; Lewis, *Women in England 1870–1950*.

42 Dyhouse, *Feminism and the Family*, 103; Lewis, "Eleanor Rathbone and the Family," 137.

43 Oakley, *Subject Women*, 285, 289; Eichler, *Double Standard*, 115.

44 Peterson, "Ethnic and Class Politics," 69, 74, 87; Wiseman, "Pattern of Prairie Politics," 305.

45 Pentland, Review of David J. Bercuson, 27.

46 Peterson, "Ethnic and Class Politics," 82.

47 Rea, "Politics of Class," 234.

48 Gray, *The Winter Years*, 128.

49 Peterson, "Ethnic and Class Politics," 101, 102, 110, 113; Wiseman, "Pattern of Prairie Politics," 315.

50 Phillips, *Divided Loyalties*, 25–8.

51 Lerner, "Reconceptualising Differences Among Women," 110.

52 Cott, *Grounding of Modern Feminism*, 3–10, *passim;* Rabine, "Feminist Politics of Non-Identity, 11–32; Poovey, "Feminism and Deconstruction," 51–66; Scott, "Deconstructing Equality-versus-Difference," 33–50; Offen, "Defining Feminism," 119–57; idem, "Liberty, Equality and Justice," 335–74; Offen, "Use and Abuse of History"; Cott, "Comment," 203–5; Dubois, "Comment," 195–7; Offen, "Reply," 198–202, 206–9; Black, *Social Feminism;* Lewis, "Essay in Revision," 5–7; Acker, "Class, Gender," 473–97. See also Maroney and Luxton, "From Feminism and Political Economy to Feminist Political Economy," in Maroney and Luxton, eds., *Feminism and Political Economy,* 5–28; Scott, "Deconstructing Equality-versus-Difference," 33–50.

53 See Cleverdon, *Woman Suffrage Movement;* Kealey, ed., *A Not Unreasonable Claim;* Kealey and Sangster, eds., *Beyond the Vote;* McClung, *In Times Like These;* McLaren and McLaren, *Bedroom and the State;* Prentice et al., *Canadian Women;* Prentice and Trofimenkoff, eds., *Neglected Majority,* vol. 2; Rooke and Schnell, *No Bleeding Heart;* Sangster, *Dreams of Equality;* Strong-Boag, *New Day Recalled* and *Parliament of Women;* Trofimenkoff and Prentice, eds., *Neglected Majority,* vol. 1.

54 Kealey, "No Special Protection," 136.

55 Silverman, "Writing Canadian Women's History," 532–3; Trofimenkoff, "Feminist Biography," 1–9.

56 Barry, *Susan B. Anthony,* 370; Barry, "New Historical Synthesis," 75.

57 VMP, Travel Scrapbook, Margaret McWilliams, Her Book, Red Journal.

58 Heilbrun, "Discovering the Lost Lives"; Heilbrun, *Writing a Woman's Life,* 25; Trofimenkoff, "Feminist Biography," 1–9; Silverman, "Writing Canadian Women's History," 532.

59 Lerner, "Where Biographers Fear to Tread."

60 *Winnipeg Free Press,* 14, 15 April 1952; *Winnipeg Tribune,* 14, 15 April 1952.

61 NAC, CFUW, MacDonnell, "A Way to Greatness," 11–13; *Canadian Welfare* 28 (15 June 1952): 21.

62 Strange, "Margaret McWilliams of Manitoba."

63 Roe, "Margaret McWilliams."

64 PAM, UWC, Cunnington and Norrie, "Margaret McWilliams," slide-tape show, 1974; Malaher, "Margaret McWilliams."

65 McWilliams and McWilliams (Stowell, pseud.), *If I Were King of Canada*; Margaret McWilliams, *Manitoba Milestones*; idem, *This New Canada*; Legislative Library of Manitoba, Margaret McWilliams, "The Battle of Wheat," incomplete typescript, n.d. (1930–31).

66 NAC, CFUW, MacDonnell, "A Way of Greatness," 13.

67 Margaret McWilliams, articles on China, *Manitoba Free Press*, 10, 12, 21, 22, 23, 27 October 1931, 26, 27 November 1931, 1, 3, 4, 5 December 1931; H.F. Angus, ed., *Canada and Her Great Neighbour*.

68 PWPW, 1943.

69 Harbord Collegiate Institute Archives; UTA, Margaret Stovel file.

70 PAM, UWC, WCC, LCW, Manitoba Historical Society; City of Winnipeg Archives, Minutes of Council; NAC, CFUW, including IFUW.

71 University of Manitoba Faculty of Education Library, *Western School Journal*, 1919–38.

72 NAC, CFUW, IFUW *Chronicle*.

73 NAC, CFUW, Minutes of the CFUW International Relations Committee, 1936.

74 *Winnipeg Free Press*, 1 November 1938.

75 For example, *Manitoba Free Press*, 20 September 1922; *Winnipeg Tribune*, 8 September 1934, 5 October 1944.

76 UTA, Margaret Stovel file.

77 MSP, Margaret McWilliams to Russell Stovel, 17 March 1952.

78 VMP, Margaret McWilliams, "The Land of the Heart's Desire," Christmas 1903.

CHAPTER TWO: FOUNDATIONS

1 MSP, Stovel Family Tree; JSP, J. Hodder Stovel, Memoirs, unpublished typescript, 15, 16.

2 JSP, J. Hodder Stovel to Helen Stearns, Christmas 1955.

3 JSP, J. Hodder Stovel, Memoirs, 30.

4 JSP, Kate Stovel, "Faversham, England: Birthplace of the Stovel Clan," unpublished paper, 20 March 1984.

5 JSP, J. Hodder Stovel, Memoirs, 21.

6 Ibid., 24; Stovel Company Ltd., *Historical Outline of the House of Stovel*, 9.

7 JSP, Tassie E. Stovel to Mrs Stewart, 11 November 1880.

8 MSP, J. Hodder Stovel, Short Memoirs, 17.

9 JSP, J. Hodder Stovel to Helen Stearns, Christmas 1955.

10 JSP, Province of Ontario, Letters of Guardianship in the Estate of Samuel Stovel, 7 March 1896.

11 JSP, J. Hodder Stovel, Memoirs, 11; MSP, J. Hodder Stovel, Short Memoirs, 2–4.

12 JSP, J. Hodder Stovel, Memoirs, 22.

13 MSP, J. Hodder Stovel, Short Memoirs, 4.

14 Ibid., 6.

15 MSP, Stovel Family Tree; J. Hodder Stovel, *A Mining Trail 1902–45*, 8.

16 Interview with Mrs W.L. Morton, 11 August 1989.

17 JSP, J. Hodder Stovel, Memoirs, 7.

18 Harbord Collegiate Institute Archives, Annual Commencement, 16 November 1894.

19 Harbord Collegiate Institute Archives, *Harbord Collegiate Review* 2, no. 1 (1 December 1893): 4, 9; 2, no. 2 (Christmas 1893): 17.

20 Woman's Supplement, *Canadian Courier*, 7 February 1914.

21 Harbord Collegiate Institute Archives, *Harbord Collegiate Review* 2, no. 1 (1 December 1893): 4.

22 Woman's Supplement, *Canadian Courier*, 7 February 1914.

23 Sissons, "Gifted – And All Canadian."

24 *University of Toronto and Its Colleges*, 99.

25 Gordon, *Postcript to Adventure*, 40.

26 UTA, *Calendar for 1894–5*, 67–69; Drummond, *Political Economy at the University of Toronto*, 30, 31–7.

27 Green, *Prolegomena to Ethics*, 458–70.

28 Armour and Trott, *Faces of Reason*, 216–22; Perkin, *Rise of Professional Society*, 124–8.

29 MacCunn, *Six Radical Thinkers*, 220, 243–4, 262.

30 McKillop, *Disciplined Intelligence*, 184–5.

31 UTA, *Sesame 1898*, 43–5.

32 *Varsity*, 23, 30 October 1895, 22 January 1896.

33 Ibid., 22 January 1896.

34 Ibid., 5 February 1896.

35 Ibid., 11 November 1896.

36 UTA, *Sesame 1898*, 56–61; Ford, *Path Not Strewn with Roses*.

37 UTA, *Sesame 1898*, 60.

38 *Varsity*, 9 December 1897, 17 February 1898.

39 JSP, J. Hodder Stovel, Memoirs, 7.

40 UTA, *Torontonensis*, 1897, 160–1; Woman's Supplement, *Canadian Courier*, 7 February 1914.

41 *Varsity*, 10 March, 21 October 1897.

42 Ibid., 21, 28 October, 4, 11, 18, 25 November, 2, 9, 16 December 1897.

43 For example, *Varsity*, 4 December 1895.

44 JSP, J. Hodder Stovel, Memoirs, 19, 12; Harbord Collegiate Institute Archives, "Notes from Willy Zimmermann."

45 NAC, CFUW, Early Women Graduates, Jessie (Holmes) Munro to Edith McColl, 23 March 1937; Fingard, "College, Career and Community," 33.

46 Woman's Supplement, *Canadian Courier*, 7 February 1914.

47 Freeman, *Kit's Kingdom*, 23, 49–53.

48 Woman's Supplement, *Canadian Courier*, 7 February 1914.

49 JSP, J. Hodder Stovel, Memoirs, 25.

50 For example, *Minneapolis Journal*, 17 December 1898.

51 *Detroit Journal*, 3 September 1903.

52 Ibid., 30 September 1899.

53 Ibid., 19 May 1900, 18 May 1901.

54 Ibid., 3 September 1903.

55 Ibid., 5 October 1901.

56 Ibid., 4 January 1902, 15 May 1903.

57 Ibid., 3 September 1903.

58 *Detroit Evening News*, 3 September 1903.

59 VMP, R.F. McWilliams, "Memorandum re Peterboro Days," 4 April 1951, 1.

60 Kidd, *Historical Sketches of Peterborough*, 60. I thank Jennifer Brown for this reference.

61 Jones and Dyer, *Peterborough*, 40–1.

62 VMP, R.F. McWilliams, "Memorandum re Peterboro Days," 3.

63 *Peterborough Examiner*, 6 January 1903.

64 Strange, "Margaret McWilliams."

65 *Peterborough Examiner*, 4 September 1903.

66 *Minneapolis Journal*, 4 September 1903.

67 *Peterborough Examiner*, 5, 15, 26 January, 2 February 1904.

68 Ibid., 8, 28, 29 October, 7 November 1904.

69 Ibid., 26 January 1905.

70 Ibid., 2 January 1906.

71 VMP, R.F. McWilliams, "Memorandum re Peterboro Days," 4.

72 *Peterborough Examiner,* 11 December 1906, 5, 8 January 1907.

73 *Peterborough Review,* 7 January 1908.

74 *Peterborough Examiner,* 3, 7 January 1908.

75 Ibid., 7, 3 January 1908.

76 Ibid., 7 November 1907.

77 Ibid., 22 November 1907; Craw, *Peterborough Story,* 73–7; Jones and Dyer, *Peterborough,* 48.

78 VMP, R.F. McWilliams, "Memorandum re Peterboro Days," 4.

79 VMP, R.F. McWilliams, unexpurgated draft memo re Peterboro Days, 1951, 6–15.

80 *Peterborough Examiner,* 8 September 1908; VMP, R.F. McWilliams, "To the Liberal and Independent Electors of West Peterborough," n.d. (1908).

81 VMP, R.F. McWilliams, "Memorandum re Peterboro Days," 4.

82 *Peterborough Examiner,* 14 December 1909; *Peterborough Directory 1909,* 295, 326.

83 VMP, R.F. McWilliams, "Memorandum re Peterboro Days," 4.

84 Ibid., 5.

85 *Peterborough Examiner,* 3 April 1907.

86 VMP, R.F. McWilliams, "Memorandum re Peterboro Days," 5.

87 Elizabeth M. Stearns to Mary Kinnear, 31 January 1989.

88 *Peterborough Examiner,* 2, 9 November 1903, 18 May 1904.

89 Ibid., 18 July 1906.

90 Ibid., 23 January 1906.

91 Ibid., 25 September 1906; Trent University Archives, Woman's Art Association Papers.

92 *Peterborough Examiner,* 26 August 1910.

93 VMP, R.F. McWilliams, unexpurgated draft memo re Peterboro Days, 1951, 11.

94 *Peterborough Review,* 9 August 1910.

95 Betty Jane Wylie Papers, R.B. McWilliams to Betty Jane Wylie, 28 February 1966.

96 VMP, R.F. McWilliams, "Memorandum re Peterboro Days," 6.

97 NAC, CFUW, CFUW *Chronicle,* 1952, 13.

98 VMP, Margaret McWilliams, "The Land of the Heart's Desire," Christmas 1903.

99 JSP, Margaret McWilliams to Helen Stovel, 5 July 1932.

100 Ibid., 28 July 1932.

101 MSP, Margaret McWilliams to Bruce Stovel, 9 April 1947.

102 MSP, R.F. McWilliams to Bruce Stovel, April 1947.

103 Interview with Velma McWilliams, 14 May 1990.

104 Interview with C. Rhodes Smith, 14 February 1989.

105 University Women's Club, Westgate, Winnipeg, Margaret McWilliams's Library. See inscriptions in, for example, Joseph Conrad, *Youth and Gaspar Ruiz*; Guy N. Pocock, ed., *Modern Poetry*; Richard Le Gallienne, *An Old Country House*; Alfred Lord Tennyson, *Idylls of the King*.

106 Interview with Velma McWilliams, 14 May 1990.

107 Interview with Douglas Campbell, 17 February 1989.

108 Interview with Helen Norrie, 31 January 1989; interview with Jean Carson, 18 January 1989; conversation with Duff Roblin, 20 March 1989; Donald Stovel MacDonald to Mary Kinnear, 16 March 1989.

109 JSP, Kate Mather to Russell Stovel, 14 April 1952.

110 PAM, R.F. McWilliams Papers, Margaret McWilliams to R.F. McWilliams, 18, 21 August 1917.

111 JSP, Margaret McWilliams to Helen Stearns, 20 December 1941.

112 JSP, Margaret McWilliams to Helen Stovel, 5 July 1932.

113 Ibid., 28 October 1929.

114 Last Will and Testament of Margaret McWilliams, 12 April 1952, 2.

115 JSP, Avis McWilliams to Helen Stearns, December 1959.

116 Harbord Collegiate Institute Archives, "Notes from Willie Zimmermann."

117 *Winnipeg Henderson Directory 1924*, 659, 1075.

118 Conversation with Virginia and Edmund Berry, 3 February 1990.

119 *University Women's Club of Winnipeg, 1909–1959*, 8–12, 16.

120 *Winnipeg Free Press*, 5 October 1953.

121 JSP, Avis McWilliams to Helen Stearns, 28 December 1958.

122 Heilbrun, *Writing a Woman's Life*, 49, 51.

123 Margaret McWilliams, speech for the women graduates at the Alumni Federation dinner for Sir Robert and Lady Falconer, *Supplement to the University of Toronto Monthly*, June 1932, 336.

CHAPTER THREE: INITIAL FORAYS

1 *Manitoba Bar News* 13, no. 2 (November 1940): 17–18. I thank Lee Gibson for her information about R.F. McWilliams's career in Winnipeg.

2 *Construction*, December 1909, April 1912.

3 Morton, *Manitoba*, 301–2.

4 *Manitoba Free Press*, 26 September 1910.

5 Morton, *Manitoba*, 302.

6 NCA, CFUW, Ursilla MacDonnell, "A Way to Greatness," CFUW *Chronicle*, 1952, 12.

7 "Winnipeg: The Gateway of the Canadian West 1912," in Artibise, ed., *Gateway City*, 265. See also Bellan, *Winnipeg First Century*, 94–117.

8 "Winnipeg: Gateway," in Artibise, ed., *Gateway City*, 270–2, 275, 277, 287; Artibise, *Winnipeg*, 132, 170.

9 "Winnipeg: Gateway," in Artibise, ed., *Gateway City*, 284.

10 "Winnipeg's Millionaires 1910," in Artibise, ed., *Gateway City*, 118.

11 Artibise, *Winnipeg*, 305, 308; Peterson, "Ethnic and Class Politics," 79–90.

12 Artibise, *Winnipeg*, 163–5.

13 "City Planning Commission 1911", in Artibise, ed., *Gateway City*, 239–44; Artibise, *Winnipeg*, 193–4.

14 PAM, Canadian Women's Press Club, Minutes, 1906.

15 Artibise, *Winnipeg*, 258.

16 *Manitoba Free Press*, 10, 11, 12, 16, 17, 21, 24, 25, 28, 29, 30 November, 1, 2, 5, 6, 9, 10, 12, 15 December 1910.

17 *Manitoba Free Press*, 8 December 1910.

18 *Manitoba Free Press*: female factory workers, 3 October 1910; suffrage news (for example), 17, 23, 26 November, 12 December 1910; Icelandic petition, 7 November 1910.

19 *Manitoba Free Press*: immigration of domestics, 5 September 1910; dower law, 21 February, 11 March 1911; protective legislation, 15 February 1911.

20 Strong-Boag, *New Day Recalled*, 41.

21 *Winnipeg Telegram*, "Women's Paper," 8 May 1907 (hereafter WP); Pedersen, "'Call to Service,'" 207; Pedersen, "'Keeping Our Good Girls Good,'"20–4.

22 WP, 18,24.

23 Ibid., 24, 32–49; Thomas, "Some Manitoba Women," 4, 19–20.

24 For example, Lady Schultz, Mrs Patterson, Mrs Hugh John Macdonald, Mrs Colin Campbell, Mrs George Bryce.

25 Strong-Boag, *Parliament of Women*.

26 WP, 38.

27 Ibid., 37–9.

28 United Church of Canada, St. Stephen's, Broadway, *St. Stephen's Silver Jubilee 1895–1920*, Winnipeg, n.d. (1920), 9–12.

29 Cook, "Francis Marion Beynon," 188–9; Cleverdon, *Woman Suffrage Movement*, 62.

30 See, for example, Margaret McWilliams, "Affair of the First Flag-Staff"; Woman's Supplement, *Canadian Courier*, 7 February 1914.

31 UTA, Margaret Stovel file, clipping, "Pen Portraits of Progressive Women: Mrs R.F. McWilliams of Winnipeg," n.d. (1920); CW, Council Minutes, 25 January, 14 June 1915.

32 PAM, Free Kindergarten Association, Manuscript History, 1910, 1.

33 PAM, Free Kindergarten Association, annual reports, 1910–14.

34 PAM, UWC, *History of the University Women's Club 1909–1959*, Winnipeg, n.d. (1959), 3.

35 PAM, UWC, Minutes, 10 November, 15 December 1911.

36 Cleverdon, *Woman Suffrage Movement*, 54; NAC, Cleverdon Papers, Margaret McWilliams to Catherine Cleverdon, 1 October 1946.

37 Hathaway, "Political Equality League," 8–10.

38 PAM, UWC, Minutes, 17 May 1912, 12 May 1913.

39 Ibid., 5, 23 March 1914.

40 Ibid., 3 October 1913.

41 Ibid., 7 November, 5 December 1913.

42 Ibid., 20 February, 2 June 1914.

43 Ibid., 24 September 1914.

44 Ibid., 7 December 1914, 15 February, 17 May 1915.

45 Cook, "Francis Marion Beynon," 196–201; Roberts, "Women's Peace Activism" 282–5; Beynon, "Wastes of War"; Beynon, "Socialism and War."

46 PAM, UWC, Minutes, 13 May 1915.

47 PAM, UWC, *The Work of Women and Girls in the Department Stores of Winnipeg* (hereafter WWG); Benson, *Counter Cultures*; Llewelyn Davies, ed., *Maternity*; Reeves, *Round About a Pound a Week*.

48 WWG, 3.

49 Ibid., 3–5.

50 Ibid., 5–11.

51 Ibid., 11–13.

52 "J.S. Woodsworth, Report on Living Standards, City of Winnipeg, 1913," Appendix D, in Artibise, *Winnipeg*, 317.

53 PAM, Department of Public Works, Sessional Papers no. 27, 7 February 1918.

54 WWG, 15.

55 Ibid., 11–18.

56 Ibid., 18–21.

57 Kealey, "Women and Labour," 76–99.

CHAPTER FOUR: THE FIRST DECADE

1 Margaret McWilliams, speech for the women graduates at the Alumni Federation dinner for Sir Robert and Lady Falconer, *Supplement of the University of Toronto Monthly,* June 1932, 336; NAC, Cleverdon Papers, Margaret McWilliams to Catherine Cleverdon, 1 October 1946.

2 Strong-Boag, *Parliament of Women,* 105.

3 PAM, WCC, Minutes, 28 December 1911, 15 August 1912.

4 Ibid., 8 December 1911, 14 October 1912.

5 Ibid., 27 January 1912.

6 Ibid., 27 April 1912.

7 Ibid., 21 September 1912.

8 Ibid., 7 February 1912.

9 Ibid., 12 March 1912.

10 Ibid., 2 March 1915.

11 Ibid., 11 November, 1916.

12 *Winnipeg Free Press,* 10 March 1962.

13 Woman's Supplement, *Canadian Courier,* 7 February 1914; PAM, Social Science Study Club, 1913–14.

14 PAM, Social Science Study Club, 1914–19.

15 *Winnipeg Free Press,* 10 March 1962.

16 PAM, Social Science Study Club, 1924, 1928, 1931, 1933–34.

17 WP, 8 May 1907; PAM, LCW, Minutes, 1912.

18 PAM, LCW, Minutes, 27 April 1915.

19 PAM, LCW, Minutes, 16 January 1911.

20 McClung, *The Stream Runs Fast,* 106.

21 PAM, LCW, Margaret McWilliams to Sir Rodmond Roblin, 28 April 1915.

22 PAM, UWC, Minutes, 22 October 1915.

23 Ibid., 20 March 1916, 25 January 1917.

24 PAM, LCW, Sub-executive Minutes, 30 April 1919–29 October 1920; Strong-Boag, *Parliament of Women,* 429–39.

25 PAM, LCW, Minutes, 30 April 1919.

26 *Manitoba Free Press*, 7 July 1917.

27 Strong-Boag, *Parliament of Women*, 432–7; McLaren, *Our Own Master Race*, 37–8; Shaw, *Proud Heritage*, 26.

28 *Manitoba Free Press*, 2, 6 July 1917.

29 Ibid., 13, 17, 20 August 1917.

30 PAM, R.F. McWilliams Papers, Margaret McWilliams to R.F. McWilliams, 20 August 1917.

31 Penner, ed., *Winnipeg 1919*, 222.

32 *Manitoba Free Press*, 12 December 1917.

33 SAB, McNaughton Papers, Margaret McWilliams to Violet McNaughton, 1 June 1919.

34 PAM, R.F. McWilliams Papers, R.F. McWilliams, "The Political Situation in Canada," December 1918.

35 SAB, McNaughton Papers, Margaret McWilliams to Violet McNaughton, 26 May 1918.

36 SAB, McNaughton Papers, Violet McNaughton to Margaret McWilliams, 9 December 1918.

37 SAB, McNaughton Papers, Margaret McWilliams to Violet McNaughton, 19 February 1919.

38 Ibid., 1 June 1919.

39 *Saturday Night*, 29 May 1920.

40 Strong-Boag, *Parliament of Women*, 389, 390.

41 PAM, Canadian Red Cross, Ladies' Auxiliary Annual Meeting, 25 October 1916; Canadian Red Cross Society, annual meetings, 1919–32.

42 Artibise, ed., *Gateway City*, 125.

43 United Church of Canada, St. Stephen's, Broadway, Constitution, 1916.

44 United Church of Canada, St. Stephen's, Broadway, Deacons' Court Minutes, 16 February 1916.

45 Ibid., 20 May, 16 December 1919.

46 PAM, Social Planning Council of Winnipeg, Minutes of the Organization Meeting of the Central Council of Social Agencies, 14 April 1919.

47 PAM, UWC, Minutes, 8 December 1916.

48 PAM, WCC, Minutes, 18 May 1918.

49 Kathryn Young, "Women's Tribute Memorial Lodge."

50 Morton, *One University*, 115.

51 Woman's Supplement, *Canadian Courier*, 7 February 1914.

52 McClung, *The Stream Runs Fast*, 62.
53 Woman's Supplement, *Canadian Courier*, 7 February 1914.

CHAPTER FIVE: "EDUCATION IN ALL ITS PHASES"

1 NAC, CFUW, *History of the CFUW 1919–1949*, 5.
2 *Western School Journal*, 1919–20, 180.
3 McKillop, *Disciplined Intelligence*, 198.
4 Ibid., 206, 197, 218, 224.
5 Margaret McWilliams, "A Constructive Philosophy for Our Time."
6 PAM, UWC, Minutes, 3 April 1917, 10 June 1918, 13 May 1919.
7 NAC, CFUW, *History*, 3.
8 Gildersleeve, *Many a Good Crusade*, 131.
9 NAC, CFUW, Minutes, 26 August 1919, 6.
10 NAC, CFUW, Executive Minutes, 25 August 1920, 28–30.
11 NAC, CFUW, Minutes, 26 August 1919, 4–6.
12 Ibid., 26 August 1920, 20–1.
13 Ibid., 25 August 1920, 12.
14 *Manitoba Free Press*, 8 September 1923.
15 NAC, CFUW, *History*, 4–5.
16 *Manitoba Free Press*, 29 August 1923.
17 NAC, CFUW, Minutes, 30 August 1921, 37.
18 *Manitoba Free Press*, 29 August, 8 September 1923.
19 NAC, CFUW, *History*, 5.
20 NAC, CFUW, Minutes, 28 August 1923, 60.
21 Roberts, "Women's Peace Activism," 276.
22 NAC, CFUW, IFUW *Chronicle*, 1920, 20.
23 NAC, CFUW, Scrapbook, 1919–23, *New York Times*, 19 May 1921.
24 *Manitoba Free Press*, 20 September 1922.
25 *Minneapolis Journal*, 29 April 1924.
26 NAC, CFUW, IFUW *Chronicle*, 1922, 83.
27 Ibid., 83–6.
28 NAC, CFUW, Minutes, 25–7 August 1926, 8.
29 Ibid., 25 August 1927, 4.
30 NAC, CFUW, transcript, 17, 18 April 1936, 1; Minutes, 27, 18 April 1936, 10–11.
31 NAC, CFUW, Minutes, 28 April 1938, 3.
32 *Winnipeg Free Press*, 27 January 1948.

33 University Women's Club, Westgate, Winnipeg, Current Events Scroll presented to Dr Margaret McWilliams, 1948.

34 Interview with C. Rhodes Smith, 14 February 1989.

35 Interview with Douglas Campbell, 17 February 1989.

36 Strange, "Margaret McWilliams."

37 *Saturday Night,* 29 May 1920.

38 United Church of Canada, St. Stephen's, Broadway, Deacon's Court Minutes, 18 May 1920.

39 PAM, UWC, Minutes, 15 September 1919.

40 *Winnipeg Free Press,* 14 April 1952.

41 PAM, UWC, Minutes, 17 November, 1 December 1919, 19 January, 12 April, 13 May 1920.

42 Ibid., 20 June, 24 August, 19 October 1920.

43 UTA, Margaret Stovel file, "Pen Potraits of Progressive Women: Mrs R.F. McWilliams," n.d. (1920).

44 Interview with Isobel Scurfield, 6 February 1989.

45 PAM, McColl Papers, circular to the members of the current events class, 2 April 1924.

46 Interview with Douglas Campbell, 17 February 1989.

47 McColl, *Vignettes of Early Winnipeg,* 47.

48 Roe, "Margaret McWilliams," 65.

49 JSP, Helen Stearns to Elizabeth Stearns, 6 July 1975.

50 *Standard* (St. Catharine's), 16 April 1923.

51 UTA, Margaret Stovel file, "Pen Portraits of Progressive Women."

52 Morton, *One University,* 108; UMA, Report of the President, 1917–18, 6–9; University of Manitoba Office of Institutional Analysis, "Numbers of Female Graduates of Faculty 1891–1942," March 1990, 1917–18.

53 UMA, Board of Governors, F.W. Crawford, "A Record of All the Members of the Boards of Governors at the University," 20 February 1948; Minutes of the Board of Governors, 3 May 1933.

54 UMA, Minutes of the University Council, 11 October 1933.

55 UMA, Presidents' Papers, Margaret McWilliams to James Maclean, 3 July 1923, 9 August 1923.

56 *Winnipeg Tribune,* 15 August 1947.

57 Green, *Lectures on the Principles,* ix, xi–xii, 129, 206–9.

58 *Western School Journal,* 1919–20, 178.

59 Cook, *Regenerators,* 4.

60 *Western School Journal,* 1919–20, 179.

61 Cook, *Regenerators*, 229.
62 Margaret McWilliams, *This New Canada*, 2.
63 Ibid., 300.
64 Ibid., 308.

CHAPTER SIX: GEOGRAPHY AND HISTORY

1 McWilliams and McWilliams, *Russia in 1926*, 9.
2 Margaret McWilliams, "A Cloud of Witnesses," 69.
3 PAM, UWC, Minutes, 12 May 1922.
4 PAM, WCC, Minutes, 17, 23 May 1922.
5 *Winnipeg Tribune*, 22 September 1922.
6 NAC, CFUW, Scrapbook 1919–23, *Telegram* (Toronto), 8 September 1922.
7 *Manitoba Free Press*, 30 September 1922.
8 Gildersleeve, *Many a Good Crusade*, 140–1.
9 *Manitoba Free Press*, 24 July, 30 September 1922.
10 Ibid., 30 September 1922.
11 NAC, CFUW, Scrapbook 1919–23, *Manitoba Free Press*, 30 September 1922.
12 NAC, CFUW, IFUW *Chronicle*, 1922, 83.
13 NAC, CFUW, Scrapbook 1919–23, *Manitoba Free Press*, 22 August 1922; *Times* (London, England), 20 August 1922.
14 Margaret McWilliams, "A Cloud of Witnesses," 69, 83.
15 VMP, Travel Scrapbook, John R. Bone to Margaret McWilliams, 24 June 1925 (should be 1924); Margaret McWilliams to R.F. McWilliams, 2 August 1924.
16 VMP, Travel Scrapbook, R.C. Wallace to Margaret McWilliams, n.d. (*ca.* 20 May 1924); Eleanor McLaren Brown to Margaret McWilliams, 30 May 1924.
17 VMP, Travel Scrapbook, Margaret McWilliams to R.F. McWilliams, 27 July 1924.
18 VMP, Travel Scrapbook, Helen F. Knight to Margaret McWilliams, n.d. (*ca.* 25 July 1925).
19 VMP, Travel Scrapbook, Margaret McWilliams to R.F. McWilliams, 27 July 1924.
20 Ibid., 2 August 1924.
21 *Winnipeg Tribune*, 22, 30 August 1924.
22 VMP, Travel Scrapbook, Margaret McWilliams to R.F. McWilliams, 9 August 1924.

23 Ibid., 6 August 1924.

24 Ibid., 17 August 1924.

25 McWilliams and McWilliams, *Russia in 1926*, v.

26 NAC, CFUW, CFUW *Chronicle*, 1926, 34.

27 McWilliams and McWilliams, *Russia in 1926*, 38, 62, 121.

28 *Leader* (Regina), 9 April 1927.

29 McWilliams and McWilliams, *Russia in 1926*, 23, 28, 32.

30 Ibid., 37, 42, 48, 52.

31 Ibid., 65, 67, 73.

32 Ibid., 76, 86.

33 Ibid., 14, 15, 110, 127, *v*.

34 *Grain Growers Guide*, 15 April 1927.

35 VMP, Margaret McWilliams, Her Book, copy of part of minutes of a meeting of the Committee of the Privy Council, PC 563, 19 March 1930.

36 JSP, Margaret McWilliams to Helen Stovel, 15 May 1930.

37 VMP, Margaret McWilliams, Her Book, Thomas Cook and Son, Estimate for Inclusive Independent Tour, 30 June 1930.

38 JSP, Helen Stovel Stearns to Elizabeth Stovel, 6 July 1975.

39 Kahn, *China Hands*, 161; PAC, CFUW, CFUW *Chronicle*, 1932, 11; Holland, "Source Materials," 91–7.

40 I thank China expert Dr Karen Minden, Department of Public Policy, University of Manitoba, for her analysis of the journalism.

41 *Manitoba Free Press*, 12 October 1931.

42 Ibid., 27 October 1931.

43 Ibid., 26 November 1931.

44 Ibid., 21 October 1931.

45 Ibid., 27 November 1931.

46 Ibid., 5 December 1931.

47 Ibid., 27 November 1931.

48 NAC, CFUW, CFUW *Chronicle*, 1932, 11.

49 Interview with Helen Monk, 7 April 1988.

50 Karen Minden to Mary Kinnear, 7 March 1989; *Manitoba Free Press*, 16 December 1931.

51 NAC, CFUW, CFUW, Scrapbook, August 1937; *Winnipeg Free Press*, 1 July, 8 September, 25 October 1937.

52 *Winnipeg Free Press*, 18 August 1937.

53 NAC, CFUW, CFUW *Chronicle*, 1937, 53, 54, 55.

54 *Winnipeg Free Press*, 8 September 1937.

55 JSP, R.F. McWilliams to Helen Stovel, 9 May 1930.

56 R.F. McWilliams, *Does History Repeat Itself?*; McWilliams and McWilliams, *Russia in 1926*, 128.

57 JSP, Margaret McWilliams to Russell Stovel, 19 February, 31 March 1952.

58 *Manitoba Free Press*, 19 November 1932; PAM, WCC, Minutes, 22 February 1922.

59 PAM, WCC, Minutes, 22 March, 17 May 1922.

60 Ibid., 27 September 1922, 30 April, 22 May, 19 September, 21 November, 28 December 1923.

61 Healy, *Women of Red River*, 32, 33.

62 Ibid., 48, 52.

63 Ibid., 47–8, 221–36.

64 PAM, WCC, press reviews of *Women of Red River*.

65 PAM, WCC, W.J. Healy to Margaret McWilliams, 16 November 1923.

66 Margaret McWilliams, *Manitoba Milestones*, vii.

67 Ross, *Red River Settlement*; Gunn, *History of Manitoba*; Hill, *Manitoba*; Begg, *History of the North-West*; Bryce, *Remarkable History*; Martin, *Lord Selkirk's Work in Canada*.

68 Wrong and Langton, eds., *Chronicles of Canada*.

69 Tait, review of *Manitoba Milestones*.

70 Morton, *Manitoba*, 420.

71 Friesen, "Manitoba Historical Society," 6.

72 Margaret McWilliams, *All Along the River*; VMP, Margaret McWilliams, Her Book, Alice Wright to Margaret McWilliams, 4 January 1931.

73 I thank Kate Hamerton for the review of *Manitoba Milestones*; Margaret McWilliams, *Manitoba Milestones*, 234.

74 VMP, Margaret McWilliams, Her Book, handwritten entry, 2 May 1930.

75 SAB, McNaughton Papers, Margaret McWilliams to Violet McNaughton, 11 September 1930.

76 SAB, McNaughton Papers, Violet McNaughton to Margaret McWilliams, 15 September 1930.

77 J.M. Dent and Sons, Ltd., agreement to publish wheat pool book, 17 January 1930.

78 Angus, ed., *Canada and Her Great Neighbour*.

79 Ibid., xii, xiv-xv.

80 *Winnipeg Free Press*, 4 April 1938.

CHAPTER SEVEN: POLITICS

1 *Winnipeg Free Press*, 18 November 1933.
2 *Saturday Night*, 29 May 1920.
3 *Woman's Century*, April 1917.
4 *Manitoba Free Press*, 22 November 1921.
5 *Canadian Annual Review*, 1925–26, 617.
6 *Manitoba Free Press*, 16, 30 November 1926.
7 Kinnear, "Women and Post-Suffrage Prairie Politics."
8 SAB, McNaughton Papers, Margaret McWilliams to Violet McNaughton, 30 June 1932.
9 *Winnipeg Free Press*, 17 October 1933.
10 *Western Home Monthly*, August 1931.
11 *Winnipeg Free Press*, 28 October 1933; PAM, LCW, Annual Report, 1933.
12 *Winnipeg Free Press*, 3, 28 November 1933.
13 PAM, UWC, IFUW clippings.
14 Interview with Mrs W.L. Morton, 11 August 1989.
15 SAB, McNaughton Papers, Margaret McWilliams to Violet McNaughton, 30 June 1932; Margaret McWilliams, speech for the women graduates at the Alumni Federation dinner for Sir Robert and Lady Falconer, *Supplement to the University of Toronto Monthly*, June 1932.
16 J.M. Dent and Sons, Ltd., agreement relating to the publication of *If I Were King of Canada*, 25 July 1931.
17 *Winnipeg Free Press*, 28 October 1933.
18 Horn, *League for Social Reconstruction*, 219–20.
19 SAB, McNaughton Papers, Margaret McWilliams to Violet McNaughton, 18 January 1933.
20 Ibid., 4 June 1923.
21 Owram, "Economic Thought," 344–77.
22 McWilliams and McWilliams (Stowell, pseud.), *If I Were King of Canada*, 35, 140.
23 Ibid., 1–5.
24 Ibid., 38, 13–17.
25 Ibid., 34–44, 80–93, 74–9.
26 Ibid., 103, 99.
27 Ibid., 109–19.
28 Ibid., 122.
29 Ibid., 125.

30 Ibid., 137, 145, 143, 67–73.

31 Ibid., 140.

32 Fraser, *Social Uplifters;* McKillop, *Disciplined Intelligence.*

33 VMP, Margaret McWilliams, Her Book, J.S. Woodsworth to Margaret McWilliams, 8 February 1932.

34 Young, *Democracy and Discontent,* 58; *Canadian Forum* 12 (1931–32): 154.

35 *Saturday Night,* 26 December 1931.

36 McWilliams and McWilliams (Stowell, pseud.), *If I Where King of Canada,* 172.

37 McKillop, "Citizen and Socialist," 51; Rea, "Politics of Conscience," 285; Rea, "Politics of Class," 232–49.

38 McKillop, "Citizen and Socialist," 64.

39 Artibise and Dahl, *Winnipeg in Maps 1816–1972,* 51.

40 *Winnipeg Free Press,* 22 November 1937.

41 McKillop, "Citizen and Socialist," 60.

42 Kinnear, "Women and Post-Suffrage Prairie Politics."

43 McKillop, "Socialist as Citizen," 66.

44 VMP, Travel Scrapbook, "Winnipeg's live-wire alderman," 4 May 1941, 4.

45 CW, Minutes of Council, 15 October 1940.

46 *Winnipeg Tribune,* 16 November 1937.

47 Helen Norrie Papers, Lila Honeyman, "An Appreciation of Margaret McWilliams," 24 February 1973.

48 CW, Minutes of Council, 4 July 1934.

49 *Winnipeg Free Press,* 26 February 1935.

50 CW, Minutes of Council, 9 March 1936.

51 Ibid., 18 March 1940.

52 Ibid., 14 January 1935; *Winnipeg Tribune,* 29 June, 20 November 1935.

53 CW, Minutes of Council, 3 January 1938.

54 Ibid., 9 May 1938, 27 December 1939, 8 January 1940; *Winnipeg Tribune,* 16 November 1937.

55 CW, Minutes of Council, 7, 21 October 1935, 3 May 1937.

56 *Winnipeg Free Press,* 18 July 1934.

57 *Winnipeg Tribune,* 8 November 1934.

58 Ibid., 16 November 1937.

59 *Winnipeg Free Press,* 10 January 1939.

60 *Winnipeg Tribune,* 8 November 1934.

61 CW, Minutes of Council, 6 March, 14 September 1939.

62 CW, Minutes of Council, 13 July 1936, "Report of the Special Committee on Unemployed Single Men's Relief Problems," 514, 519.

63 Interview with C. Rhodes Smith, 14 February 1989.

64 CW, Minutes of Council, 13 July 1936, "Report ... Unemployed Single Men's Problems," 519.

65 VMP, Travel Scrapbook, "Winnipeg's live-wire alderman," 4 May 1941, 5.

66 *Winnipeg Tribune*, 8 November 1934.

67 Ibid., 18 November 1935.

68 CW, Minutes of Council, 20 September 1937.

69 Ibid., 22 March, 14 June 1937.

70 Ibid., 19 April 1937, 24 January 1938.

71 Ibid., 24 July 1938.

72 PAM, CW, City Health Department, "An Investigation into Certain Social Conditions in Winnipeg," prepared for Alderman Margaret McWilliams by A.G. Lawrence, May 1935, 2. I thank Judy Kendle for this reference.

73 *Winnipeg Tribune*, 23 October 1937.

74 CW, Minutes of Council, 16 May 1938; report, "The Need for Housing."

75 Gray, *The Winter Years*, 219–20.

76 *Winnipeg Tribune*, 25 January 1939.

77 Ibid., 8 September 1934.

78 Ibid., 8 November 1934.

79 Ibid., 16 November 1937.

80 PAM, UWC, press clippings, January 1939.

81 *Winnipeg Tribune*, 8 November 1934.

82 Ibid., 16 November 1937.

83 JSP, Margaret McWilliams, "Where Art Thou, Eve?" November 1938.

84 *Winnipeg Tribune*, 5 October 1944.

CHAPTER EIGHT: GOVERNMENT HOUSE

1 Interview with Douglas Campbell, 17 February 1989.

2 University of Manitoba Faculty of Law, Archives of Western Canadian Legal History, R.F. McWilliams file. I thank Lee Gibson for this reference.

3 *Winnipeg Free Press*, 15 October 1940.

4 JSP, Margaret McWilliams to Helen Stearns, 20 December 1941.

5 *Winnipeg Tribune*, 5 October 1944.

6 JSP, Margaret McWilliams to Helen Stearns, 20 December 1941.

7 JSP, Margaret McWilliams to Russell Stovel, 31 October 1951.

8 Conversation with Marjorie Morley, 4 August 1989.

9 JSP, Hodder Stovel to Russell Stovel, 20 April 1952.

10 Inverview with Douglas Campbell, 17 February 1989.

11 Interview with Doris Saunders, 7 April 1988.

12 Interview with C. Rhodes Smith, 14 February 1989.

13 Conversation with Emily Garson, 3 March 1989.

14 Interview with Mrs W.L. Morton, 11 August 1989.

15 JSP, Margaret McWilliams to Helen Stearns, 20 December 1941.

16 Ibid.

17 PAM, R.F. McWilliams Papers, addendum to memorandum for Honourable E.F. Willis, 3 December 1946.

18 For example, in 1941, 1942, 1945. PAM, R.F. McWilliams Papers, "Earl of Athlone" file.

19 VMP, Red Journal, R.F. McWilliams, "Special Events," 1940; PAM, R.F. McWilliams Papers, Visitors' Book for the Lieutenant-Governor and Mrs McWilliams, 12 February 1941; VMP, Travel Scrapbook, "Winnipeg's live-wire alderman," 4 May 1941, 7.

20 Interview with Mrs W.L. Morton, 11 August 1989.

21 Conversation with Emily Garson, 3 March 1989.

22 VMP, Travel Scrapbook, "Winnipeg's live-wire alderman," 4 May 1941, 7; interview with Douglas Campbell, 17 February 1989.

23 *Winnipeg Free Press*, 22 May 1941.

24 VMP, Red Journal, R.F. McWilliams, "Trip to Swan River," 27 May–3 June 1942.

25 VMP, Red Journal, R.F. McWilliams, "Trip to Gladstone and Birtle," 27 June–2 July 1942.

26 JSP, Margaret McWilliams to Helen Stearns, 20 December 1941.

27 VMP, Red Journal, R.F. McWilliams, "The First Visit to Winnipeg of HRH the Duke of Kent," 3 August 1941.

28 *Saturday Night*, 2 August 1941.

29 *Winnipeg Tribune*, 4 August 1941.

30 Conversation with Marjorie Morley, 4 August 1989.

31 Interview with Doris Saunders, 7 April 1988.

32 SAB, McNaughton Papers, Margaret McWilliams to Violet McNaughton, 4 June 1923.

33 JSP, Margaret McWilliams to Helen Stearns, Christmas 1949.

34 PAM, R.F. McWilliams Papers, memorandum for Honourable E.F. Willis, 3 December 1946; R.F. McWilliams to E.F. Willis, 20 April 1946.

35 JSP, Margaret McWilliams to Russell Stovel, 21 March 1952.

36 Ibid., 11 September 1951.

37 Ibid., 21 October 1951.

38 Ibid., 26 October 1951.

39 Ibid., 21 October 1951.

40 Ibid., 31 October 1951.

41 Ibid., 4 February 1952.

42 "What can the women of Canada do to help win the war," radio talk, *Winnipeg Free Press*, 3 February 1941; *Winnipeg Free Press*, 14 August 1941.

43 JSP, Margaret McWilliams to Helen Stearns, 20 December 1941.

44 Bumsted, "Developing a Canadian Disaster Relief Policy," 347; JSP, Margaret McWilliams to Helen Stearns, Christmas 1950.

45 *Winnipeg Free Press*, 15, 27 May 1950.

46 VMP, Red Journal, Margaret McWilliams, entry 26 April 1941.

47 VMP, Red Journal, World Events, 15–16 October 1941.

48 Ibid., 21 January 1942.

49 Ibid., 16–17 December 1942.

50 Brandt, "Pigeon-Holed," 241.

51 Government of Canada, Advisory Committee on Reconstruction, *Report of the Subcommittee on the Post-War Problems of Women* (hereafter PWPW), 30 November 1943, 3.

52 Brandt, "'Pigeon-Holed,'" 245, 254.

53 Pierson, "'Home Aide,'" 89, 95.

54 PWPW, 7.

55 Brandt, "'Pigeon-Holed,'" 258.

56 Ibid., 247.

57 PWPW, 9–10.

58 Brandt, "'Pigeon-Holed,'" 259.

59 PWPW, 10.

60 Pierson, "'Home Aide,'" 85–97.

61 PAM, Government of Manitoba, Advisory Committee on the Co-ordination of Post-War Planning, *Report of the Subcommittee on Women's Services*, January 1945, 2, 4–6, 7, 1.

62 NAC, CFUW, Ursilla MacDonnell, "A Way to Greatness," CFUW *Chronicle*, 1952, 12.

63 MSP, clippings, n.d. (September 1944).

64 Woodbridge, *UNRRA*, vol. 1, 4, 7, 78.

65 *Winnipeg Tribune*, 5 October 1944.

66 VMP, Travel Scrapbook, radio talk, Mary David, 13 October 1944.

67 *Winnipeg Tribune*, 7 October 1944.

68 NAC, CFUW, MacDonnell, "Way to Greatness," 13.

69 PAM, Junior League Papers, Kathleen Lightcap, "The Origination of the Junior League of Winnipeg," January 1949, 1.

70 Budnick, "Performing Arts," 20.

71 Interview with Mrs W.L. Morton, 11 August 1989.

72 Malaher, "Margaret McWilliams," n.p.

73 Interview with Mrs W.L. Morton, 11 August 1989.

74 Ibid.

75 Malaher, "Margaret McWilliams."

76 Conversation with Rachel Ross, 25 August 1989; Grace Olson to Rachel Ross, 12 October 1970.

77 NAC, CFUW, President's Report, 1944.

78 Interview with Anne Loutit, 3 April 1989.

79 *Canadian Annual Review*, 1928–29, 578.

80 Friesen, "Manitoba Historical Society," 5, 6.

81 PAM, Manitoba Historical Society, Minutes, 9 February 1944.

82 PAM, Manitoba Historical Society, treasurer's reports, 5 May 1945, 29 May 1947; President's Report, 5 May 1945.

83 Morton, "President's Address," 4; Friesen, "Manitoba Historical Society," 7.

84 VMP, National Council of Women Life Membership Certificate, 1945.

85 *Winnipeg Tribune*, 15 May 1946.

86 Ibid., 2 March 1925; *Winnipeg Free Press*, 4 June 1946.

87 NAC, CFUW, president's file, 1920–50, Margaret McWilliams to Mrs R.B. Crummy, 14 April 1948.

88 *Telegram* (Toronto), 2 June 1948.

89 NAC, CFUW, president's file, 1920–50, Margaret McWilliams to Mrs R.B. Crummy, 14 April 1948.

90 PAM, LCW, annual general meeting, 25 September 1945.

91 *Saturday Night*, 28 June 1947.

92 *Varsity*, 19 November 1949.

93 UTA, Margaret Stovel file, clipping, September 1950.

94 *Globe and Mail* (Toronto), 19 April 1952.

95 *Winnipeg Tribune*, 22 March 1952.

96 Conversation with Duff Roblin, 20 March 1989.

97 Interview with Jean Carson, 18 January 1989.

98 JSP, Helen Stovel Stearns to Elizabeth Stovel, 6 July 1975.

99 JSP, Margaret McWilliams to Russell Stovel, October 1951– April 1952; MSP, Margaret McWilliams to Russell Stovel, December 1950–April 1952.

100 *Winnipeg Tribune*, 14 April 1952.

101 JSP, Hodder Stovel to Russell Stovel, 20 April 1952.

102 JSP, Roland McWilliams, "What Happened," n.d. (April 1952).

103 JSP, Hodder Stovel to Russell Stovel, 20 April 1952.

104 JSP, Roland McWilliams, "What Happened."

105 JSP, Roland McWilliams to Hodder Stovel, 6 May 1952.

106 JSP, Hodder Stovel to Russell Stovel, 20 April 1952.

107 *Manitoba Press, Winnipeg Tribune*, 14, 15 April 1952.

108 JSP, Hodder Stovel to Russell Stovel, 20 April 1952.

CHAPTER NINE: MARGARET MCWILLIAMS, WOMEN, AND FEMINISTS

1 NAC, CFUW, CFUW *Chronicle*, 1932, 11.

2 VMP, Velma McWilliams, "Margaret McWilliams," 14 May 1990.

3 NAC, CFUW, Ursilla MacDonnell, "A Way to Greatness," CFUW *Chronicle*, 1952, 14.

4 VMP, Margaret McWilliams, "Opportunities for women in public service," *Quotarian*, 16, no. 8: 14.

5 NAC, CFUW, president's file, 1920–50; Margaret McWilliams to Mrs R.B. Crummy, 14 April 1948.

6 Vickers, "Feminist Approaches," 20.

7 *Winnipeg Free Press*, 18 April 1936.

8 VMP, Velma McWilliams, "Margaret McWilliams," 14 May 1990.

9 McKillop, *Disciplined Intelligence*, 206, 217, *passim*.

10 *Winnipeg Tribune*, 8 September 1934.

11 NAC, CFUW, Minutes, 26 August 1919, 2; CFUW *Chronicle*, 1926, 32; IFUW *Chronicle*, 1926, 42–52.

12 NAC, CFUW, clippings, *Gazette* (Montreal), 20 May 1934.

13 *Winnipeg Free Press*, 1 January 1939.

14 *Winnipeg Free Press*, 17 January 1944.
15 Strange, "Margaret McWilliams."
16 JSP, Margaret McWilliams, "Eve," November 1938.
17 Freeman, "What Happened to Feminism," 329.
18 VMP, Margaret McWilliams, "Opportunities for Women," 13–16.
19 NAC, Cleverdon Papers, Margaret McWilliams to Catherine Cleverdon, 1 October 1946.
20 Government of Canada, Advisory Committee on Reconstruction, *Report of the Subcommittee on the Post-War Problems of Women* (PWPW), 30 November 1943, 19.
21 Rooke and Schnell, *No Bleeding Heart*, 199, 202.
22 Ibid., 202, 203.
23 JSP, R.F. McWilliams to Russell Stovel, 6 May 1952.
24 Interview with Mrs W.L. Morton, 11 August 1989.
25 *Winnipeg Tribune*, 23 October 1937.
26 Strange, "Margaret McWilliams."
27 Margaret McWilliams, "A Constructive Philosophy for Our Time."
28 UTA, *Calendar*, 1894–5, 69; Cook, *Regenerators*, 230–2.
29 Bacchi, *Liberation Deferred?* 146–9.
30 UTA, Margaret Stovel file, "Leader in Manitoba Life," January 1949.
31 Margaret McWilliams, *This New Canada*, 304.
32 Miller, "Writing Fictions," 49.
33 Heilbrun, "Non-Autobiographies," 70, 65.
34 NAC, CFUW, MacDonnell, "A Way to Greatness," 13.
35 Kathleen Bowley Papers, Samuel R. Stovel to Annabelle Langdon, 9 April 1979.
36 JSP, Margaret McWilliams, "Eve," November 1938.
37 For example, see Angela Davis, "Mary Barrett Speechly"; Freeman, *Kit's Kingdom*; French, *Isabel and the Empire*; Haig, *Brave Harvest*; Kealey and Sangster, eds., *Beyond the Vote*; Kinnear, "Women and Post-Suffrage Prairie Politics"; Knowles, *First Person*; Latham and Kess, eds., *In Her Own Right*; Latham and Pazdro, eds., *Not Just Pin Money*; MacDonald, *Adelaide Hoodless*; MacEwan, *And Mighty Women Too*; McDowell, "Some Women Candidates"; Pennington, *Agnes McPhail*; Prentice et al., *Canadian Women*; Rooke and Schnell, eds., *No Bleeding Heart*; Strong-Boag, *New Day Recalled*.

Bibliography

PRIMARY SOURCES

PRIVATE COLLECTIONS
Kathleen Bowley Papers
J.M. Dent and Sons, Ltd.
Velma McWilliams Papers
Helen Norrie Papers
Jack Stovel Papers
Margaret Stovel Papers
Betty Jane Wylie Papers

BRITISH COLUMBIA ARCHIVES
Nellie McClung

CITY OF WINNIPEG ARCHIVES
Minutes of Council

GLENBOW INSTITUTE
Irene Parlby Papers

HARBORD COLLEGIATE INSTITUTE
Harbord Collegiate Review
Notes from Willie Zimmermann
Archives

NATIONAL ARCHIVES OF CANADA
Cleverdon Papers
Canadian Federation of University Women
National Council of Education

PROVINCIAL ARCHIVES OF MANITOBA
Canadian Red Cross
Canadian Women's Press Club
City of Winnipeg
Free Kindergarten Association
Junior League
Local Council of Women
Manitoba Historical Society
McColl Papers
R.F. McWilliams
Social Science Study Club
Social Planning Council of Winnipeg
University Women's Club
Women's Canadian Club

SASKATCHEWAN ARCHIVES BOARD
McNaughton Papers

TRENT UNIVERSITY ARCHIVES
Women's Art Association

UNITED CHURCH OF CANADA
St. Stephen's, Broadway. Deacon's Court Minutes

UNIVERSITY OF MANITOBA ARCHIVES
Board of Governors
Faculty of Law, Western Canadian Legal History Archives
Presidents' Papers
University Council

UNIVERSITY OF TORONTO ARCHIVES
Margaret Stovel file
Sesame
Torontonensis
University of Toronto calendars
University of Toronto Monthly

UNIVERSITY WOMEN'S CLUB, WINNIPEG
Margaret McWilliams memorabilia

GOVERNMENT OF CANADA
Report of the Advisory Committee on Reconstruction, Subcommittee
on the Post-War Problems of Women, 1943

GOVERNMENT OF MANITOBA
Department of Public Works, Sessional Papers, 1918.
Report of the Advisory Committee on Post-War Planning, Subcom-
mittee on Women's Services, 1944.

NEWSPAPERS AND PERIODICALS
Canadian Annual Review
Canadian Courier
Canadian Forum
Canadian Home Journal
Canadian Parliamentary Guide
Canadian Welfare
Canadian Woman Studies
Chatelaine
Construction
Country Guide
Detroit Journal
Feminist Studies (College Park, Maryland)
Grain Growers' Guide
Henderson's Directories
Journal of Canadian Studies
Manitoba Bar News
Manitoba/Winnipeg Free Press
Minneapolis Journal
New Society
Pacific Affairs
Peterborough Examiner
Peterborough Review
Queen's Quarterly
Quotarian
Red River Valley Historian
Saturday Night
Signs (University of Chicago Press)
Varsity (University of Toronto)

Western Home Monthly
Western School Journal
Winnipeg Telegram
Winnipeg Tribune
Woman's Century

INTERVIEWS
Frances Bowles, 22 May 1989
Genevieve Brownell, 7 April 1988
Douglas Campbell, 17 February 1989
Jean Carson, 18 January 1989
Anne Loutit, 3 April 1989
Velma McWilliams, 14 May 1990
Olive Morgan, 7 April 1988
Helen Monk, 7 April 1988
Mrs W.L. Morton, 11 August 1989
Helen Norrie, 31 January 1989
Doris Saunders, 7 April 1988
Isobel Scurfield, 6 February 1989
C. Rhodes Smith, 14 February 1989
Eleanor Suttie, 15 February 1989
Betty Watson, 7 April 1988

CONVERSATIONS
Virginia and Edmund Berry, 3 February 1990
Emily Garson, 3 March 1989
Margaret Gow, 16 February 1989
Elva Humphries, 16 February 1989
Edith MacIntosh, 20 February 1989
Marjorie Morley, 4 August 1989
Duff Roblin, 20 March 1989
Rachel Ross, 25 August 1989

SELECT BIBLIOGRAPHY OF
SECONDARY SOURCES

Acker, Joan. "Class, Gender and the Relations of Distribution." *Signs* 13, no. 3 (Spring 1988): 473–97.
Adamson, Nancy, Linda Briskin, and Margaret McPhail. *Feminist Organising for Change: The Contemporary Women's Movement in Canada*. Toronto: Oxford University Press 1988.

Alberti, Johanna. *Beyond Suffrage: Feminists in War and Peace 1914–28*. London: Macmillan 1989.

Allen, Richard. *The Social Passion: Religion and Social Reform in Canada, 1914–28*. Toronto: University of Toronto Press 1971.

All Saints Anglican Church, Winnipeg. *History*, Winnipeg, n.d. (1983).

Angus, H.F., ed. *Canada and Her Great Neighbour: Sociological Surveys of Opinions and Attitudes in Canada Concerning the United States*. 1938. Reprint. New York: Ryerson Press 1970.

Armour, Leslie, and Elizabeth Trott. *The Faces of Reason: An Essay on Philosophy and Culture in English Canada 1850–1950*. Waterloo: Wilfrid Laurier University Press 1981.

Artibise, Alan F.J. *Winnipeg: A Social History of Urban Growth, 1874–1914*. Montreal and Kingston: McGill-Queen's University Press, 1975.

–, ed., *Gateway City: Documents on the City of Winnipeg 1873–1913*. Vol. 5. Winnipeg: Manitoba Record Society 1979.

Artibise, Alan F.J., and Edward H. Dahl. *Winnipeg in Maps, 1816–1972*. Ottawa: James Lorimer 1975.

Atlantis: A Women's Studies Journal. Halifax, NS: Mount St Vincent University.

Axelrod, Paul, and John G. Reid, eds. *Youth, University and Canadian Society: Essays in the Social History of Higher Education*. Montreal and Kingston: McGill-Queen's University Press 1989.

Bacchi, Carol Lee. *Liberation Deferred? The Ideas of the English-Canadian Suffragists, 1877–1918*. Toronto: University of Toronto Press 1983.

Barry, Kathleen. *Susan B. Anthony: A Biography of a Singular Feminist*. New York: New York University Press 1988.

– "The New Historical Synthesis: Women's Biography." *Journal of Women's History* 1, no. 3 (1990): 75–105.

Begg, Alexander. *History of the North-West*. Toronto: Hunter, Rose 1894.

Bellan, Ruben. *Winnipeg First Century: An Economic History*. Winnipeg: Queenston House Press 1978.

Benson, Susan Porter. *Counter Cultures: Saleswomen, Managers and Customers in American Department Stores 1890–1940*. Urbana: University of Illinois Press 1986.

Berger, Carl, and Ramsay Cook, eds. *The West and the Nation*. Toronto: McClelland and Stewart 1976.

Beynon, Francis. "Socialism and War." *Grain Growers Guide*, 19 April 1916.

– "The Wastes of War." *Grain Growers Guide*, 3 March 1915.

Black, Naomi. *Social Feminism*. Ithaca: Cornell University Press 1989.

Brandt, Gail Cuthbert. "'Pigeon-Holed and Forgotten': The Work of the Subcomittee on the Post-War Problems of Women, 1943." *Histoire Sociale/Social History* 15 (1982): 239–59.

Brodzki, Bella, and Celeste Schenck, eds. *Life/Lines: Theorising Women's Autobiography*. Ithaca: Cornell University Press 1988.

Bryce, George. *Remarkable History of the Hudson's Bay Company.* London: W. Briggs 1900.

Budnick, Carol. "The Performing Arts as a Field of Endeavour for Winnipeg Women, 1870–1930." *Manitoba History* 11 (Spring 1986): 15–21.

Bumsted, J.M. "Developing a Canadian Disaster Relief Policy: The 1950 Manitoba Flood." *Canadian Historical Review* 68 (1987): 347–73.

– "The Quest for a Usable Founder: Lord Selkirk and Manitoba Historians, 1856–1923." *Manitoba History* 2 (1981): 2–7.

Canadian Historical Review. Toronto: University of Toronto Press.

Cleverdon, Catherine C. *The Woman Suffrage Movement in Canada.* 1950. Reprint. Toronto: University of Toronto Press 1974.

Cook, Ramsay. "Francis Marion Beynon and the Crisis of Christian Reformism." In Berger and Cook, eds. *The West and the Nation,* 187–208.

– *The Regenerators: Social Criticism in Late Victorian English Canada.* Toronto: University of Toronto Press 1985.

Cott, Nancy. "Comment on Karen Offen's 'Defining Feminism.'" *Signs* 15, no. 1 (Autumn 1989): 203–5.

– *The Grounding of Modern Feminism.* New Haven: Yale University Press 1987.

– "The Limits of 'Social Feminism'; or, Expanding the Vocabulary of Women's History," *Journal of American History* 76, no. 3 (December 1989): 809–29.

Crathern, Alice Tarbell. *In Detroit, Courage Was the Fashion: The Contribution of Women to the Development of Detroit from 1701 to 1951.* Detroit: Wayne State University Press 1953.

Craw, G. Wilson. *The Peterborough Story: Our Mayors, 1850–1951.* Peterborough: Peterborough Examiner 1967.

Davies, Margaret Llewelyn, ed. *Maternity: Letters from Working Women Collected by the Women's Co-operative Guild.* 1915. Reprint. London: Norton 1978.

Davis, Allen F. *The Life and Legend of Jane Addams.* Boston: Oxford University Press 1973.

Davis, Angela. "Mary Barrett Speechly, 1873–1968: A Practical Feminist." Unpublished paper, University of Manitoba, 1988.

Drummond, Ian. *Political Economy at the University of Toronto: A History of the Department, 1888–1982*. Toronto: University of Toronto Press 1983.

Dubois, Ellen Carol. "Comment on Karen Offen's 'Defining Feminism.'" *Signs* 15, no. 1 (Autumn 1989): 195–7.

– *Feminism and Suffrage: The Emergence of an Independent Women's Movement in America 1848–1869*. Ithaca: Cornell University Press 1978.

Dyhouse, Carol. *Feminism and the Family in England 1880–1939*. Oxford: Basil Blackwell 1989.

Eichler, Margrit. *The Double Standard: A Feminist Critique of Feminist Social Science*. New York: St. Martin's Press 1979.

Feminist Studies.

Fingard, Judith. "College, Career and Community: Dalhousie Co-eds 1881–1921." In Axelrod and Reid, eds., *University and Canadian Society*, 26–50.

First, Ruth, and Ann Scott. *Olive Schreiner*. London: André Deutsch 1980.

Ford, Anne Rochon. *A Path Not Strewn with Roses: One Hundred Years of Women at the University of Toronto 1884–1984*. Toronto: University of Toronto Press 1985.

Fraser, Brian J. *The Social Uplifters: Presbyterian Progressives and the Social Gospel in Canada, 1875–1915*. Waterloo: Wilfrid Laurier Press 1988.

Freeman, Barbara M. *Kit's Kingdom: The Journalism of Kathleen Blake Coleman*. Ottawa: Carleton University Press 1989.

Freeman, Estelle. "What Happened to Feminism in the 1920s?" In Mary Beth Norton, ed., *Major Problems in American Women's History*, 329–40. Lexington, Mass.: D.C. Heath 1989.

French, Doris. *Ishbel and the Empire*. Toronto: Dundurn Press 1988.

Friesen, Gerald. *The Canadian Prairies: A History*. Toronto: University of Toronto Press 1984.

– "The Manitoba Historical Society: A Centennial History." *Manitoba History* 4 (1982): 2–9.

Gildersleeve, Virginia Crocheron. *Many a Good Crusade*. New York: Macmillan 1955.

Gordon, Charles W. *Postcript to Adventure: The Autobiography of Ralph Connor*. New York: Farrar and Rinehart 1938.

Gray, James H. *The Winter Years*. 1966. Reprint. Toronto: Macmillan 1976.

Green, T.H. *Lectures on the Principles of Political Obligation*. 1882. Reprint. London: Longmans 1963.

– *Prolegomena to Ethics*. 1882. Reprint. Oxford: Clarendon Press 1906.

Gunn, Donald. *History of Manitoba*. Ottawa: Maclean, Roger 1880.

Haig, Kennethe M. *Brave Harvest*. Toronto: Allen 1945.

– "E. Cora Hind." In Innis, ed., *The Clear Spirit*, 120–41.

Harrison, Brian. *Prudent Revolutionaries: Portraits of British Feminists Between the Wars*. Oxford: Clarendon Press 1987.

Hathaway, Debbie. "The Political Equality League of Manitoba." *Manitoba History* 3 (1982): 8–10.

Healy, W.J. *Women of Red River*. 1923. Reprint. Winnipeg: Peguis Publishers 1970.

Heeney, Brian. *The Women's Movement in the Church of England 1850–1930*. Oxford: Clarendon Press 1988.

Heilbrun, Carolyn G. "Discovering the Lost Lives of Women." *New York Times Book Review*, 24 June 1984, 1, 26.

– "Non-Autobiographies of 'Privileged' Women: England and America." In Brodzki and Schenck, eds. *Life/Lines*, 62–76.

– *Writing a Woman's Life*. New York: Norton 1988.

Hill, Mary A. *Charlotte Perkins Gilman: The Making of a Radical Feminist*. Philadelphia: Temple University Press 1980.

Hill, Robert. *Manitoba: History of Its Early Settlement, Development and Resources*. Toronto: W. Briggs, 1890.

Holland, William L. "Source Materials on the Institute of Pacific Relations." *Pacific Affairs* 58, no. 1 (1985): 91–7.

Horn, Michiel. *The League for Social Reconstruction: Intellectual Origins of the Democratic Left in Canada, 1930–1942*. Toronto: University of Toronto Press 1980.

Innis, Mary Q., ed. *The Clear Spirit: Twenty Canadian Women and Their Times*. Toronto: University of Toronto Press 1966.

Jackel, Susan. "Canadian Women's Autobiography: A Problem of Criticism." In Barbara Godard, ed., *Gynocritics/Gynocritiques: Feminist Approaches to Canadian and Quebec Women's Writing*, 97–110. Toronto: ECW Press 1987.

– Introduction, Georgina Binnie Clark, *Wheat and Woman*. 1914. Reprint. Toronto: University of Toronto Press 1979.

Jones, Elwood, and Bruce Dyer. *Peterborough: The Electric City*. Burlington, Ont.: Windsor Publications 1987.

Journal of Women's History. Bloomington: Indiana University Press.

Kahn, E.J., Jr. *The China Hands: American's Foreign Service Officers and What Befell Them*. New York: Viking 1975.

Kealey, Linda. "No Special Protection – No Sympathy: Women's Activism in the Canadian Labour Revolt of 1919." In Deian R. Hopkin and Gregory S. Kealey, eds., *Class, Community and the Labour Movement: Wales and Canada 1850–1931*, 134–59. St. John's, Newfoundland: Canadian Committee on Labour History 1989.

– "Women and Labour during World War I: Women Workers and the Minimum Wage in Manitoba." In Kinnear, ed., *First Days, Fighting Days*, 76–99.

–, ed. *A Not Unreasonable Claim: Women and Reform in Canada, 1880s–1920s*. Toronto: Women's Press 1979.

Kealey, Linda, and Joan Sangster, eds. *Beyond the Vote: Canadian Women and Politics*. Toronto: University of Toronto Press 1989.

Kidd, Martha Ann. *Historical Sketches of Peterborough*. Peterborough: Broadview Press 1988.

Kinnear, Mary, *Daughters of Time: Women in the Western Tradition*. Ann Arbor: University of Michigan Press 1982.

– "The Icelandic Connection: 'Freyja' and the Manitoba Woman Suffrage Movement." *Canadian Woman Studies* 7, no. 4 (1986): 25–28.

– "Women and Post-Suffrage Prairie Politics: Female Candidates in Winnipeg Municipal Elections, 1918–39." *Prairie Forum* 16, no. 1 (1991).

–, ed. *First Days, Fighting Days: Women in Manitoba History*. Regina: Canadian Plains Research Centre 1987.

Kinnear, Mary, and Vera Fast. *Planting the Garden: Annotated Archival Bibliography for the History of Women in Manitoba*. Winnipeg: University of Manitoba Press 1987.

Knowles, Valerie. *First Person: A Biography of Cairine Wilson*. Toronto: Dundurn Press 1988.

Latham, Barbara, and Cathy Kess, eds. *In Her Own Right: Selected Essays on Women's History in B.C.* Victoria, BC: Camosun College 1980.

Latham, Barbara, and Roberta J. Pazdro, eds. *Not Just Pin Money: Selected Essays on the History of Women: Work in British Columbia*. Victoria, BC: Camosun College 1984.

Lerner, Gerda. *The Creation of Patriarchy*. New York: Oxford University Press 1986.

– "Reconceptualising Differences Among Women." *Journal of Women's History* 1, no. 3 (1990): 106–22.

– "Where Biographers Fear to Tread." *Women's Review of Books* 4, no. 12 (1987).

Lewis, Jane. "Beyond Suffrage: English Feminism in the 1920s." *Maryland Historian* 6, no. 1 (Spring 1975): 1–18.

– "Eleanor Rathbone and the Family." *New Society*, 27 January 1983.

– "Essay in Revision." *Social History Society of the U.K. Newsletter* 14, no. 1 (Spring 1989): 5–7.

– *Women in England 1870–1950: Sexual Divisions and Social Change.* Bloomington: Indiana University Press 1984.

–, ed. *Labour and Love: Women's Experience of Home and Family 1850–1940.* Oxford: Blackwell 1986.

MacCunn, John. *Six Radical Thinkers.* London: Edward Arnold 1910.

MacDonald, Cheryl. *Adelaide Hoodless: Domestic Crusader.* Toronto: Dundurn Press 1986.

MacEwan, Grant. *And Mighty Women Too.* Saskatoon: Western Producer Prairie Books 1975.

Malaher, Rosemary. "Margaret McWilliams." Paper presented to the University Women's Club, Winnipeg, 1985.

Manitoba History. Winnipeg: Manitoba Historical Society.

Manitoba Pageant. Winnipeg: Historical and Scientific Society of Manitoba.

Maroney, Heather Jon, and Meg Luxton, eds. *Feminism and Political Economy.* Toronto: Methuen 1987.

Martin, Chester. *Lord Selkirk's Work in Canada.* Toronto: Clarendon Press 1916.

McClung, Nellie. *In Times Like These.* Introduction by Veronica Strong-Boag. 1914. Reprint. Toronto: University of Toronto Press 1974.

– *The Stream Funs Fast.* Toronto: Thomas Allen 1965.

McColl, Frances V. *Vignettes of Early Winnipeg: 1912–1926.* Winnipeg: Frances McColl 1981.

McDowell, Linda. "Harriet Dick: A Lady Ahead of Her Time?" *Manitoba Pageant*, 1975, 11–13.

– "Some Women Candidates for the Manitoba Legislature." *Transactions of the Historical and Scientific Society of Manitoba* 3, no. 32 (1975–76): 5–20.

McKillop, Brian. "Citizen and Socialist: The Ethos of Political Winnipeg, 1919–35." MA history thesis, University of Manitoba 1970.

– *A Disciplined Intelligence: Critical Enquiry and Canadian Thought in the Victorian Era.* Montreal and Kingston: McGill-Queen's University Press 1979.

McLaren, Angus. *Our Own Master Race: Eugenics in Canada 1885–1945.* Toronto: McClelland and Stewart 1990.

McLaren, Angus, and Arlene Tigar McLaren. *The Bedroom and the State: The Changing Practices and Politics of Contraception and Abortion in Canada 1880–1980.* Toronto: McClelland and Stewart 1986.

McWilliams, Margaret. "The Affair of the First Flag-Staff." *Saturday Night*, 16 March 1912.

– *All Along the River*. Winnipeg: Russell-Lang 1930.

– "A Cloud of Witnesses." *Western Home Monthly*, December 1922.

– "A Constructive Philosophy for Our Time: What Must I Do?" *Saturday Night*, 28 June 1947.

– *Manitoba Milestones*. Toronto: J.M. Dent and Sons 1928.

– *This New Canada*. Toronto: J.M. Dent and Sons 1948.

McWilliams, Margaret, and R.F. McWilliams (Oliver Stowell, pseud.). *If I Were King of Canada*. Toronto: J.M. Dent and Sons 1931.

– *Russia in 1926*. Toronto: J.M. Dent and Sons 1927.

McWilliams, R.F. *Does History Repeat Itself?* Toronto: J.M. Dent and Sons 1932.

Miller, Nancy K. "Writing Fictions: Women's Autobiography in France." In Brodzki and Schenck, eds., *Life/Lines*, 45–61.

Morton, W.L. *Manitoba, A History*. Toronto: University of Toronto Press 1957.

– *One University: A History of the University of Manitoba*. Toronto: McClelland and Stewart 1957.

– "President's Address on the Occasion of the 75th Anniversary of the Historical and Scientific Society of Manitoba, 1879–1953." *Transactions of the Historical and Scientific Society of Manitoba* 3, no. 9 (1954): 3–5.

Oakley, Ann. *Subject Women*. New York: Pantheon 1981.

Offen, Karen. "Defining Feminism: A Comparative Historical Approach." *Signs* 14, no. 1 (1988): 119–57.

– "Liberty, Equality and Justice for Women: The Theory and Practice of Feminism in Nineteenth Century Europe." In Renate Bridenthal, Claudia Koonz, and Susan Stuard, eds. *Becoming Visible: Women in European History*, 335–74.

– "Reply to Comments of Cott and Dubois on 'Defining Feminism.'" *Signs* 15, no. 1 (Autumn 1989): 198–202, 206–9.

– "The Use and Abuse of History." *Women's Review of Books* 6, no. 6 (1989).

Owram, Doug. "Economic Thought in the 1930s: The Prelude to Keynesianism." *Canadian Historical Review* 66, no. 3 (1985): 344–77.

– *The Government Generation: Canadian Intellectuals and the State 1900–1945*. Toronto: University of Toronto Press 1986.

Pedersen, Diana. "'The Call to Service': The YWCA and the Canadian College Woman, 1886–1920." In Axelrod and Reid, eds., *Youth, University and Canadian Society*, 187–215.

– "'Keeping Our Good Girls Good': The YWCA and the 'Girl Problem,' 1870–1930." *Canadian Woman Studies* 7, no. 4 (1986): 20–4.

Penner, Norman, ed. *Winnipeg 1919*. Toronto: James Lewis and Samuel 1973.

Pennington, Doris. *Agnes Macphail: Canada's First Female M.P.* Toronto: Simon & Pierre 1989.

Pentland, Clare. Review of David J. Bercuson, "Confrontation at Winnipeg: Labour, Industrial Relations and the General Strike." *Red River Valley Historian*, Summer 1976, 27.

Perkin, Harold. *The Rise of Professional Society: England Since 1880.* London: Routledge 1990.

Peterson, T. "Ethnic and Class Politics in Manitoba." In Martin Robin, ed., *Canadian Provincial Politics: The Party Systems of the Ten Provinces*, 69–115. Scarborough: Prentice-Hall 1972.

Phillips, Anne. *Divided Loyalties: Dilemmas of Sex and Class.* London: Virago 1987.

Pierson, Ruth. "'Home Aide': A Solution to Women's Unemployment after the Second World War," *Atlantis* 2, no. 2 (1977): 85–97.

Poovey, Mary. "Feminism and Deconstruction." *Feminist Studies* 14, no. 1 (Spring 1988): 51–66.

Prentice, Alison, et al. *Canadian Women: A History.* Toronto: Harcourt Brace Jovanovich 1988.

Rabine, Leslie Wahl. "A Feminist Politics of Non-Identity." *Feminist Studies* 14, no. 1 (Spring 1988): 11–32.

Rea, J.E. "The Politics of Class: Winnipeg City Council, 1919–45." In Berger and Cook, eds., *The West and the Nation*, 232–49.

– "The Politics of Conscience: Winnipeg after the Strike." Canadian Historical Association, *Historical Papers*, 1971, 276–88.

Reeves, Maud Pember. *Round About a Pound a Week*. 1913. Reprint. London: Virago 1979.

Richards, Janet Radcliffe. *The Sceptical Feminist*. 1980. Reprint. Harmondsworth: Pelican 1982.

Roberts, Barbara. "Women's Peace Activism in Canada." In Kealey and Sangster, eds., *Beyond the Vote*, 276–308.

Roe, Amy. "Margaret McWilliams." *Country Guide*, May 1952.

Rooke, P.T., and R.L. Schnell. *No Bleeding Heart: Charlotte Whitton, a Feminist on the Right.* Vancouver: University of British Columbia Press 1987.

Rose, Phyllis. *Writing of Women: Essays in a Renaissance.* Middletown: Wesleyan University Press 1985.

Ross, Alexander. *The Red River Settlement*. London: Smith, Elder 1856.

Sangster, Joan. *Dreams of Equality: Women on the Canadian Left 1920–1950*. Toronto: McClelland and Stewart 1989.

Scott, Joan. "Deconstructing Equality-versus-Difference: or, the Uses of Poststructuralist Theory for Feminism." *Feminist Studies* 14, no. 1 (Spring 1988): 33–50.

Shaw, Rosa L. *Proud Heritage: A History of the National Council of Women of Canada*. Toronto: Ryerson 1957.

Silverman, Eliane. "Writing Canadian Women's History, 1970–82." *Canadian Historical Review* 63, no. 4 (1982): 513–33.

Sissons, Constance Kerr. "Gifted – And All Canadian." *Western Home Monthly*, May 1931.

Stocks, Mary D. *Eleanor Rathbone, A Biography*. London: Gollancz 1949.

Stovel, J. Hodder. *A Mining Trail 1902–45*. Privately published, n.p., n.d. (1945).

Stovel Company Ltd. *Historical Outline of the House of Stovel*. Winnipeg: Stovel Company Ltd. 1931.

Strange, Kathleen. "Margaret McWilliams of Manitoba." *Canadian Home Journal*, August 1951.

Strong-Boag, Veronica. "Canadian Feminism in the 1920s: The Case of Nellie L. McClung." *Journal of Canadian Studies* 12, no. 4 (1977): 58–68.

– *The New Day Recalled: The Lives of Girls and Women in English Canada, 1919–39*. Toronto: Copp Clark Pitman 1988.

– *The Parliament of Women: The National Council of Women of Canada, 1893–1929*. Ottawa: National Museums of Canada 1976.

– "'Wages for Housework': Mothers' Allowances and the Beginnings of Social Security in Canada." *Journal of Canadian Studies* 14, no. 1 (1979): 24–34.

Tait, J. Wilfrid. Review of Margaret McWilliams, *Manitoba Milestones*. *North Dakota Historical Quarterly* 5, no. 3 (1929): 185–7.

Thomas, Lillian Beynon. "Some Manitoba Women Who Did First Things." *Transactions of the Historical and Scientific Society of Manitoba* 3 (1947–48): 13–25.

Transactions of the Historical and Scientific Society of Manitoba. Winnipeg: Manitoba Historical Society. Annual publication.

Trofimenkoff, Susan Mann. "Feminist Biography." *Atlantis* 10, no. 2 (1985): 1–10.

– "Thérèse Casgrain and the ccf in Quebec." In Kealey and Sangster, eds., *Beyond the Vote*, 139–68.

Trofimenkoff, Susan Mann, and Alison Prentice. *The Neglected Majority: Essays in Canadian Women's History.* 2 vols. Toronto: McClelland and Stewart 1977.

Underhill, Frank. Review of *If I Were King of Canada. Canadian Forum* 12 (1931–32): 154.

The University of Toronto and Its Colleges 1827–1906. Toronto: University of Toronto 1906.

The University Women's Club of Winnipeg 1909–1959. Winnipeg: University Women's Club n.d. (1959).

Vickers, Jill. "Feminist Approaches to Women in Politics." In Kealey and Sangster, eds., *Beyond the Vote,* 16–36.

Wexler, Alice. *Emma Goldman in America.* Boston: Beacon Press 1984.

Wiseman, Nelson. "The Pattern of Prairie Politics." *Queen's Quarterly* 87 (1981): 298–315.

Women's Review of Books. Wellesley, Mass: Wellesley College Center for Research on Women.

Woodbridge, George. UNRRA: *The History of the United Nations Relief and Rehabilitation Administration.* New York: Columbia University Press 1950.

Woolf, Virginia. "The Art of Biography." In Virginia Woolf, *Collected Essays,* 221–28. Vol. 4. London: Hogarth Press 1967.

Wrong, George M., and H.H. Langton, eds. *Chronicles of Canada.* 32 vols. Toronto: Glasgow Brook and Co. 1914–20.

Wylie, Betty Jane. "Margaret McWilliams." In Innis, *Clear Spirit,* 279–98.

Young, Kathryn. "Women's Tribute Memorial Lodge." Paper for the City of Winnipeg Historic Buildings Committee, February 1987.

Young, Walter. *Democracy and Discontent: Progressivism, Socialism and Social Credit in the Canadian West.* Toronto: Ryerson Press 1969.

Zunz, Olivier. *The Changing Face of Inequality: Urbanisation, Industrial Development and Immigrants in Detroit, 1880–1920.* Chicago: University of Chicago Press 1982.

Index